LONDON

WORLD CITY

DEPARTMENT OF PLANNING,
HOUSING AND DEVELOPMENT
SOUTH BANK POLYTECHNIC
WANDSWORTH ROAD, SW8 2JZ

This Book and its accompanying Report of Studies are published for information and discussion. Its views and recommendations are those of the team of consultants led by Coopers & Lybrand Deloitte, and publication does not necessarily indicate that they are accepted by any or all of the co-sponsors. Neither co-sponsors, nor the consultant can be liable for any loss or damage however substantial by others ensuing from reliance upon the contents of the Report.

Photo Titles and Acknowledgements

Front end paper
The City and Westminster looking west
CHORLEY & HANDFORD LTD

Back end paper
Docklands and The City looking west
LDDC

© Crown copyright 1991
Applications for reproduction should be made to HMSO
First published 1991
ISBN 0 11 701558 X

HMSO publications are available from:

HMSO Publications Centre
(Mail and telephone orders only)
PO Box 276, London, SW8 5DT
Telephone orders 071–873 9090
General enquiries 071–873 0011
(queuing system in operation for both numbers)

HMSO Bookshops
49 High Holborn, London, WC1V 6HB
071–873 0011 (counter service only)
258 Broad Street, Birmingham, B1 2HE
021–643 3740
Southey House, 33 Wine Street, Bristol, BS1 2BQ
(0272) 264306
9–21 Princess Street, Manchester, M60 8AS
061–834 7201
80 Chichester Street, Belfast, BT1 4JY
(0232) 238451
71 Lothian Road, Edinburgh, EH3 9AZ
031–228 4181

HMSO's Accredited Agents
(see Yellow Pages)

and through good booksellers

£24.95 net

ISBN 0-11-701558-X

9 780117 015586

LONDON

WORLD CITY MOVING INTO THE 21ST CENTURY

A RESEARCH PROJECT

CO-SPONSORED BY

THE LONDON PLANNING ADVISORY COMMITTEE

with

The Corporation of London
Greater London Arts
The London Docklands Development Corporation
London Transport
Westminster City Council

from

COOPERS & LYBRAND DELOITTE

WRITTEN BY RICHARD KENNEDY

with material from
The MVA Consultancy
The Greater London Group
The Local Economy Policy Unit
Comedia
Richard Ellis

London: HMSO

I NEVER TIRE OF
COMING TO LONDON – IT IS ONE
OF MY FAVOURITE PLACES. A CITY,
IF IT IS TO SURVIVE, MUST CHANGE AND
ADAPT TO NEW SITUATIONS. SOMETIMES IN
MY BLACKEST MOODS I WONDER WHY SAD THINGS
ARE HAPPENING TO LONDON – I FEAR THIS
BELOVED CITY IS IN TERMINAL DECLINE.
THEN I ARRIVE, AND THE PLACE WORKS
THE MAGIC THAT KEEPS ME COMING
BACK FOR MORE.

Carlo Ripa Di Meana, European Environment Commissioner, 1991

St. Pauls Cathedral
BRITISH TOURIST AUTHORITY

Contents

	ACKNOWLEDGEMENTS	iv
	FOREWORD	ix
	PREFACE	xi
1	LONDON: WORLD CITY	1
2	WEALTH CREATION	21
3	JOBS AND INCOME	67
4	QUALITY OF LIFE	89
5	ENABLING INFRASTRUCTURE	125
6	PROSPECTS AND POLICY	171
7	STRATEGIES FOR THE 21ST CENTURY	195
	BIBLIOGRAPHY	217
	INDEX	231

PROJECT TEAM

LPAC	Robin Clement	Leader and LPAC Deputy Chief Planner
	Amer Hirmis	Principal Economist/Planner
	Steve Cox	Planner
	Pamela Yates	Assistant Secretary
	Jeremy Peters	Administrative Officer
	Jane-Louise Head	Personal Assistant

CONSULTANTS

Coopers & Lybrand Deloitte	Francis Plowden	Partner in Charge of Government Services Division
	Jeremy Brown	Partner, Economic Development & Housing
	Geoff White	Principal of Policy & Economics
	Sean Duggan	Associate Policy & Economics
	Vince Taylor	Associate Policy & Economics
	Martin Wall	Associate Policy & Economics
	Heather Lynch	Personal Assistant
The MVA Consultancy	William Wyley	Director
	Peter Guest	Associate
The Greater London Group (LSE)	Derek Diamond	Chairman
	Tony Travers	Research Director
Local Economy Policy Unit South Bank Polytechnic	Sam Aaronovitch	Director
	Peter Brayshaw	
Comedia	Charles Landry	Chairman
Richard Ellis	Iain Reid	Head of Research
	Gillian Eleftheriou	Associate
	Mike Straw	Senior Research Analyst

STEERING GROUP AND ADVISORY PANEL

Martin Simmons — Chief Planner, London Planning Advisory Committee, Chairman

STEERING GROUP

Keith Gardner	LPAC Assistant Chief Planner (Transport)
John Lett	LPAC Assistant Chief Planner (Policy)
Peter Wynne Rees	City Planning Officer, Corporation of London
Adam Hilton	Corporate Director (Policy), Westminster City Council
Bill Hodgson	Team Leader (Strategy), Westminster City Council
Seonna Reid	Deputy Director, Greater London Arts
and later Brian Matcham	Deputy Director, Greater London Arts
and J Jean Horstman	Director of Strategy, London Arts Board
Peter Turlik	Director of Strategic Affairs, LDDC
Julia Heynat	Corporate Information Manager, LDDC
Michael Bishop	Corporate Information Analyst, LDDC
Fitzroy Ambursley	LDDC

ADVISORY PANEL: made up of the Steering Group, and the

Association of London Authorities	John McDonnell, Secretary
Bank of England	Nigel Carter, Senior Manager, Financial Markets and Institutes Division
Confederation of British Industry	Jane Calvert-Lee, Director, London Office
	Julie Yorke, Policy Co-ordinator
The Greater London Group	Professor Derek Diamond, Chairman
London Boroughs Association	John Hall, Secretary
London Chamber of Commerce and Industry	David Senior, former General Manager
	Jacqueline Ginnane, Head of Economics
London Tourist Board	Tom Webb, Managing Director
	Robert Chenery, Head of Borough Liaison and Development
PA Cambridge Economic Consultants	Barry Moore, Director
Reading University	Professor Paul Cheshire, Dept of Economics
	Professor Ian Gordon, Dept of Geography
University of California	Professor Peter Hall (corresponding member)
	Derek Gowling (corresponding Member)

and, as observers

Department of the Environment	Archie Buchanan, Controller, London Regional Office
Department of Transport	Jag Chadha, London Transportation Unit

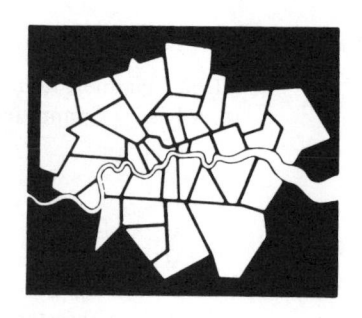

WORLD CITIES ARE
THOSE WHICH ARE CENTRES
OF GOVERNMENT, FINANCE AND BUSINESS,
CULTURE AND LEARNING, NATIONAL AND INTERNATIONAL
TRANSPORT, AND TELECOMMUNICATIONS AND
THE MEDIA. THEY COMPETE WITH
OTHER WORLD CITIES
IN THESE FIELDS.

World City Project, Consultants' Brief, October 1990

London's 33 Planning Authorities
LPAC'S LOGO

FOREWORD

For over a thousand years, London has been building a unique role as a world city. As we look forward to the 21st Century we are proud of the part which the organisations we represent take in our city's life. We acknowledge the need to review London's place in the international economy – and how this affects the people who live, work or visit here; or are customers for the services and goods we provide for the world.

We believe that a strategic approach is important in helping to create wealth, employment and income, sustaining and improving the quality of life and environment in the capital, and providing the infrastructure to enable this to happen.

In recognition of this, we commissioned Coopers & Lybrand Deloitte with a team of other consultants to investigate London's future competitiveness as a world city, and how this can be sustained and enhanced. Their analysis is set in a social and economic context, and considers how we can learn from the successes and failures of other world cities like New York, Tokyo, Paris and Berlin.

This book sets out to inform the debate on the urban policies needed to enable London to continue to evolve as a successful world city. It considers how they can best be agreed and implemented. We invite all those who care for our city to respond to our initiative by positive participation in the debate.

BARONESS HAMWEE OF RICHMOND UPON THAMES
Chairman of the London Planning Advisory Committee

BRIAN JENKINS
Lord Mayor of London

DAME SHIRLEY PORTER
Lord Mayor of Westminster

DAVID HARDY
Chairman of the London Docklands Development Corporation

BRIAN MATCHAM
Deputy Chief Executive, London Arts Board

C.W.R. NEWTON
Chairman of London Transport

November 1991

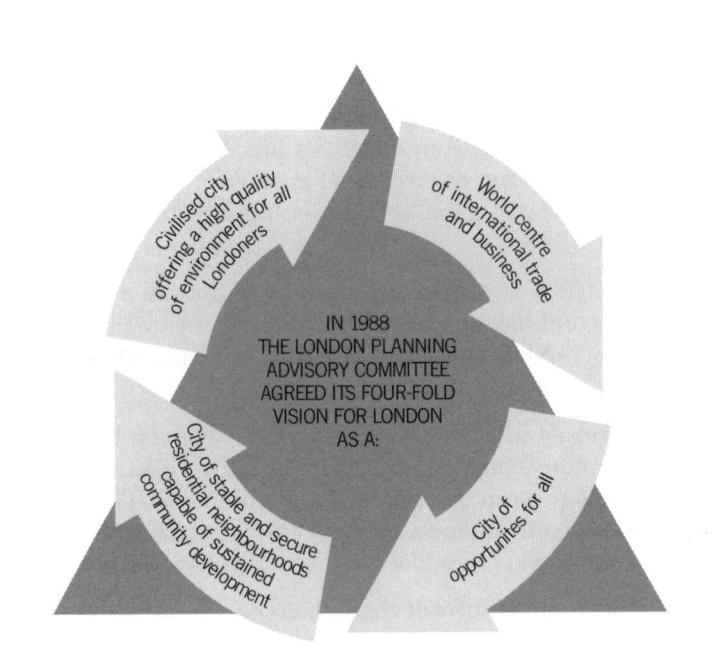

IN 1988
THE LONDON PLANNING
ADVISORY COMMITTEE
AGREED ITS FOUR-FOLD
VISION FOR LONDON
AS A:

- Civilised city offering a high quality of environment for all Londoners
- World centre of international trade and business
- City of opportunites for all
- City of stable and secure residential neighbourhoods capable of sustained community development

PREFACE

MARTIN SIMMONS
LPAC Chief Planner
Chairman of the Project Steering Group and Advisory Panel

The London Planning Advisory Committee (LPAC) is the only official London-wide forum for addressing planning and development issues. It was established under the Local Government Act 1985 which, in abolishing the Greater London Council, created a new planning system for the capital. The Committee has three functions: first, to advise the London Boroughs on matters of common planning and transport interest; secondly, to advise the Government on the Borough's common views on these matters, and as requested; and thirdly, to liaise on behalf of London with the wider South-East region, mainly through the work of the South East Regional Planning Conference (SERPLAN).

Its first main task was to advise the Government on the strategic planning framework considered necessary London-wide. The Committee agreed this, with all-party support, in Autumn 1988. At its heart was a Four-fold Vision for London, from which was derived 33 interlinked objectives and 132 policies to achieve them.

Following this, it became clear that London's future role as a world city was a matter of general concern to a wide spectrum of involved London opinion. There was, however, no technical work being undertaken on a broad co-ordinated basis to consider what London could or should do to sustain and enhance its position in an increasingly competitive world, or what could be learnt from other world cities' successes or failures. The Committee therefore agreed that a research project should be mounted, using its Four-fold Vision as the starting point, that the work should be carried out by consultants, and that other co-sponsors and supporters contributing financial support and work in kind should be sought. This book is the outcome of the consultants' work; their Report of Studies will also be published.

It is inevitable with a brief as wide as they were given, with a programme as short as twelve months, and with a very limited budget, that the consultants have had to take a very strictly focused approach to the work. There was much to be learnt from work being carried out by others – both in London and in other World Cities. This was often difficult to focus into a single picture, and there was a problem in compiling directly comparable information. But I believe that the consultants led by Coopers & Lybrand Deloitte have produced not only a fresh overview of the problems and opportunities, but more importantly have set out a basis for what London should do, in looking forward to the 21st century, to review its framework of urban policies.

I would like to thank all of those who have given us help, support and encouragement over the last year. This has not been an easy project – but it will have succeeded if it stimulates debate. If Londoners do not care, plan and work for our future, who else will?

THE FATE OF LONDON,
ONE OF THE GREATEST CITIES
THE WORLD HAS EVER KNOWN, WILL BE
ONE OF THE SIGNS BY WHICH POSTERITY WILL JUDGE US.

THERE IS A LONG ROAD TO TRAVEL BEFORE LONDON
CAN BECOME THE CITY SHE OUGHT TO BE.
THEREFORE LET US
START NOW.

*The Rt Hon Lord Latham, Leader of the London County Council
Foreword to 'The County of London Plan' 1943.*

Westminster Palace Clock Tower
JOANNE O'BRIAN, FORMAT

1
LONDON: WORLD CITY

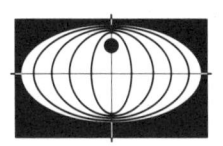

London 2000. To a greater or lesser degree, the turn into the third millennium seems set to colour our thinking until the close of the century. Whether we like it or not, the approach of the 21st century encourages reflections on the past and anticipations of almost every aspect of life in the future – including the life and times of cities in general and our capital city in particular. This seems an appropriate juncture at which to assess London's strengths and weaknesses, the lessons of the past and the prospects for the city in the year 2000 and beyond.

While a caprice of the calendar has made this a natural moment for such an assessment, social and economic considerations have lent urgency to the task. The year 2000 holds resonances for a new era, but in practice it is likely to be 1992 which marks the real turning point in the future development of Europe and its cities. The full implications of the Single European Market in 1992 and of the changes taking place on the European Community's northern and eastern boundaries are far from certain. However, it is clear that London cannot risk losing its international competitive position for want of an appreciation of the strategic planning options which might help sustain and enhance it. It is the intention of our work to provide insights which will assist in the development of such options and in the process describe and establish London as a world city with few equals.

The future development of cities

This assessment of the capital comes at a turning point in our perceptions of cities in general and London in particular. For the best part of three decades, commentators have predicted the death of the city. Initially such views appeared to be supported by the decline of inner city populations, decaying and under-resourced infrastructures, and a dispersal of economic and cultural activity to the regions. As New York City lurched into bankruptcy at the end of the 1970s and again staggered at the end of the 1980s, a death knell seemed to sound across the collective urban landscape. As Peter Sellars, the opera director and film maker, has said: "New York is the capital of the world. But they're dimming the lights on Broadway by 25 per cent and the Mayor is cutting 29,000 municipal jobs. Fun City just isn't fun any more".

These days, however, such proclamations of doom appear for London at least outdated and uninformed. While none would argue that the problems have disappeared, the stabilisation or growth of urban populations coupled with a growing appreciation of the central role played by cities in the economic and cultural life of a nation have encouraged the view that cities should be supported and developed. And positively planned rather than simply resigned to decline. In addition, after thirty years of population fall and radical physical and economic restructuring, London's economy is somewhat stronger than it was during the 1960s and 1970s. Its potential as an international capital of finance, knowledge, the arts and tourism, and as the gateway to the British economy, has probably never been greater this century. English is rapidly strengthening its position as the primary global language.

London remains the country's principal centre of government, higher education, retailing, arts, publishing, advertising and international and national communications. Furthermore, the city boasts a rich cultural and multi-ethnic diversity, a population which, given adequate housing, education and training, has the potential to take the capital and the country into a leading role in an economically and politically reformed Europe.

Since the rest of the world shows no sign of sitting back while London girds its resources for the 21st century, it is essential that we know and learn from the competition; that we consider the capital's strengths and weaknesses alongside those of other world cities like New York and Tokyo, alongside major European centres such as Paris, Frankfurt and Berlin. This book is an attempt to establish the foundations for such an assessment.

In our analysis, we felt that it was important to adopt a holistic approach which avoided consideration of only those factors which have a direct bearing on economic activity. In other words, any useful analysis of London's standing as a world city would also have to include an evaluation of those areas which have an indirect effect on economic performance – factors such as the quality of life, social framework and environment of the capital. We have assessed not only the objective facts, but also how they are perceived.

London's competitors

Liberalisation of economic activities in Eastern Europe, radical changes in the USSR and German reunification are certain to have a considerable impact on the international competitive climate. The effect of such developments on the movement of people and goods and the competition to provide services between Britain and the rest of Europe will be augmented by the opening of the Channel Tunnel and subsequent improvements to cross-Channel transport in the course of the decade. The opening up of the world, both capitalist and formerly communist, developed or developing, oriental and occidental may well provide a single service global market for goods and services.

Thus while the impact of 1992 may still be uncertain, it seems clear that anticipated changes in the competitive climate will pose both a threat to and opportunity for some of London's major exporting activities. An obvious strength and target for London's competitors is the pre-eminence of its financial centre – the City – in the West-European time-zone, a dominance which is already being eroded by competition from Paris, Frankfurt and Amsterdam. One of the main aims of this study is to provide an analysis which will illuminate London's potential to exploit its strengths and the changes in its wider environment and strengthen its competitive position in the longer term. In this respect, we must take note of the kind of strategies currently being put in place by other world cities.

On the one hand, New York, Paris and Tokyo are already exploring ways and means of enhancing their positions in the global economy. On the other hand, European cities are trying positively to take over London's role as an international centre for finance and business, and mounting an assault in the fields of communications, culture and tourism. For example, the main objective behind the Ile de France 2000 project is to enable Paris to lend substance to its claim to be "the economic and cultural capital of Europe".

Although other cities are already taking steps to ensure their economic future in the global market, our studies have concluded that at present London has few competitors as the pre-eminent global city. At the leading edge of the opposition, both Tokyo and New York are particularly afflicted by problems of scale compounded by a somewhat inhibiting national insularity in the former and seemingly intractable financial difficulties in the latter. As far as Europe is concerned, to compete with London, other cities must grapple with either significant internal adjustments – as is the case for Frankfurt and Berlin with German reunification – or the expense and upheaval inherent in the drive from national to truly global status – as is the case with Paris, Frankfurt and Milan. The world city of the future must secure the advantages of global command and creativity. It is our intention to examine just how well London succeeds in each of these areas.

In any study of this kind, it is all too easy to allow the facts, figures and analysis to smother the reality of the city as experienced by its residents and visitors. London is not just a concatenation of brick, stone, glass, steel and asphalt; or businesses and services; or a shopping list of problems and opportunities; but a living, breathing and dynamic community of people and their environment. At times exasperating, at others exciting, London can only ever be partially captured by or understood through the abstractions of research. In the words of Peter Hall "The first problem with London is to define it. London has never taken kindly to attempts at delimitation, whether by people who wanted to govern it, or by those who just wanted to fix it statistically: every time this was done London promptly outgrew its administration or its figures." Like all the cities discussed in this book, London refuses to stand still long enough to be captured in statistics.

Above all else, *London: World City* is a collection of questions, propositions and research through which we seek to describe London's status and future in the global community. This is not a book which pretends to provide all the answers. Our main concern is to offer a source of new and authoritative comparative data which will enable an informed assessment of the city and, in the process, illuminate the policy implications of such research. We have drawn widely on the work of others for our study. This will be apparent from the lengthy bibliography supporting this book. An even more extensive list of sources is available from the London Planning Advisory Committee who commissioned the study, together with reports on the detailed work carried out for it.

It is hoped that this portrait of our city will lay the foundations of a new agenda for London and initiate a debate about what needs to be done by the development of land-use transport and other policies, and the implementation of those policies in the broader context of their social and economic framework.

WHAT IS A WORLD CITY?

Academics have grappled with this question for the best part of a century. We should make it clear from the outset that it is a debate we shall touch upon but never systematically address. Our objective is to assess London's standing in the global community; to place its strengths and weaknesses alongside those of its competitors. Given that we argue the case for London as a world city, pragmatic rather than pedagogic reasoning compels us to identify other world cities with which it can be compared. In other words, in order to initiate our investigation, we were obliged to form a set of assumptions which would be tested in the course of the analysis.

In 1951, Patrick Geddes, the pioneer of city planning, noted that certain cities conducted a disproportionate percentage of the world's business. This observation has been elaborated by Friedmann and Woolff who describe "the spatial articulation of the emerging world system of production and markets through a global network of cities". London's role as a world city was firmly reflected in Abercrombie's thinking in 1943 and in the Greater London Development Plan of 1976.

Economists maintain that world cities are centres for the concentration and control of the world's active capital and serve as "banking and financial centres, administrative headquarters, centres of ideological control. ..." This idea is vividly brought to life by Ross and Trachte who describe cities like London, New York and Tokyo as "the headquarters of the great banks and multinational corporations. From these headquarters radiate a web of electronic communications and air travel corridors along which capital is deployed and redeployed, and through which the fundamental decisions about the structure of the world economy are sent. In these global cities work – but not necessarily reside – the cadre of officials and their staff who, in their persons and their official capacities, embody the concentration and centralization of capital that now characterises the global system."

So world cities are about concentrations of capital and the generation of wealth. But they are also about command and control. The Agnelli Foundation describes such cities as "'the brains' of the European urban system", the concentration of economic, financial and industrial command centres in a limited number of metropolitan areas. The Foundation characterises such cities as having an "infrastructure of the highest level, centres for the production and accumulation of knowledge."

LONDON: WORLD CITY

Lewis Mumford once likened big cities to museums where "every variety of human function, every experiment in human association, every technological process, every mode of architecture and planning can be found within its crowded area". Although the image is compelling, successful cities are *not* museums – they do not need to embody such variety. World cities may control the global economy, but there is no reason why they themselves should play a leading participatory role across the full spectrum of economic endeavour. World cities need to specialise to capitalise on their strengths.

In recent years, developments in communications technology and low-cost, high-speed travel have reduced the need for concentration of diverse economic activity and increased the choices open to businesses. It was this situation, combined with the decentralisation of activity brought about by changing international specialisation, which led to the prospect of urban decline in the 1960s and 1970s and created urban problems for those left behind.

The much heralded demise of the urban economy was premature. There emerged a new role for world cities – or, more precisely, the resurrection of an old role. The Agnelli Foundation offers a partial description of this role when it defines "pure global command cities" as those in which there are command functions but no industrial or production system. Paul Cheshire argues that the functions of the contemporary world city "are likely to be much closer to those they had before the industrial revolution – as commercial and administrative centres, as cultural centres in the broadest sense of cultural, and as providers of higher level services and urban amenities".

While we have yet to formulate a precise definition of what we mean by a world city, it is apparent that the attractions of such a place are essentially two-fold. A world city must serve as a place in which international business can be conducted efficiently and operate as a nodal point for the co-ordination and control of global economic activity. In addition, the attractions of such cities must be world-class; they must offer desirable residential areas and diverse and cosmopolitan cultural activity which satisfy, not just the needs of residents or people from other parts of the country, but also those of the international community.

Commentators like Panayotis Soldatos, the director general of the Institute for the Study of International Cities in Montreal, have adopted the "checklist" approach to identifying world cities, citing a minimum of characteristics a metropolis must possess in order to achieve international status. For example, Soldatos suggests that the media of a global city "must have an international presence and/or audience abroad" and that its population must be characterised by its "international composition". Although we considered this approach too inflexible for our purposes (not least because the two conditions cited exclude any major Japanese city from consideration), certain important world city attributes can be identified.

It should be clear that a world city will have the capacity to adjust to the changing demands of international wealth creation. In the past, such flexibility tended to be associated with a city's size, but today – as a result of structural changes in regional and global economies which will be discussed in subsequent chapters – smaller cities have the capacity to compete for global markets and status.

World cities also must be a source of employment both for people who prefer or are obliged to live outside the city, but also for those whose residential choice is constrained, for whatever reason, to the inner city. The successful world city must remain an attractive place to live and work across all social and ethnic groups and for workers from all over the world.

Finally, world cities must attend more closely than ever to the quality of life they offer. With the declining social and economic imperative of centralisation, quality of life becomes a more important variable in the equation, yielding advantage in the competition for world city status to those cities whose social and environmental fabric is less constrained by the requirements of another age.

Given that this is an ambitious study with almost unlimited scope for intriguing but ultimately distracting enquiry, we decided from the outset to constrain our investigation within a conceptual framework based on a handful of simple organising principles. This framework is illustrated in Figure 1.1.

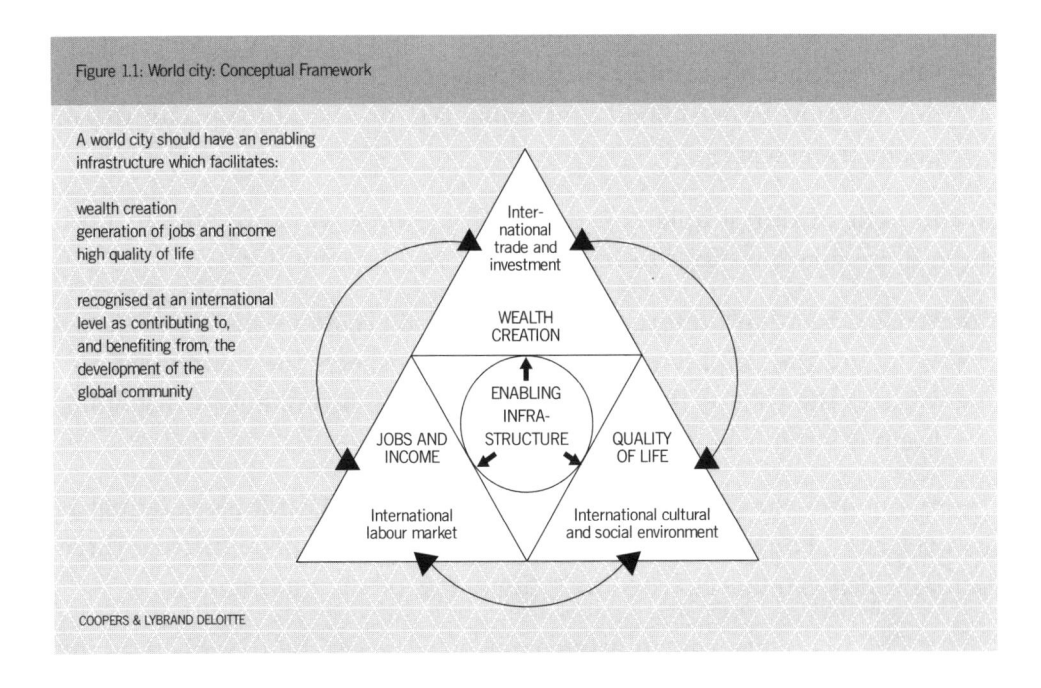

Figure 1.1: World city: Conceptual Framework

A world city should have an enabling infrastructure which facilitates:

wealth creation
generation of jobs and income
high quality of life

recognised at an international level as contributing to, and benefiting from, the development of the global community

[Diagram showing triangular framework with WEALTH CREATION at top, JOBS AND INCOME at bottom left, QUALITY OF LIFE at bottom right, and ENABLING INFRASTRUCTURE in the centre. External labels: International trade and investment, International labour market, International cultural and social environment.]

COOPERS & LYBRAND DELOITTE

Firstly, we have taken the view that there are essentially three interlinked and interdependent components critical to the sustainability of a city – its ability to create wealth; the capacity to generate jobs and income for residents; and an environment which offers a high quality of life, work and leisure. Secondly, we decided that for a city to work effectively, there has to be a balance between these interrelated components, since a significant weakness in one might well jeopardise the sustainable growth of the city as a whole. Thirdly, it seemed apparent that to merit world city status, each of the components of an individual city and the balance between them needed to bear comparison at the highest international level – a relative weakness in one and/or a relative imbalance between them could jeopardise world city status. Finally, we concluded that it was likely that the growth and maintenance of world city status is likely to be enhanced if each component grows in a balanced and interactive manner. This then establishes the ground rules of our study. At the centre of our investigation lies a single question.

- What is London's future competitiveness as a world city and how can this position be sustained and enhanced by the appropriate urban policy framework?

In the light of our simple conceptual framework we were able to raise three subsidiary questions to be addressed by our enquiry:

- What is London's international capacity to create wealth?
- What are the employment and income prospects for Londoners?
- What is the role of the quality of life and environment in sustaining London's status as a world city?

These inquiries comprise the core of our analysis of London's potential as a world city. They are augmented by consideration of a further three factors which can be regarded as refinements of the questions.

The first concerns an assessment of what can be described as the "enabling infrastructure" – the networks of transport and communications; the cost and availability both of property (public and private) and the provision of education and training. In short, the raw physical, social and cultural material which enables a city to work and evolve. Second, we must consider the global context of our enquiry – how our city is perceived by and what it contributes to the global community. Is there a sense in which a world city may need to be engaged in a mutually supportive relationship with the global community? Would it contribute to our understanding of the requirements of a world city to consider the ways in which such a city might disengage itself from the national economy and establish a separate relationship with the global community? The final factor, which is essentially an extension of our last point, centres on the recognition that a world city should operate effectively across a broad range of spatial dimensions – in other words, globally, nationally, regionally and at local levels.

It is important that a world city commands a significant position in the global market. This refers primarily to the scale of control of global economic activity rather than the holding of a commanding *participatory* position across a broad range of productive enterprise. But this is by no means an exclusive criterion. For example, there are regions of the world which cities can come to command and, as a result, achieve global status. In this respect, the Single European Market will have important implications for all existing and aspirant world cities.

In order to command global or large regional markets, the world city will need to secure economies of scale by making efficient use of its economic hinterland. We shall elaborate this point in the next chapter on wealth creation. For the moment, it should simply be noted that such a requirement might well imply the decentralisation of certain types of economic activity in order that the limited space of the city and particularly its centre be used more efficiently. However, it is equally important that a world city should encourage the *recentralisation* of those activities which gain a competitive edge from a city centre location. Without this recentralisation, the core of a city can degenerate – a process which could be observed in many urban economies during the 1960s and 1970s. Of course, the recentralisation of the appropriate enterprises will only be viable in cities which are able to provide the labour, services and infrastructure capable of sustaining such activities.

WHICH WORLD CITIES?

In order to make the study manageable, it was clearly necessary to limit the number of world city contenders with which London had to be compared.

The historical and political development of many significant cities provide obvious grounds for exclusion. For example, the economic foundations of cities in what used to be the Eastern Bloc differ so radically from those of the West as to render comparisons almost meaningless. Cities in the Third World can be excluded for similar reasons. For example, Mexico City might be one of the largest cities in the world, but at present its ability to command global markets is virtually non-existent.

To a large extent, the selection of cities was based on our own *a priori* judgement. It was obviously impractical to attempt a selection on the basis of all the world city attributes outlined above. In practice, the application of such a process would amount to the completion of the study! Instead, we based the selection on an approximate assessment of how world cities were positioned in relation to three key features of their global performance – their status as centres of financial and commercial activity; communication and administration; and culture and knowledge. We imagined these attributes as three over-lapping templates shown in Figure 1.2.

As Figure 1.2 illustrates, lying on the area of overlap – and consequently satisfying all three of the selected key world city attributes – were London, Tokyo, New York and Paris. Given that our intention was to assess the current status and *potential* of London against other world cities, it seemed shortsighted to ignore impending changes in the global economy – for example, the development of the Single European Market – which, over the next ten to fifteen years, might well bring other players into the area of overlap. With this in mind, we included Frankfurt and Berlin in our selection (although it was clear that recent changes in Germany would, especially in the case of Berlin, make comparisons difficult).

As we shall have cause to regret in the course of this analysis, international comparative data are often extremely difficult or even impossible to obtain. Statistical information is normally designed, collated and presented to serve national rather than international comparative purposes. In order to facilitate our study and make a significant contribution to the debate, we commissioned our own market research survey carried out by Richard Ellis to address a variety of issues related to the

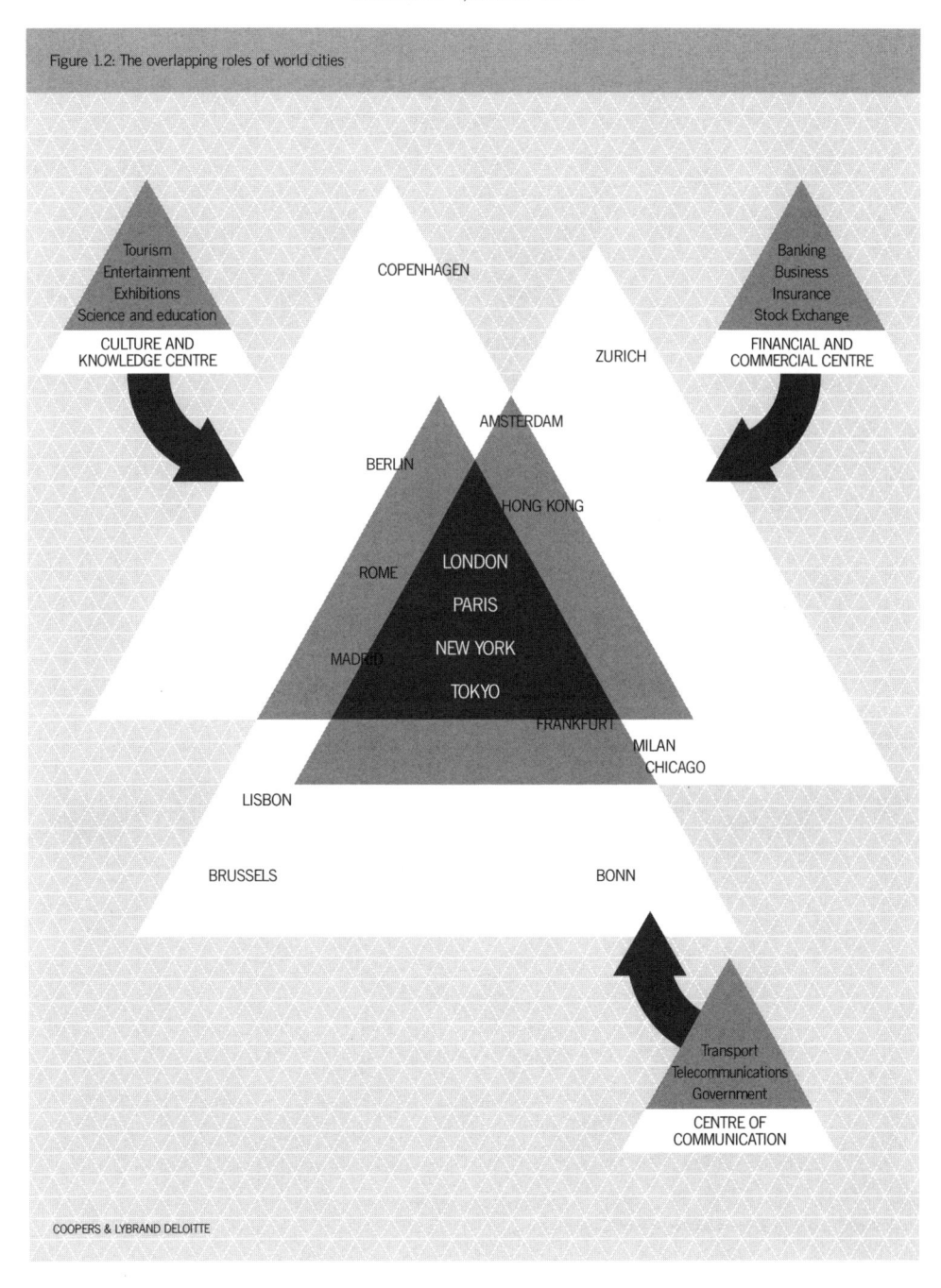

LONDON: WORLD CITY

Figure 1.2: The overlapping roles of world cities

Tourism
Entertainment
Exhibitions
Science and education
CULTURE AND KNOWLEDGE CENTRE

Banking
Business
Insurance
Stock Exchange
FINANCIAL AND COMMERCIAL CENTRE

Transport
Telecommunications
Government
CENTRE OF COMMUNICATION

COPENHAGEN
ZURICH
AMSTERDAM
BERLIN
HONG KONG
ROME
LONDON
PARIS
NEW YORK
TOKYO
MADRID
FRANKFURT
MILAN
CHICAGO
LISBON
BRUSSELS
BONN

COOPERS & LYBRAND DELOITTE

LONDON: WORLD CITY MOVING INTO THE 21ST CENTURY

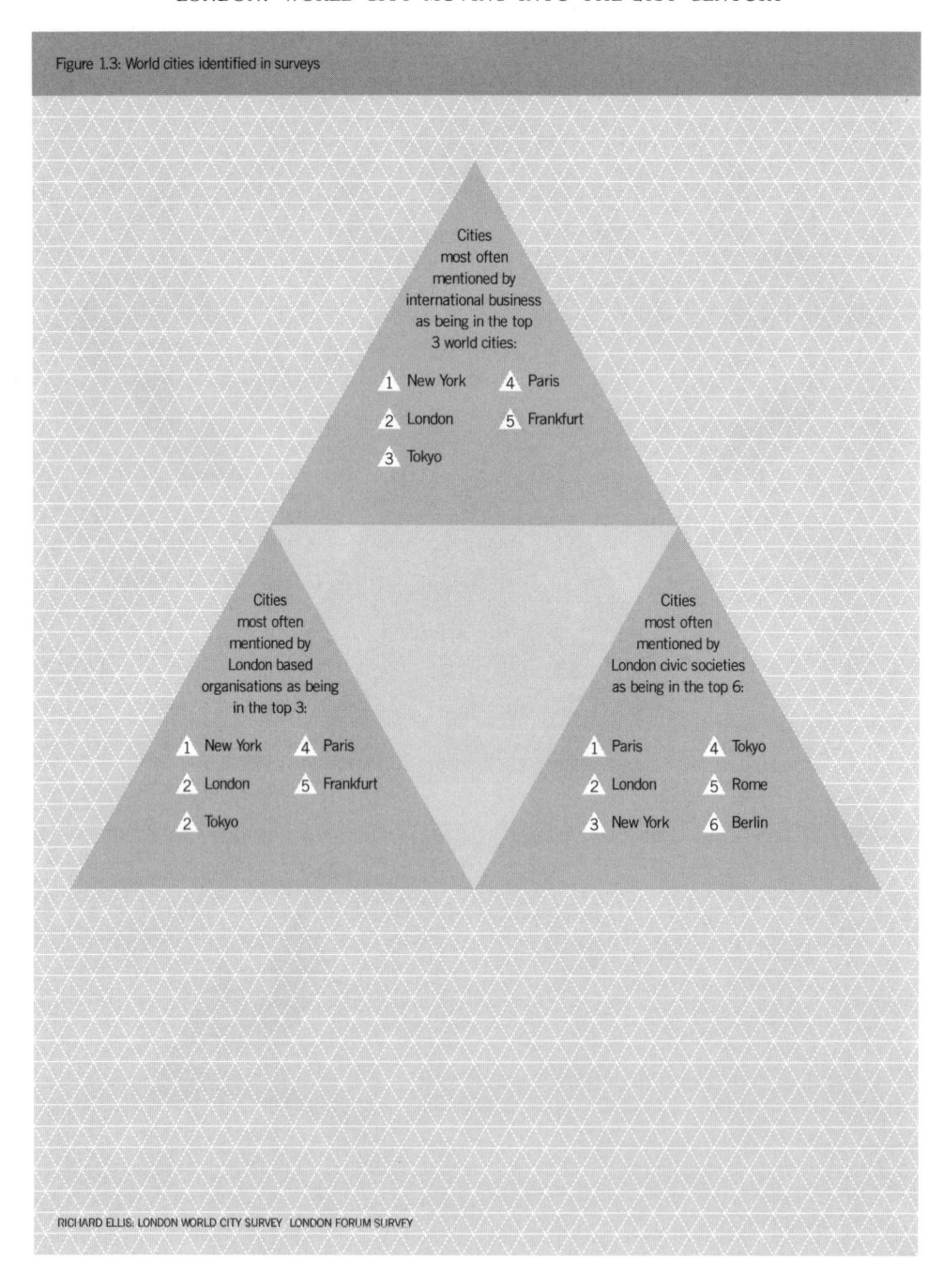

Figure 1.3: World cities identified in surveys

Cities most often mentioned by international business as being in the top 3 world cities:
1. New York
2. London
3. Tokyo
4. Paris
5. Frankfurt

Cities most often mentioned by London based organisations as being in the top 3:
1. New York
2. London
2. Tokyo
4. Paris
5. Frankfurt

Cities most often mentioned by London civic societies as being in the top 6:
1. Paris
2. London
3. New York
4. Tokyo
5. Rome
6. Berlin

RICHARD ELLIS: LONDON WORLD CITY SURVEY LONDON FORUM SURVEY assessment of London's competitiveness as a world city. The survey targeted two specific groups of respondents. The first group comprised key decision makers within the global headquarters of major multinational companies – half of the sample of 156 companies were based in London, the others in the world cities of New York, Tokyo, Paris, Frankfurt and Berlin. The second group was made up from senior executives in thirty London-based organisations which represent interests critically affected by London's status as a world city. In addition, another survey approached a range of London's civic and amenity societies which were questioned through the London Forum. A third survey carried out by the London Chamber of Commerce examined the attitudes and perceptions of a hundred foreign banks based in London.

Figure 1.3 illustrates the cities identified as having global status by the respondents to the first two of our surveys.

The results strongly confirm our initial selection of world cities. New York, London and Tokyo were placed amongst the top world cities by over 70 per cent of respondents. And, just below the front-runners, Paris and Frankfurt were considered to be up and coming contenders for world city status. A third tier of outsider candidates comprised Berlin, Los Angeles, Brussels and Singapore.

While their own economic and commercial strengths vary to some considerable extent, in terms of size and their control of global markets London, New York and Tokyo are definitively first league players. Frankfurt and, to a lesser degree, Paris fall into the second tier of cities with a claim to global status. Certainly, in terms of population (as shown in Figure 1.4) both Berlin and especially Frankfurt are considerably smaller than the other cities in our sample. As we have already suggested, size *per se* is not a defining characteristic of global status. Nevertheless, given the disparity between the populations of the cities in our sample, it is useful to bear in mind their relative dimensions when considering the implications of statistical comparisons to our analysis.

While the relative size of city populations may, on occasion, have implications for our analysis, few of the international businesses and

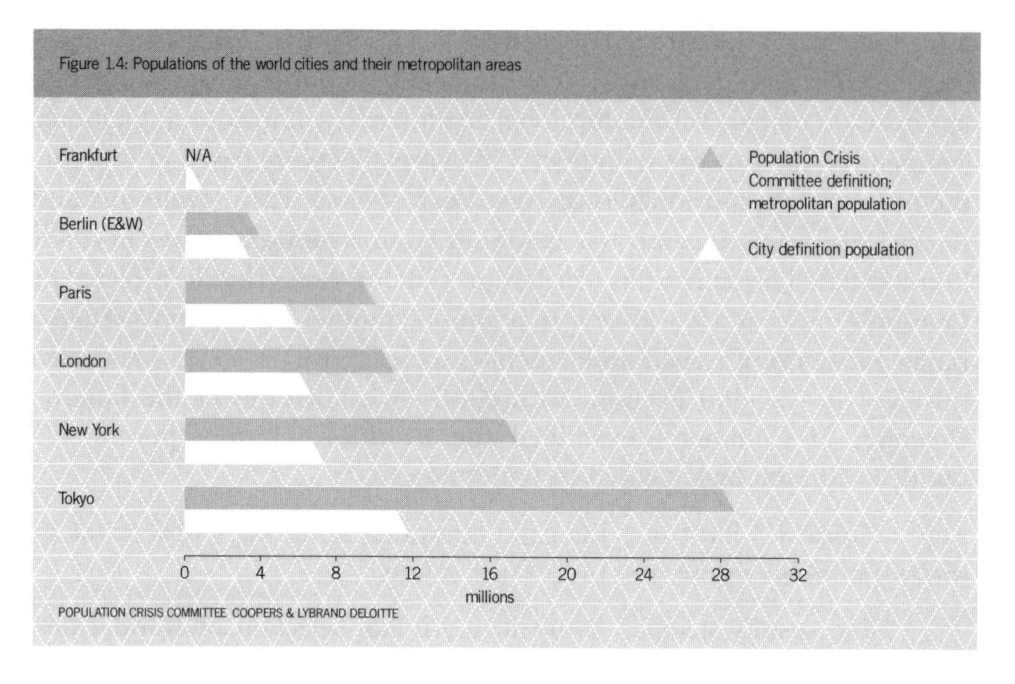

Figure 1.4: Populations of the world cities and their metropolitan areas

- Frankfurt: N/A
- Berlin (E&W)
- Paris
- London
- New York
- Tokyo

▲ Population Crisis Committee definition; metropolitan population
△ City definition population

POPULATION CRISIS COMMITTEE COOPERS & LYBRAND DELOITTE

London organisations in our surveys considered a large, well-balanced population to be a critical feature of a world city. However, as Figure 1.5 illustrates, the majority of our survey respondents considered that wealth creation, and the infrastructure of transport and communications which supports it, to be the overwhelming important characteristics of a successful world city. More than a third (but less than half) of respondents rated access to large markets and intra-city mobility as critical attributes as well as the status of the city as a world player and the strength of its national economy.

Because of the weight attached by survey respondents to the wealth creation attributes of world cities, we will began our analysis in the next chapter with wealth creation. We will follow this with Chapters 3, 4 and 5 devoted respectively to jobs and income, the quality of life and the enabling infrastructure in world cities. Chapter 6 will review the prospects

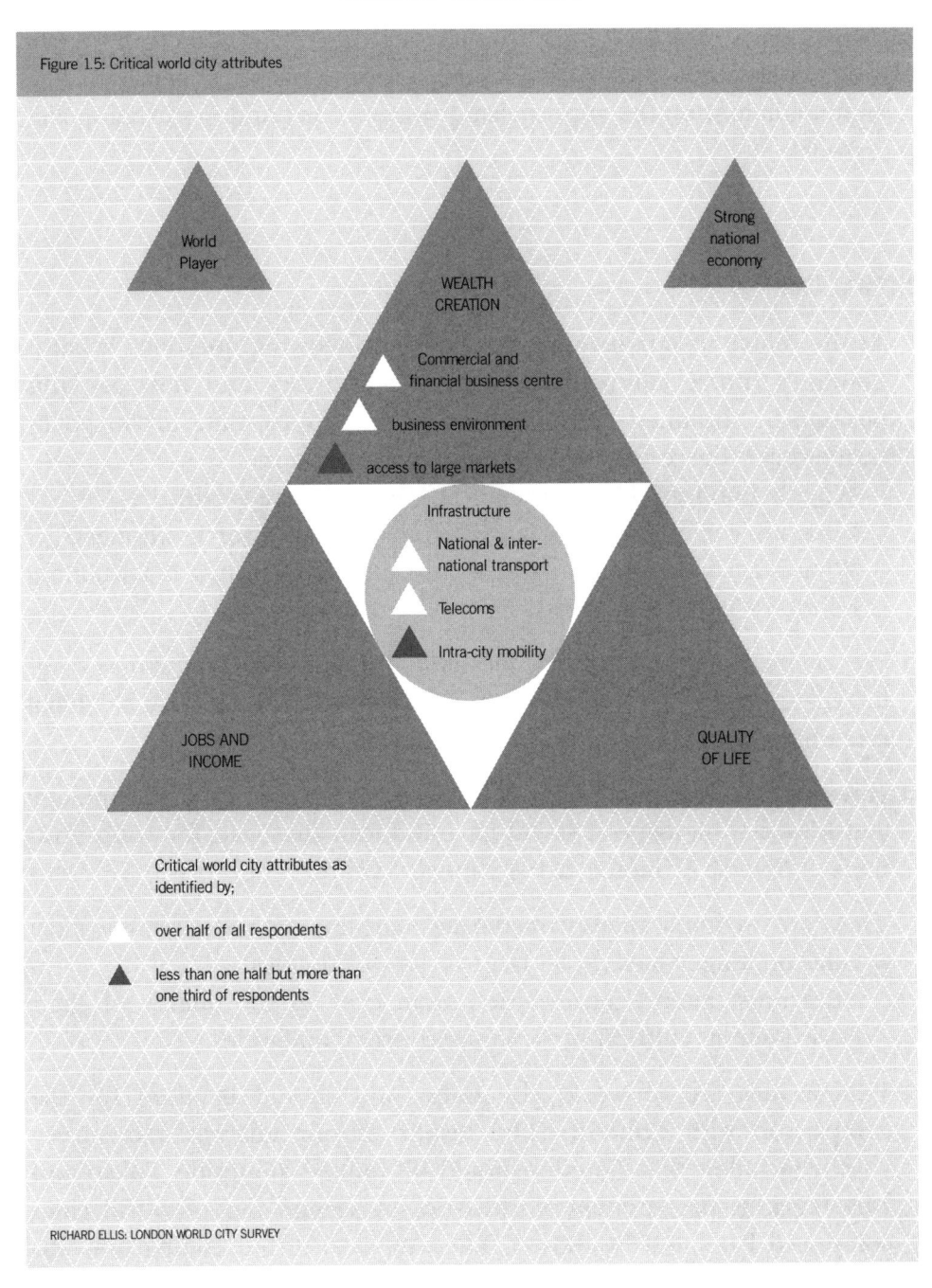

LONDON: WORLD CITY

Figure 1.5: Critical world city attributes

- World Player
- Strong national economy

WEALTH CREATION
- △ Commercial and financial business centre
- △ business environment
- ▲ access to large markets

Infrastructure
- △ National & international transport
- △ Telecoms
- ▲ Intra-city mobility

JOBS AND INCOME

QUALITY OF LIFE

Critical world city attributes as identified by:

△ over half of all respondents

▲ less than one half but more than one third of respondents

RICHARD ELLIS: LONDON WORLD CITY SURVEY

17

for world cities and the policy framework adopted in each to influence urban development. The final chapter will present our conclusions and recommendations on the appropriate priorities for London's urban policy framework.

SUMMARY

- At the centre of our investigation lies the following question: What is London's future competitiveness as a world city and how can this position be sustained and enhanced by the appropriate urban policy framework? There were three subsidiary questions:
  - What is London's international capacity to create wealth?
  - What are the employment and income prospects for Londoners?
  - What is the role of the quality of life and environment in sustaining London's status as a world city?

- We defined world cities as locations for the efficient conduct of international business and for the co-ordination and control of global economic activity.

- However, we recognised that advances in communications technology and low-cost, high-speed travel have reduced the need for concentrations of diverse economic activity in world cities.

- There are two implications from the declining imperative for centralisation:
  - cities no longer have to be large to be world cities;
  - cities must attend more closely than ever to the quality of their environment, cultural provision and urban amenities.

- Which cities are of world city status and should be used for the comparison with London? The results of our analysis and survey work concluded that London should be ranked alongside Tokyo and New York as pre-eminent world cities. A second tier of world cities comprised Paris and Frankfurt. The wild card in our comparison was Berlin.

☐ Our survey made it clear that, although the economic imperatives for centralisation in world cities may have declined, the view of international business respondents was still that the critical attributes of a world city were its wealth creation capacity and the infrastructure of transport and communications which supported it.

THE CITY'S
STRENGTH HAS DEEP
HISTORICAL ROOTS, BUT ONLY
RESPONSE TO CHANGE WILL SAFEGUARD ITS
FUTURE. CITY ACTIVITIES NOW OCCUPY APPROACHING
TEN PER CENT OF THE UK LABOUR FORCE, AND CONTRIBUTE
MORE THAN TEN PER CENT OF GROSS DOMESTIC PRODUCT. IT IS
ONE OF THE BANK OF ENGLAND'S RESPONSIBILITIES TO PROMOTE
LONDON AND THE UK AS A PLACE TO CONDUCT INTERNATIONAL
BUSINESS — BUT EACH FINANCIAL CENTRE WILL
HAVE TO WORK HARDER FOR ITS SHARE
OF GLOBAL BUSINESS.

Robin Leigh Pemberton, Governor of the Bank of England, July 1991

The Bank of England, Royal Exchange and Stock Exchange
BANK OF ENGLAND

2
WEALTH CREATION

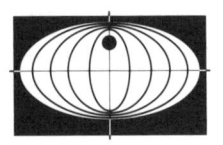

The continuing ability to create wealth in world markets is one of the key factors in sustaining a world city's development and growth. Indeed, it was the view of the majority of respondents to our survey that the attributes of wealth creation, coupled with the infrastructure that supports them, were critical to the durability of a city's global status.

Wealth creation is not the preserve of manufacturing or financial services, but also derives, for example, from leisure and recreational services, cultural facilities and the provision of education. It is also important to bear in mind that the wealth creation activities of a world city must be proven and sustained in global markets.

WEALTH CREATION IN WORLD CITIES

A distinctive characteristic of world cities is that they host businesses and activities which are significant in world terms and derive their competitive advantage from being in a world city. This sounds tautological. But then the advantages of a world city location come precisely from the network of interlocking and supportive firms and organisations whose business and services are linked in supplying the world market. There is also considerable prestige associated with a world city location, along with access to international communications and transport, and the convenience of face-to-face interaction in a community of mutual interests.

These advantages are by no means immutable. Technological change and global economic developments modify the benefits in respect of particular activities. For example, the advantage of locating in a world city location has diminished for sectors like manufacturing and wholesale distribution which are space and land-intensive and involve the bulk handling of goods. This has come about as a consequence of changes in the economics of location and from the shifting patterns of international trade and investment.

Such transformations emphasise the need for flexible response in order for a world city to survive. This will emerge as a recurring theme throughout our analysis. World cities must have the capacity to adjust to changing world conditions and to competition within them for resources of urban land, property and labour and for proximity to world markets. In the course of adjustment, cities will inevitably lose some sectors of activity to their hinterland, or even beyond. For the most part, such a process is an essential component of a world city's development and growth. But it should be noted that the loss of certain activities – especially those associated with headquarters and control functions – could be regarded as a threat to the long-term future of any world city.

So what has been the pattern of adjustment in our sample of world cities? Figures 2.1–2.4 present the change over the last twenty years in the shares of manufacturing, distribution and financial and business services in total employment in the world cities and the relative position in the late 1980s. The most notable trends are the decline of manufacturing's share of employment and the growth in services. London is distinguished by a particularly marked decline in manufacturing share and growth in the share of financial services in the 1980s. New York shares London's manufacturing decline. Tokyo has shown similar growth to London's in financial services.

Much can be learned from a search behind these statistics in an effort to identify the kind of activities which will continue to be located in the cities in our sample. This is easier to accomplish for some cities than

WEALTH CREATION

Figure 2.1: Changes in the share of manufacturing in total employment, 1970-1989 (1970= 100)

- Berlin
- Tokyo
- Ile de France
- Frankfurt
- Paris
- London
- New York

COOPERS & LYBRAND DELOITTE

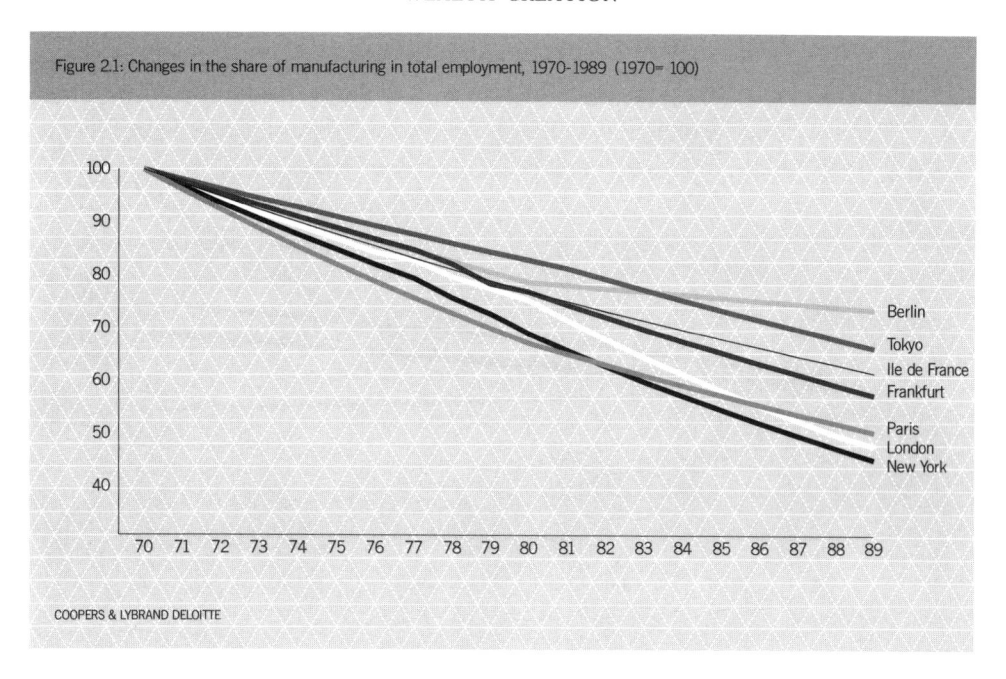

Figure 2.2: Changes in the share of distribution in total employment, 1970-1989 (1970= 100)

- London
- Tokyo
- Berlin
- Ile de France
- New York
- Frankfurt
- Paris

COOPERS & LYBRAND DELOITTE

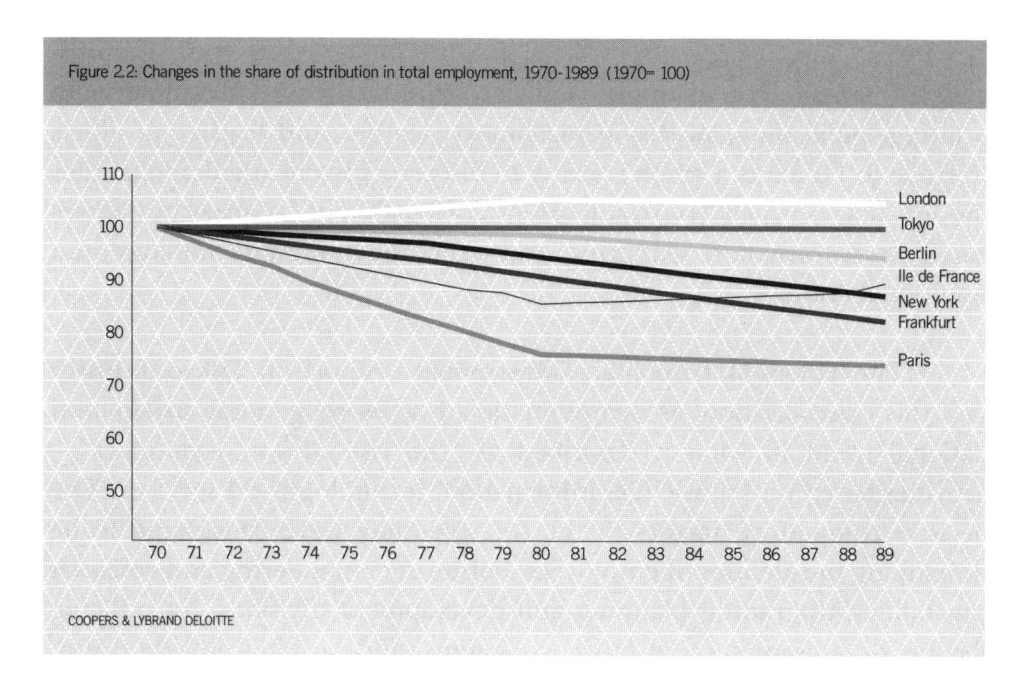

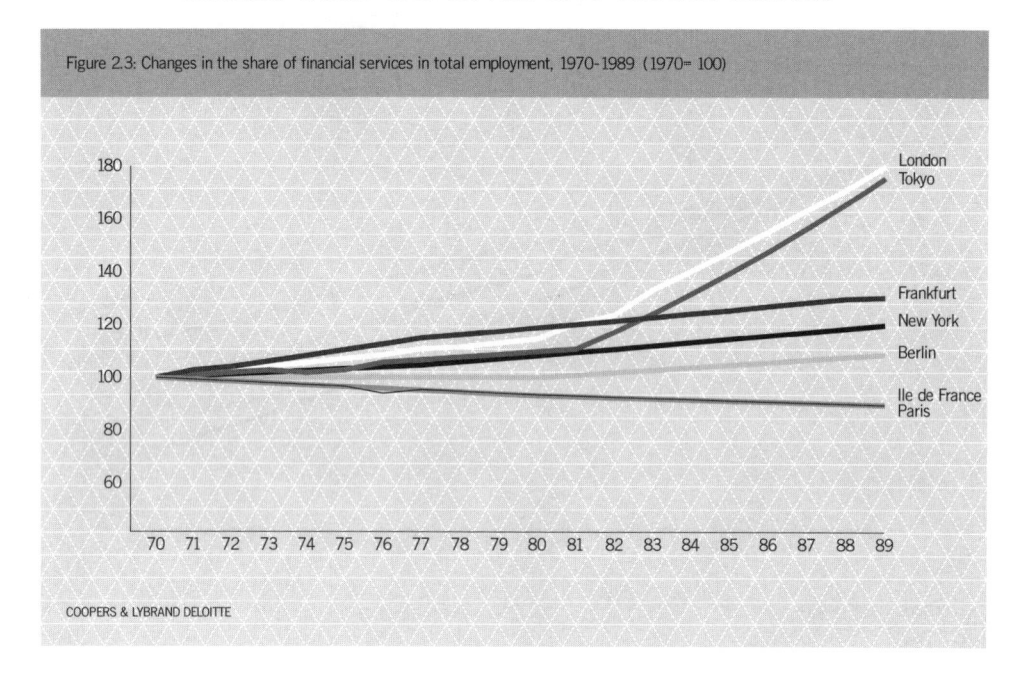

Figure 2.3: Changes in the share of financial services in total employment, 1970-1989 (1970= 100)

London
Tokyo
Frankfurt
New York
Berlin
Ile de France
Paris

COOPERS & LYBRAND DELOITTE

it is for others. For example, Tokyo's manufacturing specialisation in printing, publishing, precision machinery, leather and leather products (relative to Japan as a whole) is easy to discern. This neatly demonstrates the advantages which Tokyo still offers as a location to Japanese businesses based on information gathering and processing, high technology and traditional crafts.

The Tokyo Metropolitan Government's report on Tokyo industry saw this specialisation as symptomatic of a more general urban and national trend in what it described as "the rise of soft economics" – activities based on knowledge, information, technology and services. The decisive competitive factors in the soft economy were considered to be developing the abilities of employees, bolstering engineering and research capabilities, upgrading planning and development divisions, introducing flexible organisational and business systems, and tapping outside talent.

WEALTH CREATION

Figure 2.4: Sectoral share in total employment, late 1980s

MANUFACTURING
- Ile de France
- Paris
- Berlin
- Tokyo
- Frankfurt
- London
- New York

DISTRIBUTION
- Ile de France
- Paris
- Berlin
- Tokyo
- Frankfurt
- London
- New York

FINANCIAL AND BUSINESS SERVICES
- Ile de France
- Paris
- Berlin
- Tokyo
- Frankfurt
- London
- New York

COOPERS & LYBRAND DELOITTE: VARIOUS SOURCES

"In short," the report concluded, "the key is human ability and above all human creativity."

The Tokyo Metropolitan Government was confident that the city could offer many locational advantages in the "soft economy". With its intense concentration of population and companies, Tokyo forms not only an enormous market in its own right, but, in the words of the Tokyo Metropolitan Government, also provides a "greenhouse for fostering new businesses that could grow in no other soil." It provides the opportunity for face-to-face communication and information exchange which is likely to become ever more precious as communications technology advances, making access to information from electronic sources effectively common currency. Thus, at least as much as the size of its population or the absolute range of its economic activities, it is the fertility and flexibility of the Tokyo-style "greenhouse" which will determine the competitiveness and sustainability of a world city's economy.

The soft-economy vision for the world city is articulated most explicitly by the Tokyo Government but we can detect echoes of the same theme in pronouncements from other world cities.

In the French Government's promotion of the Paris-Ile de France region as "the political, financial, economic and cultural capital of France", the significance of the size of the home market is, once again, emphasised – 100 million residents in a radius of 500km. But, like the Tokyo Metropolitan Government, the French are keen to stress the agglomeration economies inherent in the soft-economy vision. Reference is made to growth and concentration of research and development personnel and facilities in the region and to the rapid spread of electronics, data processing, pharmacy and energy – sectors in which employment in the region has increased by more than 50 per cent in the last decade. But all the while the emphasis is on the concentration and flexibility of resources, the development of a fertile and innovative business environment.

In 1988 a report from New York's Regional Plan Association stressed the importance of a world-class knowledge base in the development of a global city's economy. Stigmatising that city's failure to develop major academic and research centres in the sciences, the report argued that "the city should begin now to establish such a technological centre, using the strengths of the city's universities and corporations. Handled properly, such an initiative should create an urban, 21st century version of California's Silicon Valley ..." All the recommendations pointed to the maintenance and development of New York as a preeminent information centre.

It seems clear also that Frankfurt's mayor is all too aware of the dangers of an over-reliance on the city's financial and business services sectors. "Frankfurt is not only a city of banks and fairs, but also a seat of important high-technology industries and firms. We should give special attention to this field in order not to be dependent exclusively on service activity."

The Commissioner for Economic Development of the City of Berlin is another who would probably align himself with the soft-economy vision set out by the Tokyo Metropolitan Government. In his introduction to the Berlin Economic Development Corporation's report on "Berlin: An Ideal Location for Business" (1991), he describes Berlin as "both the largest Germany industrial city and the greenest ... Its cultural attractions are second to none, and its location in the centre of Europe makes it a convenient place to conduct business and to perform research and development, whether in microelectronics and software, biogenetics or medical equipment, communications or environment."

In these declarations from the cities and in the broad statistical trends, we can see evidence of the perceived new urban agglomeration economies based on access to large markets, diversity and creativity. When we examined the specialisation of the Greater London economy relative to the UK as a whole in 1989, we found as might have been anticipated from Figures 2.1–2.4 the dominating influence of financial and business services. However, the pattern of specialisation of London *within* manufacturing (relative to the rest of the UK) was much the same as we observed for Tokyo – a mixture of high-technology manufacture (office machinery and electronic data processing equipment), craft based industry (leather goods) and information processing and dissemination (printing and publishing). So, on this basis, London appears to have a specialisation structure within manufacturing which could build on potential new agglomeration economies. However, London is different from the other world cities on two counts. First, the manufacturing sector is a very much smaller share of the London economy than in other world cities except New York. Second, there is no clearly defined wealth creation strategy articulated in or for London which integrates manufacturing into the soft-economy vision expressed for example by the Tokyo Metropolitan Government.

COMMAND AND CREATIVITY IN WORLD CITIES

To an outsider, a successful world city will appear as an urban economy which manages to accommodate external pressures and shocks smoothly and readily. In reality, we suggest that the secret of such an economy is that it is a dynamic combination of highly turbulent but mutually reinforcing activities. It is bolstered and battered by a wide range of determinants – local, regional, national and global – but in the final analysis growth and competitiveness depend on the capacity to achieve and sustain global command through scale and agglomeration economies and to maintain momentum and growth through creativity and innovation.

Global command

One of the characteristics of a world city is that it has attained the urban equivalent of an absolute critical mass. Scale is combined with close and productive networking of supply, subcontracting and intermediate services and production. Such a clustering of economic activity forms the basis of what we have referred to as agglomeration economies. It creates a significant market of itself whose needs must be met, a large pool of human resources and a flexible enterprise structure, all of which are crucial to an effective response to the unpredictable demands of global markets.

The durability of world cities will depend in part on the market they themselves create. Generally, such cities tend to occupy a dominant position within their national economies. For example, a business survey conducted by *The Economist* concluded that it was the existence of a large market within Tokyo itself (rather than global economic considerations), which influenced most companies to base themselves in the city. In the world city league table, Tokyo has the greatest dominance of its national economy, followed by London, Paris and New York. At present, partly a result of the postwar division of Germany and partly due to their limited economic portfolios, Frankfurt and Berlin dominate the German economy to a much lesser degree.

Any appreciation of a world city's ability both to generate and serve the scale of its own market needs must take account of the relationship between the central city area and its economic hinterland. The latter both provides a market and a source of labour, goods and services for the more centralised operations. At its best, the relationship with the hinterland expands the economies of scale and increases the dynamic potential of the city. At its worst, it can lead to diseconomies of scale and polarisation.

If we take population estimates for the wider metropolitan areas and relate them to the more narrowly defined city population figures, we can get some idea of the multiplier effect of the cities on their economic hinterland. On that basis, Tokyo and New York have the largest multiplier effect (a ratio of metropolitan to city populations of about 2.4) with London and Paris in a second category (a ratio of 1.6) and the German cities in the third category (a ratio of not much more than 1.0).

It can be inferred that Tokyo and New York are potentially in the best position to achieve scale economies through effective allocation of resources between the cities and their hinterland. However, with any inadequacy in infrastructure and particularly transport provision, both cities are also potential victims of the most disruptive diseconomies of scale. By contrast, the German cities seem less likely to incur such damaging diseconomies.

In the years ahead, the concept of a physically identifiable economic hinterland is likely to mutate with the emergence of what amounts to an "electronic" hinterland. In some sectors the spread of hi-tech communications will enable the development of a new kind of hinterland which will have less to do with its geographical relationship to the city, and particularly its centre, and more to do with time zones, common language and business and other relationships.

A further aspect of the command features of world cities is their combination for the national and global economy as centres of command, communications and control.

To varying degrees, all our world cities can be regarded as concentrations of economic, financial, cultural and political power. While the economic life of other cities tends to be based around branches and subsidiaries, the world city accommodates front- and head-office activities of multinational companies as well as international stock markets (New York, London, Tokyo, Paris and Frankfurt) and/or seats of political or administrative power (London, Berlin – in the past and future – Tokyo and Paris). It is the kind of place with a recognisable image, culture or style where any international retailer must have a branch or its name on its perfume bottle.

These command elements are important to the status of a world city – not least because they attract further business and activity. As we have seen, the Agnelli Foundation divides world cities into "complete" global cities, which unite command functions with a superior industrial or production capacity, and "pure" global cities which have much less significant industry or production. According to this categorisation, Paris and Frankfurt emerge as complete global cities, while London is cited by the Foundation as the prototypical "pure" command city. In other words, London has achieved a very high command and control capacity, but the deterioration of its industrial base may threaten its completeness as a world city.

New York's problems are more pronounced than London's since a significant number of its corporate headquarters have begun to move out to the suburbs or even into other states. Although in the recent past the subsequent loss of employment was masked by the growth of the financial services sector, the trend must be regarded as a significant loss of control and decision-making capacity from the heart of that city.

Global creativity

A world city is likely to be characterised by a dynamic diversity of economic activity. A broad spectrum of business activity enables a city to exploit effectively a diversity of opportunities, to respond flexibly and efficiently to competitive threats and to some extent insulate itself against the shocks and tribulations of the national and global economy. What is important is not the absolute range of economic activity in a given city, but the existence of dynamic diversity in those areas of economic, social and political activities that benefit from urban agglomeration economies.

The capacity for creativity and innovation through urban agglomeration is thought by many commentators to be the key to success for world cities. The reasons are fairly obvious. In order to be able to adjust effectively to the greater variety of external shocks and trends to which a world city is likely to be vulnerable, it will need to continue to be creative and innovative in both the development of existing sectors of the economy and in the pursuit of new enterprise. Such qualities will also enable a city to maintain and augment its position at the leading edge of global developments.

In the "complete" command city, one in which command and production centres co-exist, the potential for innovation is high. It is activated by the positive interaction between the command functions of government, commerce, research and knowledge-based organisations and the location within the city; and of the strategic centres of international business networks, knowledge creation, distribution and communications.

Creativity and innovation, and the factors which promote them, are extremely difficult to identify and measure. They are most likely to be recognized only when they can be applauded. For example, the highly innovative character of London's financial sector is exemplified by its successful development of the eurobond market. Creative failure can also be observed but much less readily because such failures are not advertised. Most difficult of all is to identify when and how creative capability is being eroded. One measure is the willingness and capability to take risks.

Risk is the constant companion of innovation. It seems clear that the ability to assess and manage risks will become ever more important as competition between the world cities becomes more acute. A 1989 survey suggested that increased competition in the financial and business services sector will force financial intermediaries to take greater risks in the drive for profitability and concluded that "the ability to accept and manage risk will be decisive" in the years ahead. While the need for innovation informed by risk management is easy to acknowledge, how it can best be delivered and by whom is considerably more difficult to discern. Skills and experience in risk management are bound to be at a premium in the years ahead and doubts have been expressed about London's ability to deliver the requisite skills through training.

We shall consider innovation and creativity as it relates to the cultural industries a little later when we discuss the wealth creation potential of this sector. For the moment, suffice it to say that the phrase "short-termism" which has been coined to describe attitudes to manufacturing, research and development and training in the UK also may be an appropriate description of the London's cultural and even commercial activities. This we believe to be a serious weakness, if London's capacity to transform creativity into production is regarded as critical to the sustainability of its status as a world city.

To illustrate the themes of command and creativity we will now take a more detailed look at London's wealth creation capabilities in financial services, manufacturing and the cultural sector relative to other world cities.

Financial Services

An efficient financial system is the backbone of a modern industrial economy. National and global economies rely on their financial sectors to facilitate and develop world trade growth and, in the process, to enhance their standard of living. A recent report conducted in the European Community concluded that financial services directly contributed 6.5 per cent of total value added to the economy and accounted for around 3 per cent of total employment within Member States.

In London, the financial and business services sector experienced a significant boom throughout the 1980s, developing faster both relative to its own historical evolution and compared to that of other sectors of the economy. The growth of financial services in London was more significant than in the United Kingdom as a whole. Over the period 1986-9, London's share of national financial and business service GDP increased from 27.5 to 28.5 per cent. This sector's share of the local economy rose from 31.5 to 37.5 per cent in the same period. In terms of the generation of income from abroad, the contribution made by London's financial sector grew rapidly from £5.2 billion in 1983 until 1986 when it peaked at £9.6 billion. It suffered a decline thereafter to £6.2 billion in 1989, although there were indications of some improvement at the beginning of 1990. Figure 2.5 highlights London's position in the financial sector. Paris and Frankfurt are relatively new rivals to New York, Tokyo and London. Thus, while they are rapidly establishing a market position, it will be many years before they can begin to match London's breadth and depth of experience and authority in this field.

It is too early to assess the causes and consequences of the global boom in financial and business services. It is unclear whether the growth in this sector has already peaked or whether the rationalisations of the early 1990s are merely a prelude to further development as the industry seeks to extend its products, refine its services and enhance its productivity. Equally, it may well emerge that the source of the boom lay more in the changing nature of domestic demand than shifts in the international

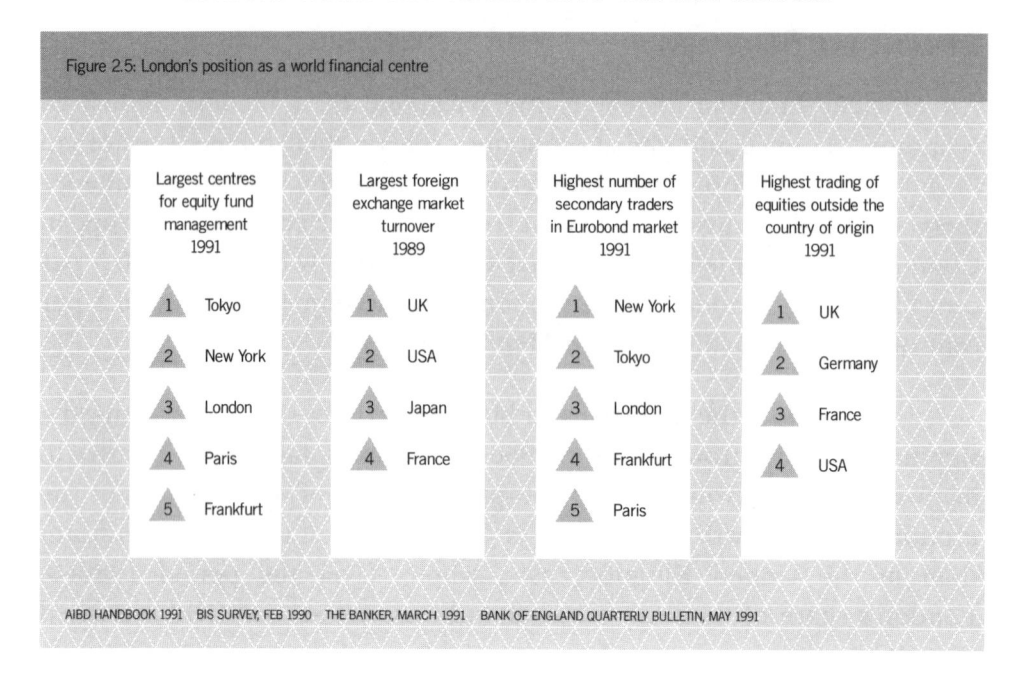

Figure 2.5: London's position as a world financial centre

Largest centres for equity fund management 1991	Largest foreign exchange market turnover 1989	Highest number of secondary traders in Eurobond market 1991	Highest trading of equities outside the country of origin 1991
1. Tokyo	1. UK	1. New York	1. UK
2. New York	2. USA	2. Tokyo	2. Germany
3. London	3. Japan	3. London	3. France
4. Paris	4. France	4. Frankfurt	4. USA
5. Frankfurt		5. Paris	

AIBD HANDBOOK 1991   BIS SURVEY, FEB 1990   THE BANKER, MARCH 1991   BANK OF ENGLAND QUARTERLY BULLETIN, MAY 1991

markets. Thus, it is not clear whether the future prospects of a world city's financial services sector will be bound up more with its national economic development or with world trade. This is important in the case of the UK because the national economy was perceived as less robust relative to other world city economies in the responses to our survey.

The liberalisation of the financial services industry has led to an expansion and, arguably, overcapacity in both securities and banking in London and New York, which in turn has precipitated moves towards rationalisation and consolidation in both cities. Over the next few years, London will undoubtedly be forced to fight to sustain its position in the market as international competition follows the UK down the path of liberalisation.

In Japan, the eradication of interest rate controls, the strength of the Japanese economy, and its dominance as a financial centre in the

Pacific Rim will strengthen Tokyo's position. In the United States, the problems of the savings and loans markets has prompted an urgent and probably far-reaching overhaul of the US banking system. There are proposals on the table which could both remove restrictions on interstate banking and sweep away the Glass Steagal Act which enforced the separation of banking and securities business. The eradication of these controls would probably enhance the ability of financial institutions in the United States to operate in both the domestic and international markets. This is likely to increase rivalry within the United States, causing New York to look over its shoulder at other US rivals as well as those abroad. Germany and France, in preparation for the long march towards monetary union within the European Community, have already taken considerable steps towards the liberalisation of their financial services and in the process enhanced the competitive challenge of both Frankfurt and Paris as European financial centres.

European Commission proposals on financial regulation and taxation may erode some of the competitive advantage so far provided by the more hospitable regime prevailing in the City of London. Such moves could well mean the repatriation of Euroguilder and EuroDM to their home markets and would also precipitate a deepening of financial markets within France, Holland and Spain. The potential for financial innovation amongst London's competition could be enhanced.

Insurance is an area of financial services where deregulation has yet to make itself felt. The arrival of the Single European Market will bring about fierce competition in this sector. The effect is likely to be that the independent domestic insurance industries will shrink and possibly become concentrated in the European Community's main financial centres.

There are many aspects of the Single European Market which may challenge London's current status as the European financial centre. But there are particular decisions which could have far-reaching symbolic and real consequences such as the location of the European Central Bank. Such an institution could attract to its host city a wide range of those

European Community financial institutions which benefit from a proximity to the seat of financial and economic power. As a consequence, the decision about the Bank's location could be crucial to all the European world cities in our sample, although we note that the World Bank location in Washington does not seem to have adversely affected New York's financial dominance.

We think the location decision will be particularly important to Frankfurt whose future European financial status will be profoundly affected. Frankfurt faces an additional insecurity as regards the future of the Bundesbank, which might well be moved from Frankfurt to Berlin. Should this move be accomplished, Frankfurt could cease to be a serious long-term competitor for London in the financial business sector. In the shorter-term London could benefit from the in-fighting between Frankfurt and Berlin which could effectively stop either from achieving a critical mass.

The decision to locate the European Bank for Reconstruction and Development in London must be regarded as a symbolic indication of London's status, political clout and its breadth of experience and expertise as a leading financial centre. However, as we indicated above, London's relatively strong position is by no means unassailable and its financial services sector faces a challenge with the approach of the Single European Market. There are strong indications that the continuing process of European economic integration benefits central regions much more that those which are geographically on the periphery. If Frankfurt remains Germany's main financial and business centre, there is good reason to fear that the Brussels-Frankfurt-Paris triangle may become the hub of economic activity.

In particular, the investment management and insurance functions of the London institutions may face a medium-term erosion of market position. The commercial and specialist banking functions are more strongly placed but will have to meet the challenge of any crisis in confidence given the hunger of alternative European locations to seize on market opportunities.

The particular importance of the future of financial services to London derives from the way in which it has come to dominate growth in the London economy. This sector accounted for the greater part of the overall growth in gross domestic product – both nationally and in London – over the 1980s and was accompanied by a massive growth of employment. Between 1986 and 1989, London's entire net increase of 155,000 jobs (ie, a 4.5 per cent rise) could have been accounted for in full by the 20 per cent growth in the financial and business services employment from 707,000 in 1986 to 847,000 in 1989.

So, there is much to play for within European financial services. But this is not an issue confined to Europe. Whosoever wins in Europe will only do so if they can challenge the dominance of New York and Tokyo in the world. Both cities are clearly aware of the threats and opportunities.

The prospects for New York's financial services are healthier than other parts of the city's economy but the last few years have seen significant job losses – 27,000 in securities and 15,000 in banking since 1987. Nevertheless, there is evidence that American companies are likely to be at the forefront of the move to apply flexible manufacturing-based techniques to improve productivity. The development and successful application of such techniques could pose a serious competitive challenge to other global financial centres especially if it is associated with changes in working practices that overcome time-zone barriers.

The huge reserves available to Tokyo's industries and the strength of the Japanese economy tend to counter the unhealthier aspects of the city's business environment – like its relentless opposition to foreign participation and the possible fragility of the property-based equity in Japanese banks and financial institutions.

Our conclusion on London's position as a global financial centre is that it is such a significant international player that it has a substantial head-start against other European competition. But the margin thus provided will get squeezed – both by the challenge from the new and aspiring European entrants, most notably in Germany and France, and by the eagerness of the New York and Tokyo institutions to increase productivity. Over the medium-term this will increase the vulnerability of London to any loss of confidence and to the likely refocusing of financial activity in Europe towards the East.

The optimistic view of London's wealth creation prospects based on financial services was expressed by one American company's response to our survey – "London has always been a major financial centre and will continue to be so." The darker view was voiced by another American business – "London won't resist the challenge of growing cities which are hungrier for progress ... the word for London is complacency."

To a large extent, these views reinforce those voiced by other surveys. For example, a survey of communications managers in financial sector organisations across Europe by Coopers & Lybrand Deloitte in 1989 for British Telecom, showed that few companies believed London would lose ground as Europe's premier financial centre in the short term. A similar survey again conducted by Coopers & Lybrand Deloitte for British Telecom of foreign financial institutions in London, which examined London's role as a financial centre in the 1990s, also concluded that it was unlikely to suffer any real change in its current status. However, London's position was under threat because it had what was considered to be a rather parochial attitude. An earlier survey of the UK financial services industry by the Bank of England in 1988 showed that European financial markets would remain fragmented for many years and, for the time being, there were still advantages to be gained from a UK location. However, there was a clear warning which emerged from the survey which suggested that competitive pressures in financial markets were increasing and these were most likely to originate from the USA and Japan.

Manufacturing

London's manufacturing has been in steady decline over many years. A comparison of our world cities reveals that only New York shares such a decline and the low proportion of total employment it now represents (see

Figure 2.6). In 1971, the capital's economy employed just over a million manufacturing workers. By 1989, only 445,000 workers were employed in manufacturing, 10 per cent of total employment as against a national figure of just over 20 per cent.

It used to be fashionable in some quarters to accept this decline as inevitable and of no consequence – manufacturing "doesn't matter". However, there are a number of reasons why a further erosion of London's manufacturing could have unfortunate results. Firstly, in contrast to the vision of a post-industrial world, there is ample evidence that there is in fact a large and growing global market for manufactured goods and one in which developed urban economies can profitably participate. The continuing process of trade liberalisation will open new markets and thus enhance this demand and render it more sophisticated. Secondly, there are economic and social considerations to be borne in mind when examining the case for urban-based manufacturing. The industry preserves blue collar employment in urban areas with unemployment problems. For example, London's residual manufacturing industry employs high proportions of less skilled manual workers drawn from particular local depressed areas. Finally, the survival of manufacturing should be considered in the context of ensuring a diversity of economic activity within a world city, most particularly in those activities which the Japanese see contributing to the urban agglomeration economies in the soft economy, notably information based, high technology and craft based sectors.

London's manufacturing employment prospects now look decidedly poor. Most commentators agree that employment potential in London's manufacturing industries are likely to deteriorate in the 1990s. Existing manufacturing industries looking for growth are sometimes constrained by the lack of adjacent land into which to grow, which effectively frustrates local development. As a result, the healthiest sections of the industry looking for growth relocate to find large, cleared and accessible, or even better greenfield sites with a potential for expansion.

Arguably the decline in London's manufacturing industries could be regarded as a natural and indeed healthy decentralisation of such activities to its economic hinterland. Greenfield sites provide greater possibilities for expansion and can enable businesses to make considerable savings in their running costs. It is certainly the case that such a trend is also in evidence in both Tokyo and Paris. However, there are indications which suggest that such an optimistic reading makes a virtue out of an unpalatable necessity. To a large extent London's manufacturing decline can be attributed to the significant restructuring and rationalisation which have taken place within its industry over the last two decades. There is also some evidence to suggest a particular decline in London's high-technology manufacturing. In 1981, this sector employed some 225,000 workers; by 1987, this figure had fallen to 187,000 – a 6.4 per cent decline as against a 5.8 per cent fall in the rest of the country. This could have significant implications for the industry's knowledge base. It could inhibit the mutually beneficial interdependence between the production and service sectors. In the process it could damage prospects for London as a whole.

How does London's situation compare with that of our other sample cities? By any standards New York is in serious trouble. Having preceded the rest of the States into the current recession, the city's economic downturn is so pronounced that it is likely to remain in a slump even after any national economic recovery in the United States is well underway. This is because the city's economy relies to such a large extent on service industries which, in the current recession, have been hardest hit. Other parts of the US which are less service-sector dominated may well prove more resilient to economic shocks.

Like London and for similar reasons, New York's manufacturing industries have been in steady decline since the 1950s, when they accounted for a million jobs or 1 in 15 of all manufacturing employment in the United States. By 1990, employment in this sector had fallen to around 345,000 and seems destined to further decline in the years to come. This rather bleak prospect appears to be echoed in most other sectors. A study by the Regional Plan Association encompassing New York City and its surrounding states (ie, New Jersey, Connecticut, New York State) indicates that, by the year 2015, only 23 per cent of employment growth will be accounted for by the city itself, while across the river New Jersey seems set to soak up around 40 per cent.

Tokyo-toh (the Tokyo metropolis) has a population of around 12 million. Manufacturing workers formed 22 per cent of the total working population of 6 million in 1985. Tokyo-toh accounted for 7.3 per cent of all Japan's output of manufacturing goods in 1988. The greater metropolitan region of the Kanto Plains contributed one quarter of total output. While the percentage of workers engaged in the manufacturing industries has declined since 1970, there appears to be a consensus amongst commentators that this sector will continue, at least in the foreseeable future, to be a significant component of Tokyo's economic structure.

There are a number of reasons why Tokyo's manufacturing base looks considerably healthier than that of London or New York. Since the 1960s, Japan's productivity growth has been extremely rapid, although there is an element of catch-up involved in this development. Japanese industry in general appears to have overcome both the slowdown in productivity growth which marked the first half of the 1980s and the accompanying exchange rate problems. Because of the enormous volume of capital created by the Japanese economy and available to Tokyo's industry, investment is high and the efficient structure of the manufacturing sector – which contains a larger percentage of small firms than the United States – facilitates flexible specialisation and subcontracting. In addition, the nature of Japanese manufacturing – with the emphasis on research, high technology and skill-intensive labour – ensures that its products are considerably more competitive than those of much of the rest of the world. Japan's high trade surplus (£109.7 billion in 1988) in manufacturing is strongly correlated to the contribution of this sector.

In the tightly defined Paris municipality, the city's 230,000 manufacturing industry workers account for around 14 per cent of its total workforce of 1.6 million. However, the industry extends deep into the wider Ile-de-France hinterland where manufacturing accounts for as much as 21 per cent of the workforce. Throughout the city, electrical and related engineering remains significant. It should be noted that the stability of this sector is intimately linked to the fortunes of a very small number of companies, since four – Renault, Talbot, Citroen and SNECMA – account for the employment of 40,000 workers.

In comparison to London and New York the manufacturing industry in Paris looks relatively healthy. It should be noted that recent years have nevertheless seen a decline in both the number and percentage of industrial jobs. However, the manufacturing sector appears to have a robust place in the economy of Paris. As in Tokyo, its contribution is seen primarily in terms of the soft economy – high technology engineering and electronics, information technology, communications and cultural and craft-related activities.

While Frankfurt tends to be discussed exclusively in terms of its financial services capacity, in reality it has a relatively well-developed industrial base with 18 per cent of the city's workforce employed in manufacturing. In 1987, the number of manufacturing workers in stadt Frankfurt was 103,000, a decline from the 1960's peak of over 160,000. An even greater percentage of the workforce in Frankfurt's hinterland are engaged in this sector, where the 106,000 manufacturing workers account for 30 per cent of the total workforce.

The economic potential of Berlin post-reunification is extremely difficult to predict. As we have already indicated, like Frankfurt, Berlin's future will be radically affected by the overall success of the re-unified Germany's economy and the ultimate location of the EC Central Bank and the Bundesbank. Commentators can do little more at this stage than identify those factors which will play a key role in determining in its development – the rate and extent to which Germany's administrative institutions are relocated to the city; the quality of the city's infrastructure and the speed and efficiency of its development from a very low base relative to other world cities; the costs of unification; the willingness of foreign companies to choose Berlin as the base of their East European

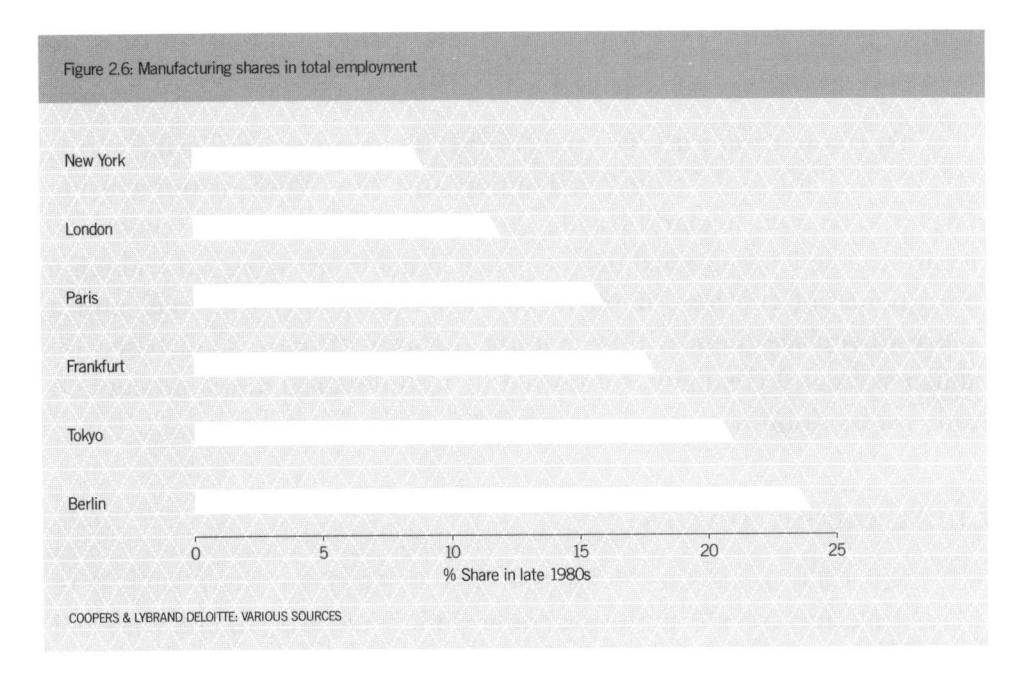

Figure 2.6: Manufacturing shares in total employment

[Bar chart showing % Share in late 1980s for New York, London, Paris, Frankfurt, Tokyo, Berlin]

COOPERS & LYBRAND DELOITTE: VARIOUS SOURCES

operations and, ultimately, their EC headquarters; and the success or otherwise of the adjacent Eastern European economies.

Prior to unification, manufacturing in West Berlin accounted for 26 per cent of total employment which in 1989 stood at 895,000, a situation which appears to have been mirrored in the East where manufacturing accounted for 25 per cent of total employment which in 1989 was 697,000. However, the economics of manufacturing in Berlin are distorted by the subsidies which in the past have supported this sector in both East and West, and the inefficiency and low-productivity of East German industry. The most that can be said with any degree of certainty is that there should be an adequate supply of both skilled and unskilled labour and considerable scope for industrial investment throughout the city and its recently expanded hinterland. Extremely tentative projections seem to suggest that the future of Berlin's manufacturing industries is likely to be relatively healthy, given that Federal and EC public policies appear inclined to encourage economic development eastwards.

By comparison with the other world cities we are considering and as revealed in Figures 2.1 and 2.6, London and New York manufacturing appears to be a particularly fragile component of their urban economies. In part, this reflects national performance in manufacturing but it also is a consequence of the loss of old urban agglomeration economies and a failure to replace them within manufacturing with new ones, based on human skills and creativity, supported by technological development and ready access to information and knowledge.

CULTURAL ACTIVITIES

> Especially since the 1880s, the arts in Germany have helped to drive and transform the economy. The visual arts, architecture and sculpture influence in important ways the development of industrial technology; and in more general ways even music and literature have effects.

As this 1903 quote from the German economist Kindermann might suggest, the theme of this section is that the cultural industries represent an often undervalued contribution to wealth creation. From the one hundred or so interviews and discussions we have held with representatives of the cultural sector in London and elsewhere for this study, we have found a difference of perception on the role of the cultural sector. Other world cities appear to subscribe to the view that *culture creates wealth*, whereas in London the prevalent view is that *wealth creates culture*. In other words, arts and culture are regarded as social window-dressing, the sector in which investment is considered once all else has been covered. As a result, there is a persistent failure to enable the cultural sector to make its full potential contribution to a creative and innovative economy.

It should be stressed throughout that arts, culture and entertainment are defined very widely. They encompass a range of creative activities which can be participatory, private or public, amateur or professional, subsidised or commercial. Many are closely linked with other activities including manufacturing, business and service industries, retailing and education. Some require special accommodation while others function in shared buildings or public places and open space. Thus we use the term "cultural activities" to include all such endeavour.

Cultural activities affect a wide diversity of functions in a world city and in significant ways. In the first place, the sector creates directly both wealth and employment, turning over some £7,500 million per annum in London alone and directly employing around 214,500 people. Employment in the sector represented 6 per cent of total employment in London and grew by around 20 per cent in the 1980s. Secondly, the cultural sector plays a pivotal role in establishing a positive image for the city, a crucial consideration in the global marketing of a metropolis. In addition, it makes a considerable contribution to the quality of life and social well-being of residents, a factor on which we shall elaborate when analysing the quality of life in the world cities. Finally, the educational value of the cultural industries extends beyond the realm of expertise associated with specific sectors, since it is generally acknowledged that this area generates a wide-range of transferable skills useful for work in disparate sectors of the economy.

The view that culture can and does create wealth has found support elsewhere. For example, the main report outlining the Arts Plan for London, prepared for Greater London Arts by Peat Marwick McLintock at the end of 1989, concluded that:

> The arts form an industry in its own right and as such play a valuable role in the economy of the UK and specifically of London. The arts are major employers in London and as many as a third of the nation's practitioners live and work in London. In addition, the cultural heritage and provision of the capital acts as a magnet to tourists both from overseas and domestically. ...

In summary, the arts in London are vital to the continuing success of the tourist industry, but they also contribute to the life and prosperity of the capital on a much broader base, both internationally and locally.

In an attempt to provide a systematic assessment of London's cultural sector, and to enable meaningful comparisons between cities, we have reviewed and discussed each sector in terms of its production chain – from the generation of ideas, to the point at which the product is consumed by an audience:

- **Beginnings** How good is London at ideas generation, how many patents, copyrights, trademarks are held by London organisations and, more generally, how creative is the city?

- **Production** What is the capacity of London to turn this creativity into production? Are the people, resources and productive capacities available to aid the transformation of ideas into marketable products? This can be measured by the level and quality of impresarios, managers, producers, editors, engineers as well as suppliers and makers of equipment such as in film or design, studios and framemakers.

- **Circulation** This concerns the quality of agents and agencies, distributors and wholesalers (in film or publishing), packagers and assemblers in London. It also includes the quality of support material such as catalogues, directories, archives, stock inventories to aid the sale and circulation of artistic products.

- **Delivery Mechanisms** These are platforms which allow cultural products to be consumed and enjoyed. It is about the places they are seen, experienced or bought and is measured by the availability of theatres, cinemas, bookshops, concert halls, TV channels, screens, magazines, museums, record shops and their national and international links.

- **Audiences and Reception** This concerns the public and critics and involves assessments of issues such as market and audience research, as well as questions of pricing and sociological targeting (eg, young and old, gender and education). How good, for example, is London at getting people from different economic and social backgrounds to experience and participate in cultural activities? How good is London at reaching foreign markets? How good is London at creating and profiting from a lively cultural life for all who live or work in or visit the capital?

WEALTH CREATION

As far as the UK is concerned, London completely dominates most sectors of the cultural industry, but when considered in relation to other world cities its performance at the various stages in the production chain was assessed by Comedia as set out in Figure 2.7:

Figure 2.7: London's performance relative to all other world cities in the cultural production chain

	BEGINNINGS	PRODUCTION	CIRCULATION	DELIVERY MECHANISM	AUDIENCE RECEPTION
Performing arts	4	3	3	5	3
Music	4	4	4	3	4
Film and TV	4	2	3	2	4
Literature	3	4	3	3	3
Visual Arts	4	2	3	3	3
Design	4	2	3	3	3
Architecture	4	1	2	N/A	2

Very weak performance = 1   Very strong proved performance = 5

COMEDIA

It is clear that London is very strong at the front end of the creative process whether at the high or popular levels. Well-known artists, designers and performers from Prince to Pavarotti all regard London as an essential global showcase for their talents. In addition, London's cultural training infrastructure remains strong, but is in danger of being eroded through a lack of investment. Although there is plenty of creative talent in the city, there are indications that ideas simply are not making the transition into profitable products often enough. This could be the consequence of failing to provide support for individual creators – ie, financial support, access to facilities, marketing and exposure – at an early enough stage in their careers. Certainly, the consequence is that many with creative arts skills and training either do not stay in London or, if they do, tend to drift away from their early careers.

Our qualitative analysis confirms that London is extremely accomplished in promoting tried and tested cultural products. But the outlets for the promotion of innovative, new wave cultural products have received uneven support and success over the last decade. As a result, the city has seen a weakening of an important avenue through which new ideas are fed into the more conservative commercial centres of production.

In terms of the delivery of product to the consumer, London has highly successful well-developed outlets for the dissemination of most mainstream cultural products. The sole exception is in the cinema, where London is relatively less well-endowed with venues in comparison with other world cities. But outside mainstream culture, there is a conspicuous deficiency in the availability of outlets. This inhibits the nurturing of new creative talent and puts a stay on creativity and innovation.

If we shift focus on to the international arena we can draw some qualitative conclusions about how each of London's cultural sectors compare with their global counterparts as shown in Figure 2.8.

New York takes top position in the cultural wealth creation league table. Its economic might in this sector is matched only by London amongst the other world cities. By way of contrast, Paris probably takes first place as the world city which has most heavily subsidised, supported and developed its cultural life across the spectrum of artistic endeavour. London takes its second position in the league table, primarily because of the strong historical foundations of its cultural heritage and the significance of English as a world language. London is imbued with a great deal of talent and experience in the cultural sector which, if more robustly supported at an early stage of the production chain, could consolidate or even improve London's position.

Tokyo's almost exclusively home-based cultural product effectively inhibits meaningful comparisons. It simply has not exported cultural

Figure 2.8: World cities' cultural performance ratings by sector

	LONDON	NEW YORK	TOKYO	PARIS	FRANKFURT	BERLIN	OTHER CITIES IN TOP THREE
Visual arts	8	9	3	8	3	4	
Theatre	9	9	N/R	8	7	N/R	Amsterdam
Film A/V	6	7	3	3	N/R	2	Los Angeles
Music	9	10	5	7	N/R	N/R	Los Angeles
Design	8	9	10	6	4	N/R	Milan
Advertising	10	10	9	7	4	3	Milan
Fashion	7	9	9	10	N/R	N/R	Milan
AVERAGE	8	9	5	7	3	1	Los Angeles Milan

Rating 1 = low performance   Rating 10 = high performance   N/R = Not rated

COMEDIA

products significantly into the global market. This said, Sony's ownership of CBS and Mitsubishi's acquisition of MGM point to the Japanese determination to buy into the sector. As far as the global market is concerned, Tokyo seems likely to be restricted primarily to the support and promotion of foreign cultural products.

Any assessment of the cultural industries of German cities is complicated by the polycentric nature of the country. If the cultural life of all Germany's cities were taken together, the ratings in the league table would be considerably higher. It seems reasonable to assume that Berlin's position will be considerably enhanced internationally over the next decade or so and the city is planning expenditure to ensure that this takes place. Frankfurt has made impressive leaps by using culture to change the image of the city. This said, it is a considerably smaller city than the others in our sample and its scope for cultural development is limited accordingly.

GLOBAL TRENDS

From our assessment of London's relative wealth creation ability, there has arisen a number of points of concern. Financial and business services are clearly a major strength of the London economy. Over the medium to longer term, we see this advantage being squeezed by rivalry with the other dominant players – New York and Tokyo – and by the competitive hunger of new entrants such as Frankfurt and Paris. There will be two main consequences of this trend. London's financial services – and hence London itself – will become more vulnerable to shocks and crises of confidence. Secondly, London's financial institutions must become more creative, developing their human skills and use of new technology to increase productivity and to innovate in the services provided.

Some disquiet may be justified about the capability of UK and London organisations to do this if we look at the history of manufacturing and even at the developments in the provision of cultural services. Our assessment of the latter as a seedbed of talent inadequately brought to commercial fruition is one which has been made about British manufacturing time and again. One wonders whether financial services will be exempt from this apparent British difficulty in taking the longer term view and in translating our undoubted creativity and innovation into commercial gain.

These points of concern must be perceived in the context of major global trends. Most obviously, there are opportunities and challenges presented by the completion of the Single European Market. An analysis by the London Planning Advisory Committee compared London's relative sectoral strengths in the European Community with the sectors thought most likely to gain from the Single European Market. It demonstrated (Figure 2.9) that, whilst manufacturing is likely to gain most within the Community, London's relative position is such that a low proportion of the gains is likely to come its way. Financial services are a London strength but will benefit comparatively less. So, while London might be expected to reap some rewards overall from the completion of the Single European

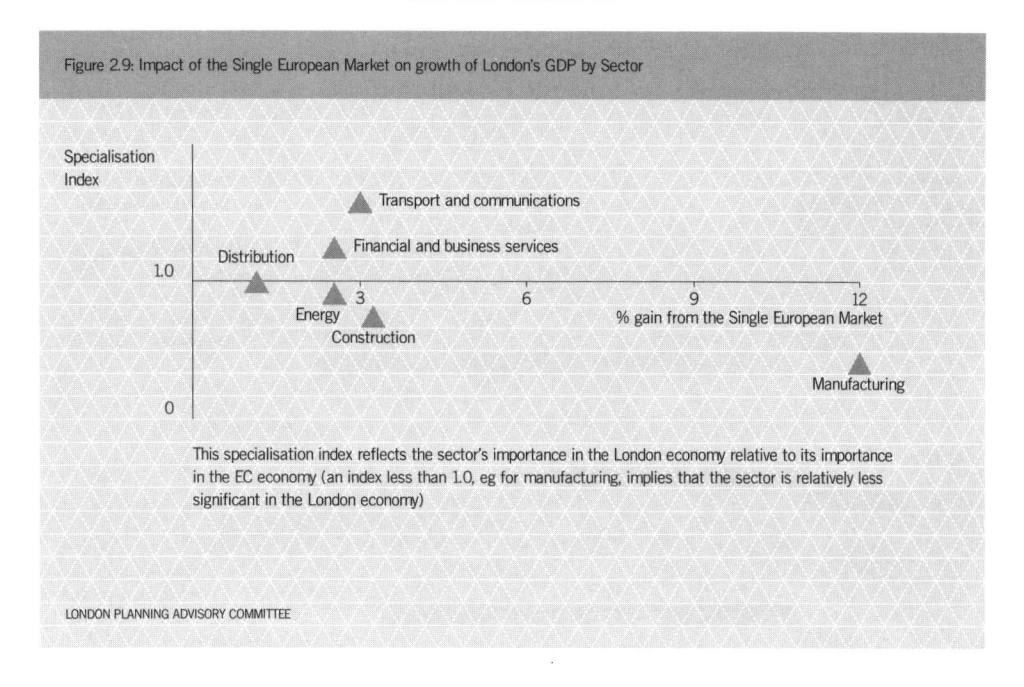

Figure 2.9: Impact of the Single European Market on growth of London's GDP by Sector

Specialisation Index vertical axis (0 to 1.0); horizontal axis: % gain from the Single European Market (3, 6, 9, 12).

- Distribution
- Transport and communications
- Financial and business services
- Energy
- Construction
- Manufacturing

This specialisation index reflects the sector's importance in the London economy relative to its importance in the EC economy (an index less than 1.0, eg for manufacturing, implies that the sector is relatively less significant in the London economy).

LONDON PLANNING ADVISORY COMMITTEE

Market, it is likely that cities with more substantial strength in those sectors with most to gain will benefit most.

But there are other global trends to consider. Developments in central and eastern Europe will open up new growth possibilities in the medium term and contribute to a shift of economic power within Europe as a whole to the east. Continued rapid growth in the Pacific Rim will exercise a powerful influence on the global distribution of economic power, enhancing the world city status of Tokyo but also increasing the potential for new entrants such as Singapore and Los Angeles.

In order to gain an insight into potential "winners" and "losers" from these global trends, we invited respondents to the special survey undertaken for this study to quote unprompted which cities they felt would either benefit or lose. The results are presented in Figure 2.10. It clearly shows that the central, mainland European cities are seen to be

LONDON: WORLD CITY MOVING INTO THE 21ST CENTURY

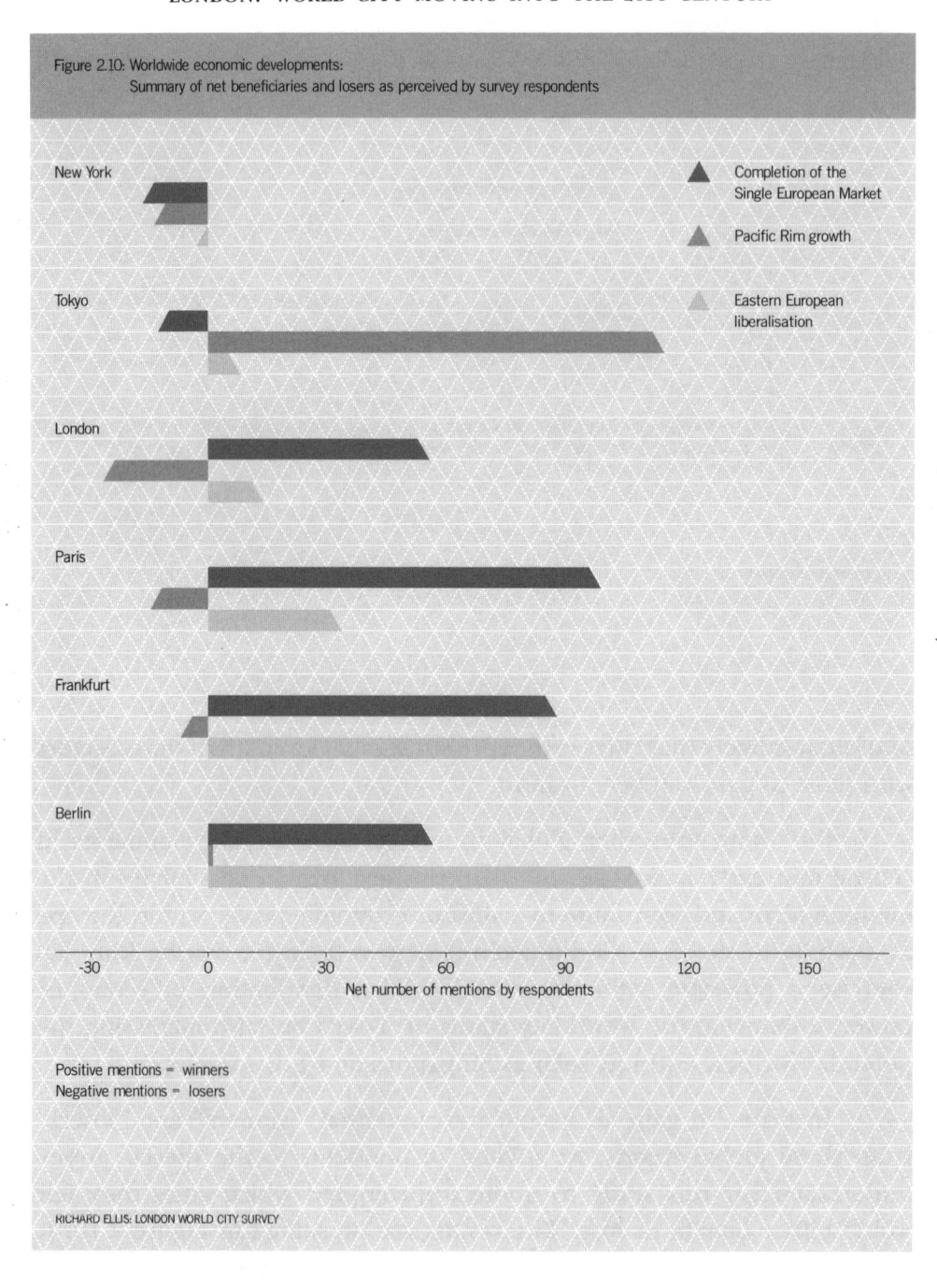

Figure 2.10: Worldwide economic developments:
Summary of net beneficiaries and losers as perceived by survey respondents

▲ Completion of the Single European Market
▲ Pacific Rim growth
▲ Eastern European liberalisation

Net number of mentions by respondents

Positive mentions = winners
Negative mentions = losers

RICHARD ELLIS: LONDON WORLD CITY SURVEY

likely to benefit most from the major world developments over the medium term. Berlin, Frankfurt and Paris are expected to benefit most significantly and London is thought likely to gain on balance but to a lesser degree. Tokyo, despite the perception that it could lose from European developments, was expected to gain significantly from its anticipated pivotal role in the Pacific Rim. The net result of these world developments was an expectation that New York will be an overall loser.

London respondents to our survey generally had a more negative view of London's ratings on wealth creation attributes and the supporting infrastructure – see Figure 2.11. We will meet this phenomenon again whenever we report our survey results. It perhaps reflects a loss of vision or pride in the city or, perhaps, the English predilection for underplaying our hands. While most respondents acknowledged London's strengths as a commercial and financial centre, there was considerable concern about shortcomings in London's infrastructure, which many regarded as inhibiting its wealth creation prospects. The weaknesses of London's *internal* transport system – "intra-city mobility" – was singled out as a particular cause for concern. But London was also seen as lagging behind other world cities in the provision of state-of-the-art telecommunications facilities. Given the generally high standard of telecommunications in London, it seems likely that this is more a problem of perception rather than a reflection of current reality, a throwback to the era of broken phone-boxes and poor international exchanges.

There was also concern amongst respondents about the long-term strength of London's national economy and the access London afforded to large markets. However, in the eyes of the international business community, London is not seen as a potential loser as a result of major economic trends in the years ahead. In other words, there is still time to take preventative action to stop our negative perception of ourselves becoming a global judgement. Obviously, if the negative self-image of London was to persist, it could be extremely damaging to future prospects.

LONDON: WORLD CITY MOVING INTO THE 21ST CENTURY

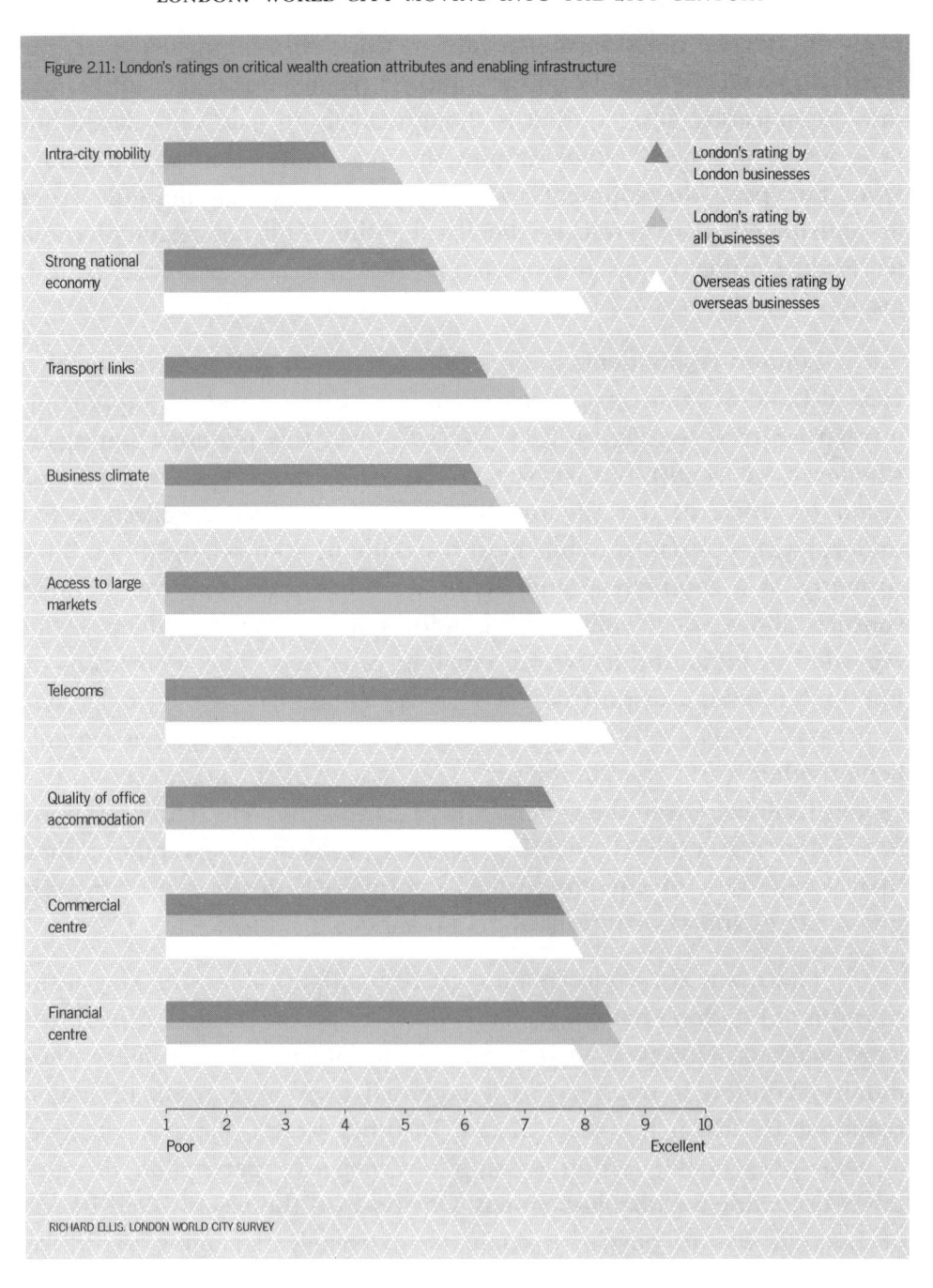

Figure 2.11: London's ratings on critical wealth creation attributes and enabling infrastructure

- Intra-city mobility
- Strong national economy
- Transport links
- Business climate
- Access to large markets
- Telecoms
- Quality of office accommodation
- Commercial centre
- Financial centre

Legend:
- London's rating by London businesses
- London's rating by all businesses
- Overseas cities rating by overseas businesses

Scale: 1 (Poor) to 10 (Excellent)

RICHARD ELLIS, LONDON WORLD CITY SURVEY

54

WEALTH CREATION

Figure 2.12 reveals how respondents to our survey viewed their city's wealth creation prospects over the next fifteen years. More than half the London sample anticipated growth in the economy, but nearly 60 per cent of the Tokyo respondents and over 80 per cent of the other European respondents expected an increase in wealth creation in their cities. This is an unsurprising result for the mainland European cities since they will be developing from a smaller economic base and thus their ability to create wealth in percentage terms is likely to be more dramatic in the short to medium term. In terms of its economic base, London is significantly more advanced than such cities and its economy does not have to grow so fast to keep ahead. Indeed, a very rapid growth of the economy is not necessarily desirable, because of the strain it is likely to impose on the city's infrastructure.

It is one thing to ask business generally about wealth creation prospects. It is something else to observe how businesses are voting with

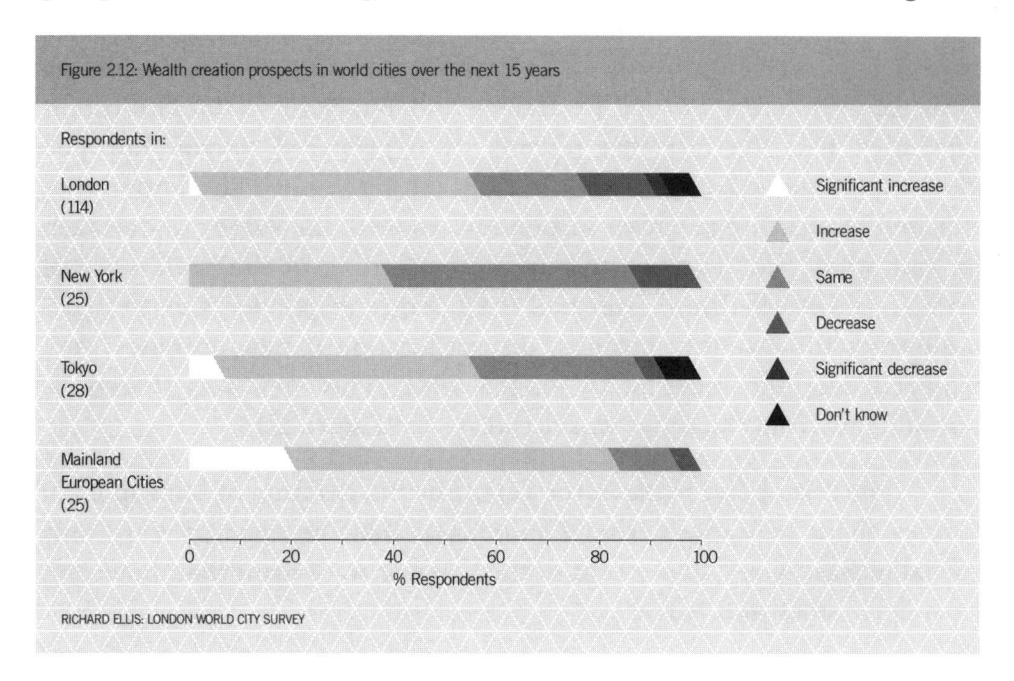

Figure 2.12: Wealth creation prospects in world cities over the next 15 years

RICHARD ELLIS: LONDON WORLD CITY SURVEY

their feet. On the latter, let us consider first the evidence on actual relocations out of London.

The recent report by Graham Lomas for the Institute for Metropolitan Studies provided a salutary reminder of some often neglected facts about relocation decisions by London organisations. First, the moves each year typically involve very few firms. Jones Lang Wootton's (1989) report showed just eighteen outward moves in 1988 involving nearly 5,000 jobs. Second, many of the moves have been to other parts of Greater London. Eleven out of the twenty-four destined known moves in 1989 were to the outer boroughs. The short distance of moves was also revealed in a Weatherall Green and Smith study of the central London office market in 1990 – over 20 per cent of all firms surveyed had moved within the last two years and most (some 70 per cent) involved moves to another address in the same postal district of the City – most firms want to stay in London, particularly in the central business district (CBD). This preference for a central London location was also demonstrated in a report examining office centres across Europe by Healey and Baker in 1989. The report concluded that the fact that tenants were prepared to pay Europe's most expensive occupation costs in London highlighted the importance attached to securing premises in London. Indeed, the survey undertaken for our study adds further support to the finding of the preference of firms for a CBD location. Over half the London respondents expressed a preference for a central business district location if new premises were required over the medium to longer term. This view was shared by respondents from the other world cities – see Figure 2.13.

The third point made in the report by the Institute of Metropolitan Studies about relocations from London was that the majority were only partial moves. "Only 40 per cent of the score or so of firms that move out, move lock, stock and barrel".

What are the factors behind relocation decisions in London and how does London compare on these with other world cities? According to the Institute of Metropolitan Studies, the dominant factors have been

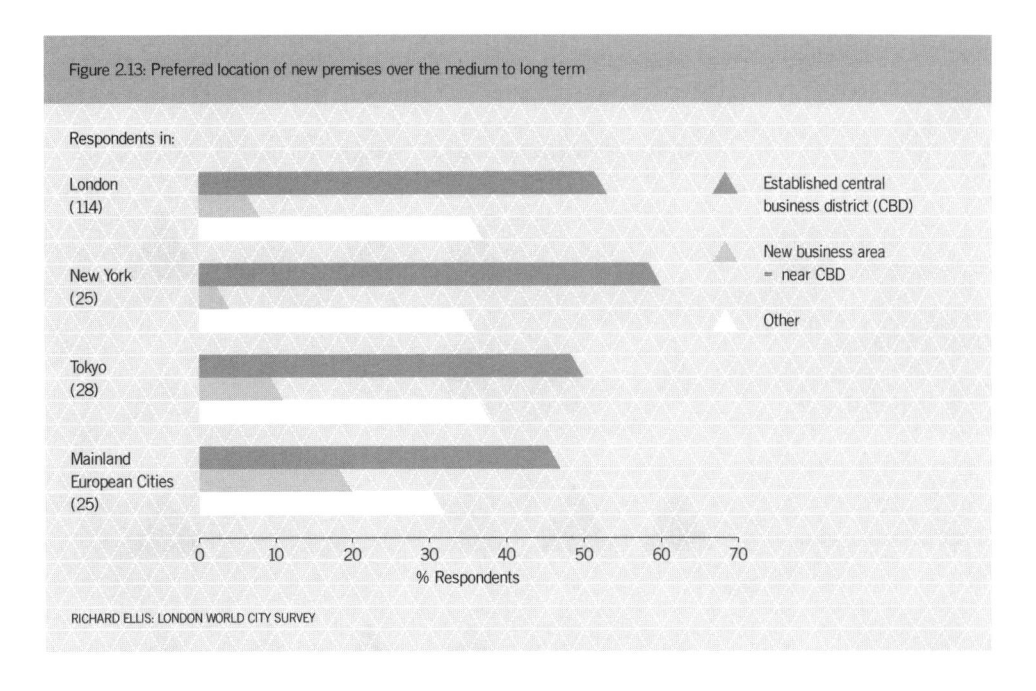

Figure 2.13: Preferred location of new premises over the medium to long term

property costs, the need to consolidate and expand and labour costs, with the latter becoming more significant over the 1980s. From our examination of the evidence on locational choice in the other world cities as well as London, we found that other significant factors were access to transport and telecommunications, the availability (as well as the cost) of suitable property and labour, the quality of life and the proximity to markets.

According to our reading of survey evidence and the comparative data, London's attractiveness as a location is attributable to the availability of property, the availability and cost of labour, access to markets and its telecommunications regime and facilities (see Figure 2.14). However, the results of our own survey cast some doubt on London's relative strength in telecommunications and market access.

On the assessment in Figure 2.14, Paris appears to be the only city offering a balance of locational advantages. Other cities have a marked

LONDON: WORLD CITY MOVING INTO THE 21ST CENTURY

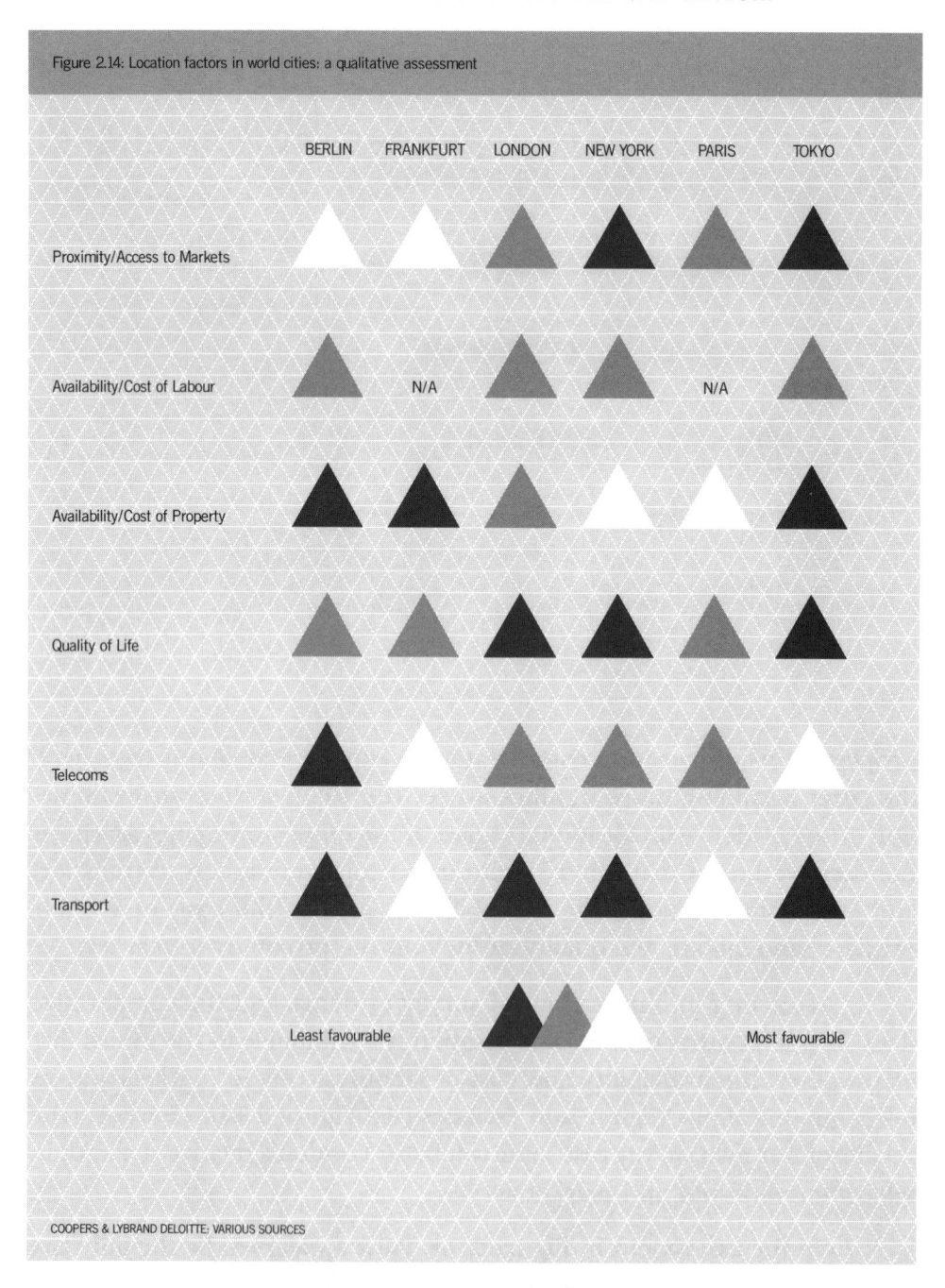

Figure 2.14: Location factors in world cities: a qualitative assessment

	BERLIN	FRANKFURT	LONDON	NEW YORK	PARIS	TOKYO
Proximity/Access to Markets	Most favourable	Most favourable	Medium	Least favourable	Medium	Least favourable
Availability/Cost of Labour	Medium	N/A	Medium	Medium	N/A	Medium
Availability/Cost of Property	Least favourable	Least favourable	Medium	Most favourable	Most favourable	Least favourable
Quality of Life	Medium	Medium	Least favourable	Least favourable	Medium	Least favourable
Telecoms	Least favourable	Most favourable	Medium	Medium	Medium	Most favourable
Transport	Least favourable	Most favourable	Least favourable	Least favourable	Most favourable	Least favourable

Least favourable ▲▲△ Most favourable

COOPERS & LYBRAND DELOITTE: VARIOUS SOURCES

58

advantage on one or more attributes relative to London. For example, an often quoted comparison is that London office costs are some 50 per cent higher than in any other world city location (except Tokyo). Not only is that differential narrowing (especially recently), but Figure 2.14 demonstrates the importance of putting this one factor into the context of the overall portfolio of locational influences including overall profitability. As the Institute of Metropolitan Studies put it, quoting survey results in an analysis by *The Banker*, "taking into account the overall cost of living, personal taxes, offices overheads, property and direct employment costs, London is a cheaper location than Paris and Frankfurt. Comparisons clearly need to take account of the full picture."

One of the surveys undertaken in support of the present study by the London Chamber of Commerce and Industry was of a hundred foreign banks based in London which were asked about the range of its locational advantages. The main strengths were seen as its regulatory regime, its position between the US and Japanese time-zones and the well-developed, English-based infrastructure which underpinned the financial services sector. Factors that might motivate transfer to another location were continued increases in the costs of operations, the loss of London's leading financial position and any further tightening of regulations. The second factor is of interest because it suggests the more than symbolic importance of key decisions such as the location of the European Central Bank.

The factors most important in exercising an influence on the cost and convenience of operations in London were cited to be congestion, airport access, living and working costs, cleanliness and education and training. When asked about alternative locations the foreign banks most often quoted Frankfurt and Paris within Europe. These two cities also appear in the list of global regions and major city locations where our sample of international businesses anticipated significant expansion over the next fifteen years. But one fifth of all businesses expecting expansion specifically quoted London. American companies, in particular, emphasised London as a focus for future growth.

Most foreign and London-based respondents to our survey of business were convinced that the trend towards decentralisation was likely to continue over the next decade in all their cities – see Figure 2.15. As far as London respondents were concerned, cost was the main factor cited for the decentralisation trend – accommodation costs (although this was prior to the current slump in property prices), general operating costs and those costs tending to affect the labour force (ie, transport, housing and living costs). Transport was deemed to be a major factor in the decision to decentralise, with many respondents making reference to traffic congestion and the disruption costs of failures in the public transport network.

By contrast, only 20 per cent of all respondents expected recentralisation trends. But what is interesting is the diversity of responses between the cities. Only 8 per cent of the New York sample believed that recentralisation was likely in their city – an impression more or less echoed by the 10 per cent response to recentralisation from London-based firms.

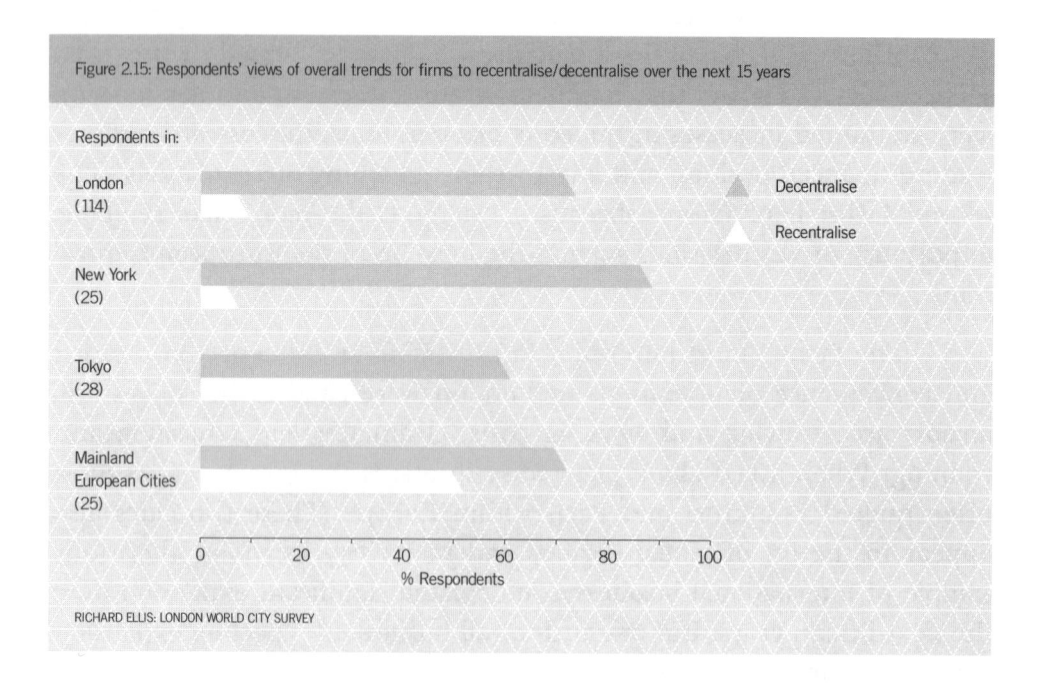

Figure 2.15: Respondents' views of overall trends for firms to recentralise/decentralise over the next 15 years

RICHARD ELLIS: LONDON WORLD CITY SURVEY

WEALTH CREATION

However, in the mainland European cities about half the respondents anticipated recentralisation trends as did one quarter of the Tokyo respondents.

The reasons given for potential recentralisation reflected the urban agglomeration economies we emphasised at the outset of this chapter. As one firm put it, "companies find that when they are out of New York, they are out of touch; they don't meet people at lunch time." In Paris, the same sentiment was expressed, "head offices and marketing services will stick to Paris as modern communications cannot replace physical contact." In London the view was expressed that previous decentralisation moves had been too hasty and total – they "will probably want to move a core element back into the centre".

The agglomeration economies were perceived to be of considerable importance by the financial and business sector. As shown in Figure 2.16, in

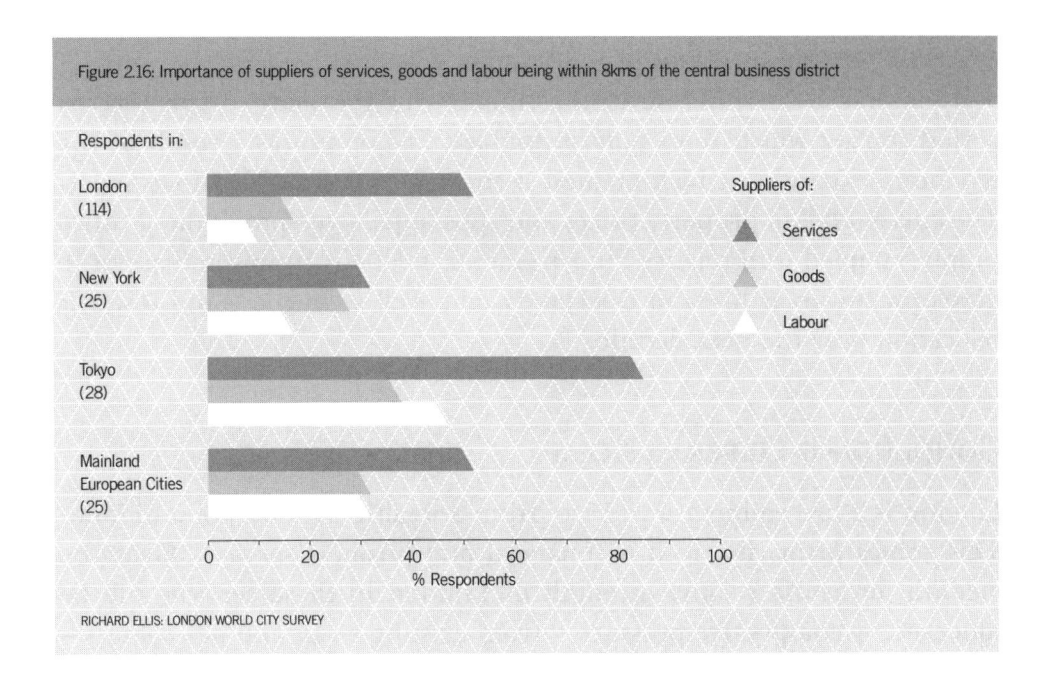

Figure 2.16: Importance of suppliers of services, goods and labour being within 8kms of the central business district

RICHARD ELLIS: LONDON WORLD CITY SURVEY

our survey over 70 per cent of respondents felt that suppliers of goods and services to this sector should be sited within five miles of the central business district with about one quarter suggesting that such supplies ought to be actually based in the area. As Figure 2.16 demonstrates, there was a difference of view between the city respondents in terms of the location of suppliers of goods and labour. London respondents were very much more doubtful than other respondents about the importance of a source of local supply of goods and labour. There is just a hint from this result, combined with the London views on recentralisation, that the agglomeration economies are less powerful in London (and, indeed, New York) than they are in the other world cities.

Certainly as far as London is concerned, the trend to relocate is likely to continue over the next couple of years. This is expected to be fuelled by the public sector, as the government's programme of dispatching selected departments to the provinces takes effect. During 1991–2, 9,000 public sector jobs will be relocated out of the city. However, it should be noted that most of the recent exodus from the city is the result of decisions taken in response to the situation in the mid- to late-1980, a period during which rents almost doubled in London as a result of the economic expansion which created a shortage of available office space. The current fall in property prices and substantial over-provision of office supply, coupled with relative improvements in labour supply and access to development areas like the Docklands may well stem the trend towards relocation over the next decade.

CONCLUDING OBSERVATIONS

London is a pre-eminent world city from a wealth creation point of view. This comes primarily from its financial and business services. Over the medium term the relative strength of London in these services will be squeezed by competitive pressure – from existing rivals and newcomers – and by global trends which will tend to favour Tokyo and the mainland European cities. In other sectors – and perhaps in financial services too – London's relative position is weakened by the difficulty encountered in translating creativity into production and commercial possibilities.

The consequence of these influences – and here we have to be conjectural – could be an erosion in London of the key attributes we have identified for a world city, namely agglomeration economies and creativity in products and services traded globally. The clustering of activities which have a mutual dependency on innovative ideas, on skills and creativity, and on new technologies is a vitalising factor in world city development. The Tokyo Municipal Government recognises this when it heralds Tokyo's role in the soft economy. If this issue is recognised in London, it is rarely articulated and does not appear to feature much in consideration of London's requirements to safeguard its competitive future. We conclude that the agenda of action for London must include not only attention to those critical attributes of international transport and communications, but also to the development of culture, education and training and innovative potential.

SUMMARY

- The wealth creating capacity of world cities is to be found in the agglomeration of activities based on knowledge, information, technology and services – the new agglomeration economies. The key to sustained competitiveness as a world city is human ability and creativity in a network of interlocking and supportive firms and organisations whose business is supplying the world market.

- London's economic structure differs from the other world cities in the combination of a marked decline in manufacturing and significant growth in financial and business services. The latter – now employing one quarter of all employees in London – dominates London's economy to an extent not matched in other world cities and now provides more than a third of London's GDP.

- London is such a significant world player in financial services that it has a substantial head-start against other European competition. But its position will be squeezed – by the challenge of aspiring European rivals and by the determination of New York and Tokyo to increase productivity and innovation.

☐ By comparison with other world cities, manufacturing in London (and New York) is a particularly fragile component of its economy. This reflects in part national weaknesses in manufacturing but also the loss of old urban agglomeration economies and a failure to replace them with new ones which are based on human skills supported by technological development and a commercially alert knowledge base.

☐ New York takes top position in cultural wealth creation matched only by London amongst world cities. London is imbued with such cultural talent and experience that improved translation of creativity into production could enhance its position in the global league even further.

☐ Our assessment that London's wealth creating prospects are generally good was shared by the majority of our survey respondents. But other world cities' growth prospects are likely to be better (except New York) for two reasons:
   – world market trends are more likely to favour other world cities; and
   – London's relative position is weakened by its poor innovative performance – especially in manufacturing.

☐ There was evidence from our examination of locational moves and intentions and from our survey results that London's agglomeration economies were seen to be weaker than in other world cities (except New York).

☐ It was clear from our comparative work that in other world cities (including New York) there was an agreed city-wide vision or strategy for wealth creation which recognised the cities' global role – this was lacking in London.

THE QUESTION IS
NOT REALLY: HOW MANY JOBS
CAN THE CITY HOLD? – BUT RATHER: HOW MANY JOBS
CAN WE HOUSE UNDER DECENT CONDITIONS AND WITHOUT MAKING TOO
MANY PEOPLE TRAVEL TOO FAR TO THEIR WORKPLACES;
AND WILL THE DEMAND FOR WORKERS
BY SEX, AGE AND SKILL REQUIREMENTS
MATCH THE AVAILABLE WORKFORCE?

Gerald Vaughan
Tomorrow's London – Essay Accompanying the GLDP, 1966

People at Work
LONDON DOCKLANDS DEVELOPMENT CORPORATION

3
JOBS AND INCOME

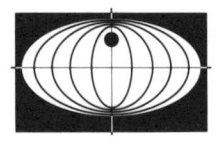

The last chapter examined the wealth creation capabilities of world cities. We acknowledged the role of creativity and innovation in economic life and considered the strengths and weaknesses of a range of economic activities within each of our sample cities. However, in the examination of business trends, it is all too easy to lose sight of the fact that, in the final analysis, it is a city's workforce which makes or breaks the wealth creation capability of world cities. In this chapter, we focus on the labour market within the world cities and the efficiency with which it operates.

LABOUR MARKET ATTRIBUTES IN WORLD CITIES

The attributes of a world city most closely related to the efficient operation of the labour market were considered by three-quarters of the business respondents to our survey to be critical or at least important to its success as a world city as shown in Figure 3.1. But only three of these attributes were considered by one quarter or more as *critical*, namely intra-city mobility, education and training and access to a diverse set of skills. Each of these three has a major influence on the efficiency with which local labour markets work within the cities – ie, the extent to which local labour can contribute to, and earn from, the wealth creation of the city.

Significant deficiencies in any of these attributes can have serious implications for both the economic and social life of the city. They can lead

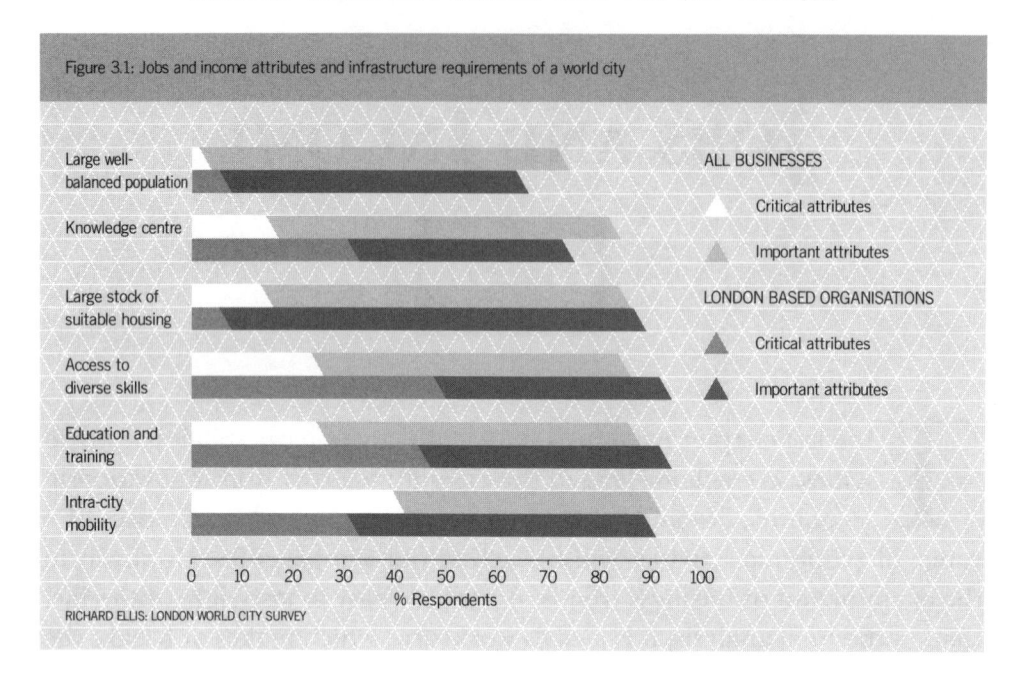

Figure 3.1: Jobs and income attributes and infrastructure requirements of a world city

to declining populations and the labour needs of central businesses being met increasingly by long distance commuting. Mismatches will increase in the labour market as revealed by the coexistence of high vacancy and unemployment rates. There will be a burgeoning of those sections of the population who exist outside the social and economic life of the community – the so-called "underclass" who can, only with the greatest difficulty, participate in the labour and housing markets or find a place in the city's political and social framework. Polarisation and multiple deprivation can set in and the process is perpetuated.

Generally, these kinds of urban labour market problems appeared during 1960s and 1970s. This was a period of urban-rural shift or decentralisation, when declining urban populations were thought to herald the end of the large "city" economy. It was a time of structural, technological and economic turbulence. There was a trend away from manufacturing and towards service industries. Each of these factors put pressure on cities' labour markets.

In the 1980s, there has been an apparent resurgence of the urban economy. In the world cities, populations were on the rise, although both economic and demographic growth was more muted or taking place over a broader geographical area in some cities than in others. But the scars from the years of declining populations and inadequate urban adjustment ran too deep to have entirely disappeared by the beginning of the 1990s. Indeed, as we shall see, not only have the numbers of disadvantaged world city residents increased, but their relative position has deteriorated.

Over the last twenty years, the labour markets in all the world cities have become considerably more complex, most relying on their economic hinterlands to compensate for the perceived deficiencies of local urban labour supply. It is difficult to avoid the conclusion that the indigenous labour markets of many world cities have become more inefficient, an inadequacy exemplified by increasingly persistent high levels of unemployment coupled with significant numbers of unfilled vacancies. Such a dichotomy highlights not only the problems of local labour markets, but also the constraints facing a city economy which relies on its hinterland for its workforce. While most world city businesses according to our survey seem surprisingly sanguine about the decentralisation of the labour force, the cost and inefficiencies of longer distance commuting, the export of income and wealth from the city and the non-productive use of local labour suggest that the issue should be a matter for debate rather than resignation.

Our assessment in this chapter will be undertaken as follows. First, we will consider the London labour market in some detail, exploring particularly the extent and impact of local labour market deficiencies. In subsequent sections, we will consider the extent to which other world cities have similar problems. Finally, we will make our own subjective judgement of the relative performance of London's labour market and compare this with how our survey respondents rated London's labour market attributes and job generation prospects.

The Labour Market in London

In 1936, London's population peaked at 8.6 million, fluctuated for the next three decades but remained around the 8 million mark until 1966. The remainder of the 1960s and 1970s saw a steep decline before the population eventually began to stabilise in the 1980s at around 6.5 million.

While London's population declined, its hinterland in the rest of the South East witnessed a population growth which spread in a wave across the region. Between 1981 and 1988, London's population declined by 70,000 while the rest of the South East gained some 403,000 residents. This dispersal had its roots in the planning policies of the 1960s and 1970s which promoted decentralisation to the New Towns. Although numbers continued to decline slightly, the widespread exodus from the city came to an end in the early 1980s, while at the same time overseas migration into the city – which in previous decades had been a key factor in population growth – declined to relatively minor significance.

Demographic projections for London tend to vary considerably, but such consensus as there is suggests that by the year 2000, or shortly after, the city's population is likely to have recovered to over 7 million. The labour force is expected to increase to slightly over 3.6 million by the year 2000, a rise of about 170,000 in a twenty year period. Between 1983 and 1990, the workforce in employment rose by 228,000. This was mostly the result of a rise in the employment of women – from 1.47 million in 1983 to 1.63 million in 1990 – and a growing number of self-employed workers. According to a report by Reading University, this trend is projected to continue, although at a slower rate as the decade progresses. As regards the composition of that labour force, current population projections indicate that in the longer-term, the much heralded "demographic time-bomb" – the long anticipated shortage of young people entering the labour market – will eventually be neutralised by the steady growth of London's population. However, in the medium term – ie, over the next five years – the current movement from surpluses to shortages in the youth market will have serious implications for the development of recruitment policies.

Most commentators acknowledge that there is likely to be considerable variation in the availability of labour within the London region. For example, growth in labour supply is likely along the riverside areas of East London. Indeed, the higher population growth amongst ethnic minorities within the inner East "crescent of deprivation" will create a significant increase in labour supply throughout the region.

For a significant proportion of workers (perhaps as much as a third), London can be regarded as a single labour market. These are people whose skills are sufficiently in demand to be marketable virtually anywhere in London. They are the "insiders", typically skilled, white, middle-class, high earning and living on the fringes of London or beyond.

But for another major component (of the order of a fifth) of the labour force, London comprises a large number of ill- defined (though by no means mutually exclusive) local labour markets, each with its own distinct characteristics. The weaknesses of these local labour markets became more conspicuous in the mid-to-late 1980s, when there were approximately 120,000 vacancies despite unemployment levels of close to 400,000 people.

Recent fieldwork (by the Local Economy Policy Unit of the South Bank Polytechnic in London) provides a specific example of the real implications of the mismatch statistics. At a time just before the current recession, the survey revealed not a single Spitalfields Bangladeshi whose place of work was in the closely adjacent City of London. This is a powerful illustration of the problems encountered by the "outsiders", typically unskilled or inappropriately skilled, an ethnic minority, either on low pay or unemployed and living in the inner city. Predictably, unemployment amongst London's ethnic minority workers is almost twice as high as it is for their white counterparts – 13 per cent compared with 7 per cent. Bear in mind that, at around 15 per cent, London's ethnic minority workers form a much higher proportion of the city's labour force than the national average (of 5 per cent). Therefore, the higher unemployment rates they experience within a much higher proportion of the workforce make a potentially potent source of "outsider" frustration and resentment.

This mismatch of skills and vacancies is partly a failure of London's training infrastructure which is generally regarded as poorly organised and underdeveloped. London's vocational training record is considerably worse than that of the country as a whole. In 1990, only 0.8 per cent of London's labour force participated in any form of work-related government training – ie, half the national average of 1.6 per cent. We consider the issue of education and training provision in a later chapter. But, to anticipate its conclusions, London's training provision appears to be quite inadequate to meet the scale of the needs of those who have become marginalised from the labour market or, indeed, have been thrust outside it. This implies not only a waste of resources and the creation of social polarisation and tension, but also requires an expensive solution – through commuting – to meet the labour requirements of central London businesses. In 1989, commuters transferred approximately £10 billion of spending power out of London to the rest of the South East – or about one-sixth of the capital's GDP. This compared with £6 billion in 1984.

In-commuting reduces the level of vacancies open to unemployed London residents. By way of illustration, the 1981 census figures showed that the numbers of in-commuters to London was around 520,000. To put this figure into perspective, consider that of the 300,000 jobs available in the City of London in 1981, over 100,000 were held by either Home County residents or workers from even further afield – for example, 38,000 from Essex; 16,000 from Kent and 14,000 from Surrey. By way of contrast, genuinely local workers played a relatively minor role in the composition of the City's labour force. The Boroughs of Hackney and Islington sit on the very borders of the City, yet in 1981 each supplied only 6,500 of its workers.

The 1991 census figures will provide a more up-to-date picture of this situation. Meanwhile, British Rail figures indicate that the number of workers commuting into the city rose by over 50,000 commuters between 1979–89, bringing the total travelling by BR alone to 473,000.

Much of any growth in demand for labour in London seems likely to be met to a large degree by non-residents rather than mobilising the under-utilised local labour force. The employment prospects will only improve for London's indigenous workforce with the development of policies specifically directed towards enhancing local labour supply. Such policies would need to include the improvement of intra-city transport, the development of local training schemes including those customised to new business requirements and the availability of affordable housing with easy access to the new areas of the employment.

We have observed in the previous chapter that the type of work carried out in London has changed faster over the last ten years than in the rest of Britain. The banking, insurance and financial sector increased its contribution to London's total employment from around 15 per cent in 1981 to 23 per cent in 1989, while in Britain this sector's share of employment grew from 8 per cent to 11 per cent over the same period. In 1990, a full 80 per cent of London's workforce was engaged in financial and business services, public administration and education. The decline in manufacturing employment has been dramatic and it is projected that by the year 2000 only 6 per cent of London's workforce will be engaged in manufacturing.

The service sector domination of London's labour market is demonstrated by the 1989 Annual Census of Employment. It indicated that 28 per cent of London's workforce were either managers and professionals, scientists or technicians. Office and sales staff accounted for a further 29 per cent and a mere 9 per cent were involved in skilled labour with an additional 21 per cent engaged in semi- or unskilled manual labour. Between 1983 and 1988 there was an increase of nearly 200,000 professional and managerial employees. "Insiders" they may be, but most of them live outside London or on its periphery.

In summary, how would we depict the operation of London's labour market? The key point, we think, is that a high and increasing proportion of the city, especially inner city, residents have become marginalised from the city's source of wealth creation. Put at its simplest, we find it difficult to justify why not one Spitalfields Bangladeshi in a recent survey had a place of work in the City of London – this must be a waste of resources.

We suggest that there are economic and social implications which flow from this situation. The economic consequences are that labour resources with diverse skills remain under-utilized within the city, that labour is imported from peripheral areas at additional expense to the employer (disruption costs), to the commuter (additional stress and fatigue), to the public purse (extra transport provision) and the overall environment. Moreover, the leakage of one sixth of wealth generated in the city to locations outside it seems an unnecessarily generous endowment, given the needs of those who live in the city but who benefit little from their proximity to the sources of wealth creation.

Potentially, the social consequences of the economic polarisation described above are equally damaging. A consideration of London wards ranked on multiple deprivation indicators is a salutary reminder of three points. First, the commercial expansion of the city to the "east" is to be welcomed if, from a jobs and income point of view, it helps to alleviate the crescent of deprivation currently experienced in that area. Second, there are other areas of similar deprivation and under-utilised human resources which deserve urban regeneration consideration, notably in the broad band just south of the River Thames and to the north west and north east of the city centre – in other words, almost forming a ring of deprivation around the central area. Third, "outsider" residential areas within the city are currently not well connected in terms of public transport – ie, north-west to north-east to east to south. As we have already noted, by far the highest proportion of the respondents to our survey (some 40 per cent) considered intra-city mobility to be a critical attribute for a world city.

JOBS AND INCOME

An urban policy framework must consider the dangers posed by widening social divisions in a city where job opportunities are polarised between high status producer services jobs for the qualified "insiders" and unstable consumer service employment for the rest. These social and employment tensions were a key factor in New York's period of economic crisis in the 1970s and the flight of headquarters from the city. There is no single and simple policy to deal with these issues. There has to be a combination of targeted education and training, public transport provision, public sector employment and other means of facilitating the deployment of lower income and disadvantaged groups to avoid their marginalisation within a prosperous and busy world city.

In the remaining sections of this chapter we will consider the extent to which other world cities have experienced similar labour market problems as London and how they have responded. We do this in three sections: for New York which has the same, more pronounced problems, as London; for the mainland European cities which either have not experienced the same problems to the same degree (the German cities) or have adopted policies to deal with them; and for Tokyo which is in a category of its own because of its cultural homogeneity, its prowess in manufacturing and its size.

THE LABOUR MARKET IN NEW YORK

According to Kornblum, the apparent numerical stability of New York City's population conceals a perpetual movement of people in and out of the metropolis. The population grew to almost 8 million in 1970, but by 1980 it had fallen to around 7 million. However, by 1986 the population had risen once again to 7.3 million.

A major contributing factor to the falling populations of the 1970s was the extensive migration from the city into the wider metropolitan region and beyond. Demographic projections suggest that the population of this wider region will continue to grow from 20 million in 1990 to around 21.5 million by the year 2000, while there is every indication that the population of the city will stabilise at around 7 million. The demographic statistics relating to New York, however, fail to convey the ebb and flow of a population in a constant state of flux. Kornblum suggested that "Since the 1960s, New York City 'exported' about 2 million white residents, most of whom were replaced with new immigrants from the Caribbean, Latin America, and now Africa ... Sometime in the mid-1990s, non-Hispanic whites will be in the numerical minority."

In September 1990, New York had a workforce of around 3.3 million of whom a rapidly decreasing proportion had been employed in manufacturing (accounting for only 9 per cent of the total employment). At the beginning of the 1990s, the dominant industries were in the service sector, government and what is known in the United States as the FIRE industries – in other words, Finance, Insurance and Real Estate. There is every indication that employment in the service sector will continue to increase, while manufacturing will persist in its decline. One of the consequences of this will be the fall in the available number of lower-skilled jobs requiring lower educational qualifications.

New York – like London – is suffering an unhealthy polarisation of its workforce, the repercussions of which are almost certain to be an increasingly inefficient labour market and rising unemployment – or, at the very least, the further development of the city's "hidden economy". New York comprises a large number of distinct local labour markets many of which are somewhat more sharply defined than their British counterparts. For example, Brooklyn still retains a significant proportion of New York's manufacturing industries, while Manhattan plainly dominates the information processing and financial services sectors.

The shifting demands of the labour market and the constant migration to and from the city puts considerable pressure on New York's weak and much-criticised educational and training institutions. In particular, the city's own school system is generally regarded as inadequate. This sits uneasily with the global wealth creating dominance which we associated with New York in the previous chapter in terms of financial and cultural business.

What we observe from our evidence on New York is that it has a similar, but very much more marked, social and employment polarisation and tension as in London. One fifth of the New York population live below the poverty line (more like one third in the Bronx). There are three points of uncomfortable similarity between New York and London which we feel obliged to note. First, both cities have a low percentage of their employment in manufacturing – in 1989 both cities employed about 10 per cent in this sector compared with over 15 per cent in the other world cities. Second, the public education and training system in both cities is poorly regarded internationally, although comparative figures are hard to establish. Third, the intra-city mobility provision in both cities is deemed by resident businesses to be poor (this will be supported by our review of transport provision in Chapter 5).

One feature of New York is the comparative open entry into its informal economy, prompted in large part by the rapid influx of immigrants and a tradition of absorption of large numbers of new immigrants for more than a hundred years; that it has a less permanently defined "outsider" or "underclass" component to its population; and that it provides much stronger political representation of its ethnic and cultural minorities.

THE LABOUR MARKET IN MAINLAND EUROPEAN CITIES

Paris

Between 1970 and 1988, the number of residents in the tightly defined metropolitan area of the City of Paris fell from 2.5 million to barely 2 million with some 4 million resident in the outer suburbs. However, the gradual move out of the city was matched by an increase in the population of the wider Ile-de-France area, which has grown from 9.9 million in 1975 to over 10.6 million in 1990. Demographic projections indicate that this trend is set to continue. The population of the wider Ile-de-France area is expected to grow to around 12.3 million over the next 25 years, while that of the City of Paris is anticipated to stabilise.

The exodus from the city and the growth of its hinterland have, as in London, been encouraged by public policies which have promoted the development of New Towns and the spread of large-scale housing projects around the periphery of the city. Current strategy is directed towards increasing the size of small peripheral municipalities and a wider dispersal of the population. Like many other world cities, Paris is moving towards a central core of service sector industries but is retaining a significant periphery of manufacturing. For this reason alone, Paris is less likely than London or New York to develop a significant "outsider" class amongst its residents.

Moreover, unlike London and New York, Paris is able to reap the benefits of a strong national education system which is augmented by an organised and well-established programme of vocational training. One of the strengths of vocational training in France is the "investment obligation", the system by which employers either finance the training of their own workforce, or else fund regional, sectoral or national training organisations.

In addition, Paris's strategically planned transportation system, coupled with the relative compactness of the central city core itself, significantly enhances the effective mobility of the labour force. The Paris mass transit system is heavily subsidised, with part of its cost being met by the employers in central Paris.

However, in spite of superior education, vocational training and a transport infrastructure which contributes to the flexibility of the labour force, some 9.5 per cent of the workforce were unemployed in 1990. Moreover, Paris too has its disadvantaged groups. Surrounding the central city are concentric rings of low-income housing providing residence for populations displaced from the centre or in-migrating from North and West Africa.

Berlin

The unified Berlin now has a population of about 3.3 million, while the city and its hinterland together have about 5 million residents. Just over

JOBS AND INCOME

2 million people in this wider area were formally inhabitants of West Berlin. Over the period 1969–89, the West of the city suffered a slight population decline, although it has increased since the mid-1980s. Demographic projections anticipate little increase over the next decade, predicting a population of just over 2 million inhabitants by the year 2000.

The Berlin Economic Development Corporation – a non-profit making organisation supported by the city, the Chamber of Commerce, the Chamber of Crafts, and two Berlin banks – estimated that the working population of the unified city was over 1.5 million in 1990. About a quarter of employees were in production industries and some 15 per cent in services. There is a clear distinction between East and West on the latter – in the Eastern part of the city only 6 per cent were employed in services in 1989 compared with over 20 per cent in the west.

West Berlin's Land Use Plan of the mid-1980s outlined public policy priorities designed to improve the flexibility of its labour force and the competitiveness of its industry. A major concern was to improve the city's research and training institutions which, coupled with Berlin's "technology programme", was intended to encourage innovation in product design and production. It was anticipated that manufacturing would be consolidated rather than expanded because of the shortage of land for industrial development. The main emphasis of the development programme was in the growth of the services sector which was regarded as "of more than regional importance". Now, the Berlin Economic Development Corporation claims that the city's "pool of 1.6m employees covers the entire spectrum of activities – from research to manufacturing, and from services to trade" all within an area of 900km^2 "comparable to the area of Greater London".

In 1989, the East Berlin labour force amounted to around 700,000 people with an equal number of male and female workers. With the withdrawal of state subsidies following reunification, closures and privatisations have led to almost 50 per cent unemployment in an economy hitherto dominated by out-dated heavy manufacturing industries and an unproductive, mostly redundant bureaucracy.

The future of Berlin's labour market is difficult to predict. There are simply too many imponderables. So much depends on the determination of the Federal government, the decisions of the Treuhand Trust and the investment strategies adopted by individual enterprises towards the modernisation of East Berlin's economy. The interactions between labour markets, the sale of land and property and the development of housing policies are all critical to the evolution of employment patterns and little can be projected until such matters are resolved. In addition, it seems likely that surplus labour will be attracted to the capital from elsewhere in eastern Germany and possibly even from ethnic German communities in other parts of Eastern Europe.

The situation in Berlin prior to reunification was one in which the only "outsider" problem was represented by the *Gastarbeiten*. However, with unemployment in West Berlin rising to about 10 per cent in the late 1980s and with the anticipated increase in unemployment in the eastern part of the city, it is difficult to avoid the implication that polarisation and social tensions will follow.

Frankfurt

In 1990 the population of Frankfurt (Stadt) was around 600,000. It lies at the centre of ribbons of urbanisation within the Darmstadt area of Hessen, a position which accounts for its reputation as the "octopus city" of Western Europe. In 1987, Frankfurt city employed some 558,000 workers – a clear indication of the extent to which people commute into the centre – while the surrounding hinterland provided jobs for an additional 349,000 workers. Unlike London, Frankfurt comprises a small number of relatively distinct labour markets with a high percentage (some 18 per cent) of the workforce engaged in manufacturing and an increasing proportion employed in the financial, business and service sectors for which the city has become predominant in Germany.

Complementing these sectors of employment are related activities, like the substantial fair and convention business and the centres of media and publishing networks. The city's airport complex alone employs 50,000 people and serves as Continental Europe's leading global nexus.

Frankfurt's industrial base appears to be considerably more robust than that of London and contributes to the economic diversity which characterises a complete global city. However, this "completeness" may be threatened if the city's financial services sector is challenged by competition from other world cities – including, perhaps, Berlin. Clearly jobs and income are likely to be shaped by such a challenge.

In economic terms, Frankfurt is frequently singled out as a global success story, its prosperity in part the product of both agglomeration economies and the considerable benefits of the excellent educational and vocational training facilities available in Germany.

Tokyo

The Tokyo region is home to no less than 25 to 30 per cent of Japan's total population. Throughout the post-war years, the city's population grew rapidly in contrast to the other world cities. This was partly the result of natural growth and partly a consequence of large-scale migration into the city during the 1950s and 1960s. By 1988, the population of metropolitan Tokyo itself had reached almost 12 million, but by this time the city had fused into a wider agglomeration which encompassed Yokohama to the south and spread eastwards around Tokyo Bay. This wider region boasted a population of 30 million people. The Tokyo Metropolitan Government anticipates a more moderate population rise over the next decade – taking the number of residents of the city proper to over 12 million by the year 2000. Tokyo's high-density housing and all-round congestion put a considerable strain on land, infrastructure and services, which in turn inhibits the efficient mobilisation of the workforce.

In the mid 1980s, Tokyo employed just over 6 million workers. The city supports a particularly high concentration of highly-skilled financial, administration and headquarters functions, businesses opting to site in Tokyo as much because of the size and economic strength of the local market as because of the city's key role in the global economy. The service and distribution sectors dominate the city's employment (some 40 per cent in all). But, as we discussed in the previous chapter, Tokyo still retains large manufacturing employment.

Day-time commuting into the city recently passed the 3 million mark and is expected to continue to rise over the next decade. It seems likely that the surplus of day-time over residential population will continue to grow for the foreseeable future. Generally speaking, the Tokyo labour market has, until recently, been constrained by the shortcomings of the city's infrastructure rather than deficiencies in the quantity and quality of skills. The convergence of high-level economic skills in the city is matched by an intense concentration of universities, technical colleges and research facilities coupled with an extremely high percentage of students.

It is age rather than training which seems set to be the cause of Tokyo's labour-supply problems in the years ahead. The population of Tokyo is aging faster than that of Japan as a whole. As a consequence, there is increasing concern about the prospect of labour shortages. Already, graduate labour is at a premium and there is mounting pressure for improvements in productivity. For example, the Tokyo subway authority has recently agreed to allow women to work as guards, while at the same time installing the system's first automatic gates. Elsewhere in the economy, there are indications that the flexibility of the labour force is becoming increasingly important in averting problems associated with skill shortages. For example, Sony has redeployed production workers to compensate for a shortfall in one of its delivery subsidiaries, while Isuzu has met shortages of showroom staff by retraining some of its assembly workers.

CONCLUDING OBSERVATIONS

On the evidence of our survey results, both London and overseas-based respondents shared some of the doubts we have identified with regard to London's labour market attributes. As Figure 3.2 shows, intra-city mobility,

JOBS AND INCOME

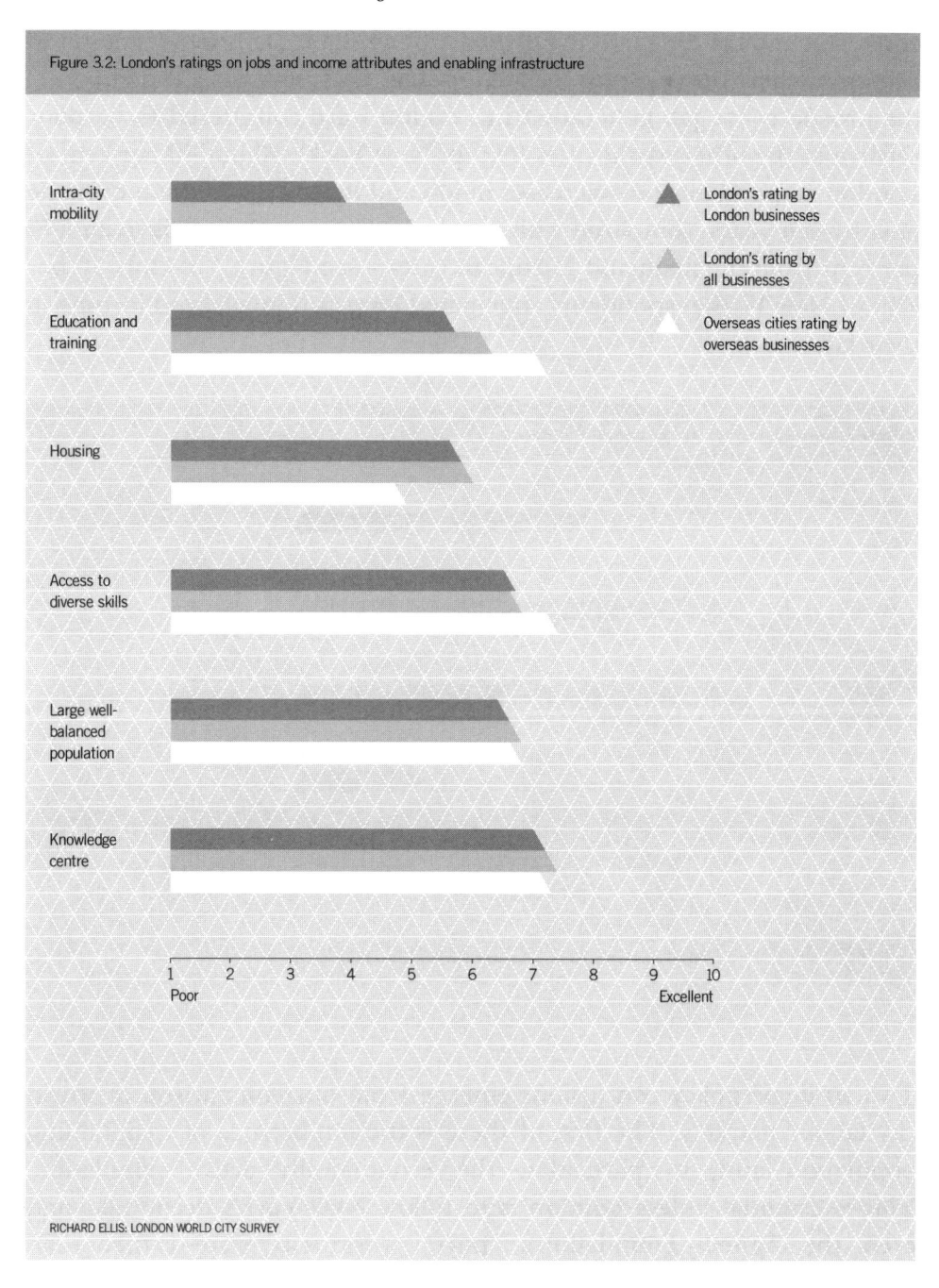

Figure 3.2: London's ratings on jobs and income attributes and enabling infrastructure

- Intra-city mobility
- Education and training
- Housing
- Access to diverse skills
- Large well-balanced population
- Knowledge centre

▲ London's rating by London businesses
▲ London's rating by all businesses
△ Overseas cities rating by overseas businesses

1 (Poor) 2 3 4 5 6 7 8 9 10 (Excellent)

RICHARD ELLIS: LONDON WORLD CITY SURVEY

education and training and the diversity of available skills were thought to be more weakly provided for in London than elsewhere. As a consequence, the prospects for job generation in London were considered to be poor relative to the other world cities (except New York). About 40 per cent of London respondents saw increases in job and income generation over the next fifteen years, compared with nearly 60 per cent from Tokyo and 75 per cent from the mainland European cities – see Figure 3.3. Only 20 per cent of New York respondents anticipated increases in jobs and income in their city.

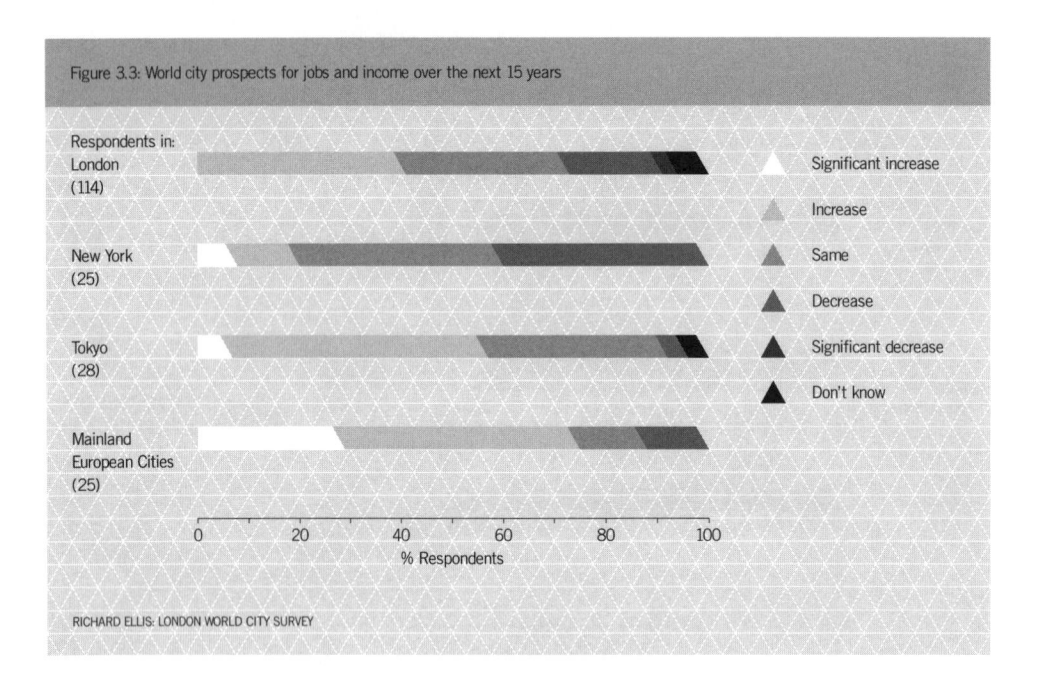

Figure 3.3: World city prospects for jobs and income over the next 15 years

RICHARD ELLIS: LONDON WORLD CITY SURVEY

Two strategic policy conclusions emerge from our comparison of world city labour markets. The first of these is the importance of maintaining population and, in particular, the economically active population. This is essential unless London is to follow New York's decline beyond even the Agnelli Foundation's "pure" world city state rather than to develop as a "complete" world city. If workplace and residence are to become still further divorced, not only will commuting requirements increase and the overheating already experienced by the rest of the south-east be exacerbated, but so too will the chance of large parts of London emerging as the "sink" estate of the region with all the attendant social problems which that implies.

Secondly, on the demand side it is tempting to posit a strategy targeted exclusively on "tradeable" and particularly internationally tradeable – goods and services and a high wage, high productivity workforce. Were London to follow the "pure" global city model the resultant economic and social impact could only accentuate the overheating in west London and the rest of the south east region's economy. Instead, we would advocate the advance of a strategy which, while recognizing the need to develop and train such a workforce, also acknowledged the significance of the many other activities which are essential to support them in both public and private sectors. This strategic policy consideration raises issues of economic diversity and training which are dealt with in Chapters 2 and 5 respectively.

SUMMARY

- The attributes of a world city in terms of jobs and income and the associated infrastructure were, according to our analysis and survey work, three-fold – education and training appropriate to commercial needs, access to a diverse set of skills, and intra-city mobility.

- The international business respondents to our survey considered that London was served less well on these three counts than other world cities.

- One consequence of this was the increasingly conspicuous mismatch of London labour demand and supply reflected in high unemployment coexisting with high vacancy rates. An increasing proportion of London, especially inner London, residents have become marginalised from the sources of wealth creation.

- The implications are that labour resources remain under-utilised within London and that labour is imported from peripheral areas at additional costs to the employer (disruption costs), to the commuter (stress and fatigue), to the public purse (transport provision) and to the overall environment (air pollution). Moreover, one sixth of wealth generated in London leaks from it as a consequence.

- Less than half our survey respondents in London and New York anticipated that jobs and income would increase over the next fifteen years compared with the majority to Tokyo and mainland European cities' respondents.

- The urban policy framework for London should consider the dangers posed by widening social divisions where job opportunities are polarised between high status producer services jobs for the qualified "insiders" and unstable consumer services employment or unemployment for the rest. These divisions were a key factor in New York's economic crisis in the 1970s and the flight of headquarters from the city.

- There is no single, simple solution to these issues. In order to address them, it will be necessary to adopt a city-wide appraisal of education and training, intra-city transport provision and other means of deploying lower income and disadvantaged groups to avoid their marginalisation within a prosperous and busy world city.

The thing about
London is not that it is the most
beautiful city in the world, or the nicest,
or the most exciting, but that it is the most inexhaustibly
interesting. It is not just the ever apparent age of the place,
but its mingled sense of knock about change and conservation —
when I look at Wordsworth's view from Westminster Bridge,
the whole metropolis from the distant towers of the City
to Chelsea reaches seemed to be undergoing perpetual
rejuvenating surgery, both cosmetic and organic,
transplants of one kind or another, century
after century.

Jan Morris
The Times Saturday Review, April 1991

Ice Skating at Broadgate
STANHOPE PLC AND ROSEHAULGH PLC

4
QUALITY OF LIFE

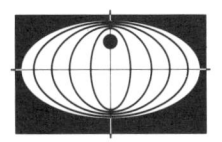

In previous chapters, we dealt with the rather more tangible requisites for the success of a world city. While objective comparisons may be problematic, at least the wealth creation capacity of a metropolis can be assessed alongside that of other world cities. Similarly, jobs and income can be quantified and compared between cities and countries.

Quality of life is something different. More than any of the other attributes of a world city, it tends to be subjectively defined and then often by its absence. In this respect, quality of life represents the paint on the canvas that is the city – its colour and texture, even the light it reflects, will effectively determine the city's perceived ability to accommodate, reflect and foster civilised values and human achievements. The quality of life, work and leisure may be elusive attributes of the urban environment, but as far as residents, employees and visitors are concerned they tend to be the means by which it is judged.

In this chapter we shall examine the key factors which determine the quality of life in our sample cities – from the availability of green space to the negative effects of noise and pollution. We will also present a comparative overview of the role and quality of culture as part of the enjoyment of life, work and leisure in the world cities.

QUALITY OF LIFE – THE KEY ELEMENTS

We have attempted to demonstrate that the sustainability of a world city requires wealth creation which, in turn, is dependant on agglomeration

Figure 4.1: Urban quality of life framework: key elements and relationships

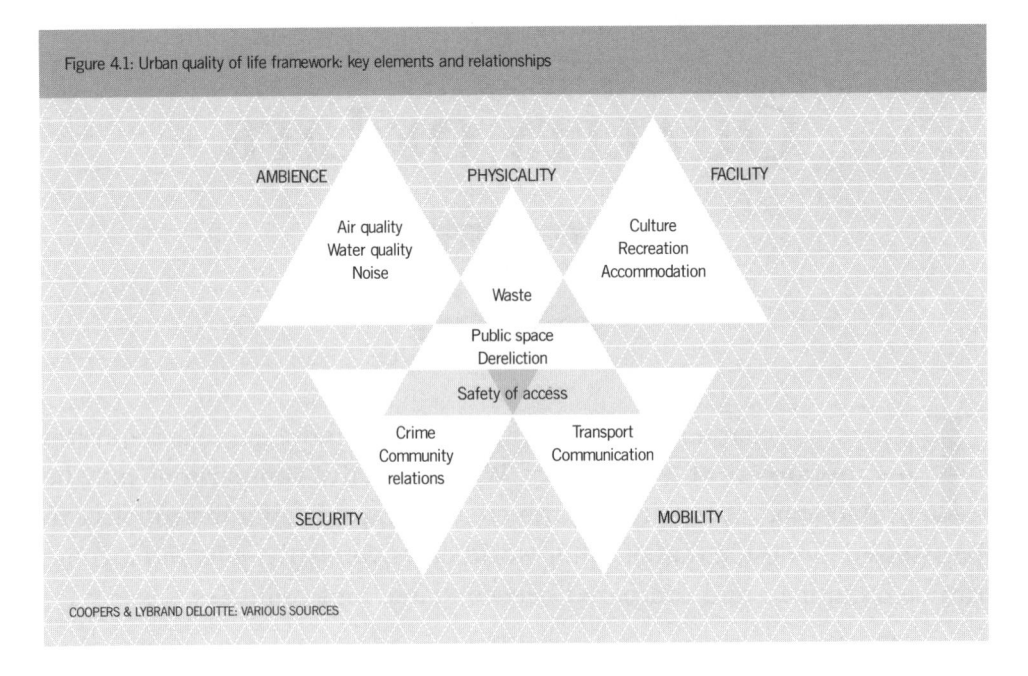

AMBIENCE — Air quality, Water quality, Noise

PHYSICALITY — Waste, Public space, Dereliction

FACILITY — Culture, Recreation, Accommodation

Safety of access

SECURITY — Crime, Community relations

MOBILITY — Transport, Communication

COOPERS & LYBRAND DELOITTE: VARIOUS SOURCES

economies and creativity. As a result, a world city is a bustling, hectic environment in which to live and work. Such an environment can induce stress. This is not an unmitigated evil, since effectively managed stress can stimulate innovation and creativity. However, beyond certain limits, and certainly in those aspects of life over which the individual has little control, stress can be dysfunctional and is likely to have an adverse effect on the city dynamic. Thus, for those living and working in a metropolis, we believe that the key consideration in the quality of life is the effective management of stress.

The elements which comprise the quality of life in a city are diverse and imprecise. Furthermore, comparative assessment of such elements is muddied by culturally determined perceptions and considerations. Nevertheless, some degree of common ground can be established. Our interpretation of the available evidence tends to suggest that the reduction of

QUALITY OF LIFE

urban stress, over which individuals have little control, must lie at the heart of any strategy to improve quality of life in the city.

Over the last few years, a number of indicators have been used to quantify the principal dimensions of the quality of life. Figure 4.1 presents those elements which most regularly appear in informed assessments of the quality of life in an urban environment.

Taken individually, it is easy to dismiss these individual elements as unimportant; often their impact is marginal at any given point in time. But, in the longer term, and taken together, their significance is considerable. The potential negative aspects of these elements can ultimately inhibit access to and mobility within the city; precipitate the degradation of, and reduction in access to, public space; and discourage residence and social activity. Conversely, their potential positive effects can create a new enlivening and enriching environment which makes the city a good place to visit, to relocate to or to stay in.

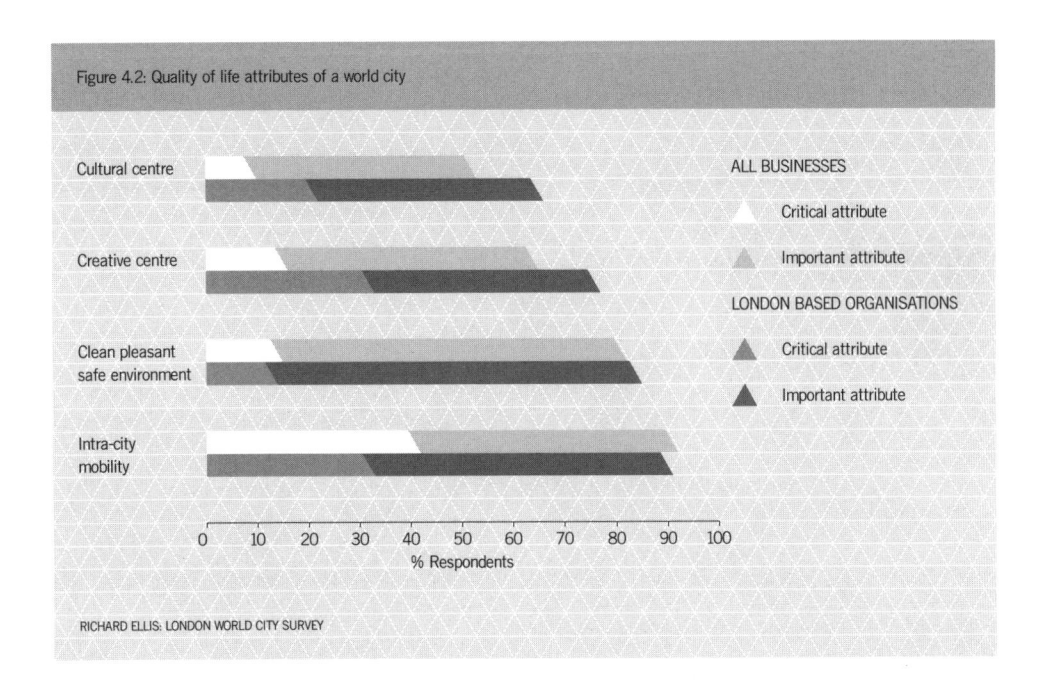

Figure 4.2: Quality of life attributes of a world city

RICHARD ELLIS: LONDON WORLD CITY SURVEY

The results of our survey strongly support certain key elements of quality of life identified in Figure 4.1. The attributes which emerged as being most important were fast and easy mobility within the city; a clean, safe and pleasant environment; a creative and innovative centre: and a well-developed cultural and historic backdrop. The survey results reveal that a significant proportion of respondents considered these factors to be critical or important attributes of a world city – see Figures 4.2 and 4.3.

A survey of members of the London Forum also carried out as part of our work examined in some depth those aspects of urban life which were considered most likely to comprise the quality of life. Members were asked to identify what they considered to be the most important factors contributing to a high quality of life in a world city. The results are similar

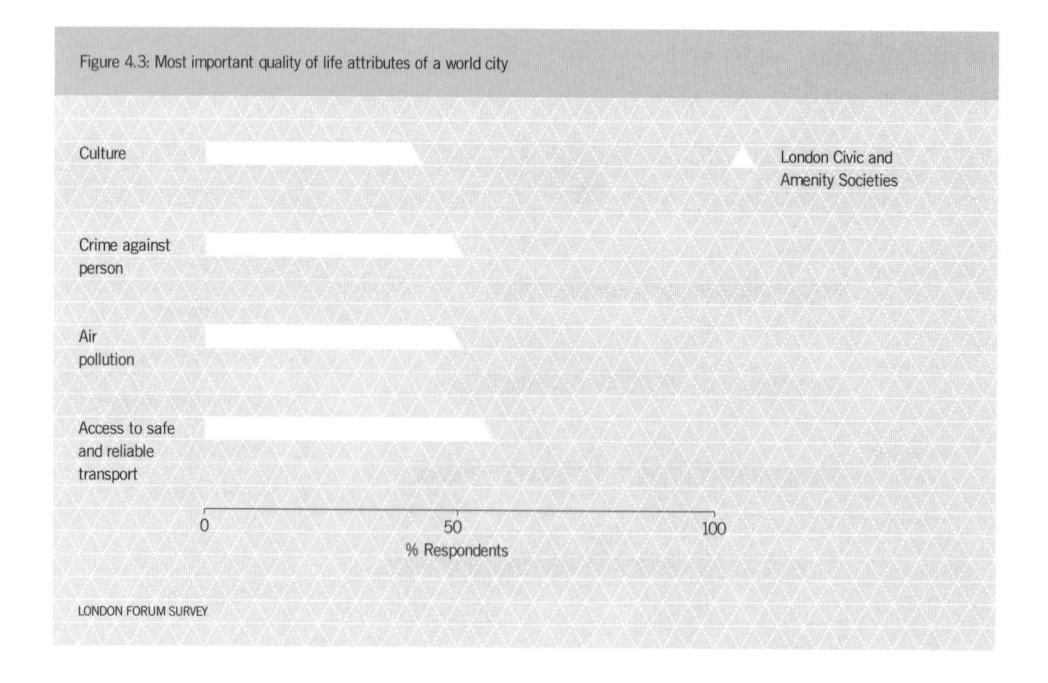

Figure 4.3: Most important quality of life attributes of a world city

- Culture
- Crime against person
- Air pollution
- Access to safe and reliable transport

% Respondents

London Civic and Amenity Societies

LONDON FORUM SURVEY

to those of our larger survey of organisations. Those factors which were identified by more than 40 per cent of the Forum members were access to safe and reliable public transport; low levels of air pollution; low levels of crime against the person; and a variety of high quality cultural activities.

On the face of it, none of these results are particularly surprising. However, it is instructive to take a look at those determinants of quality of life which were considered by London Forum members to be *less* important. The factors which emerged were low levels of water pollution (11 per cent); low levels of crime against property (11 per cent); high levels of visible policing (11 per cent); short travel to work times (11 per cent); good local shopping facilities (6 per cent); and good local social and leisure facilities (6 per cent).

As a result of our survey findings and our reading of previous evidence we feel justified in concentrating on the following quality of life elements:

☐ pollution, especially that related to transport;

☐ pleasant environment, particularly that which is afforded by public space and the design of the built form;

☐ personal safety; *and*

☐ cultural provision.

QUALITY OF LIFE

In this section we shall examine in detail those factors identified above which are most closely associated with stress in world cities. The assessment is largely qualitative because of the limited amount of comparative data at the city level that appears to be available.

Pollution

Air Pollution The relationship between the sources of air pollution and the various forms of atmospheric pollutant that is emitted can, in general terms, be classified as follows:

- sulphur dioxide and other sulphurous compounds are chiefly emitted from stationary sources such as factories, offices and homes;

- carbon dioxide, carbon monoxide, nitrogen oxides, lead and hydrocarbons are primarily emitted by mobile sources such as cars, buses, lorries etc;

- stationary sources are also significant contributors of nitrogen oxides and carbon dioxide; and

- particulate matter (dust) is most closely associated with mobile and stationary combustion and crushing activities.

Sulphur dioxide emissions A number of factors have contributed to the relatively recent decline in sulphur dioxide pollution which has been noted in all of the world cities. In part, the fall in sulphur dioxide emissions is a result of the strengthening of controls on the sulphur content in fuel (particularly following the widespread reporting of the adverse impact of sulphur dioxide emissions in the form of acid rain). The effect of these controls has been supported by the use of fuels which are generally lower in sulphur – for example, fuel oils and, more particularly, natural gas. Finally, improvements in energy efficiency and conservation, largely driven by the rising cost of fuel during the 1970s and early 1980s, have significantly reduced fuel consumption.

Figure 4.4 reveals that London's relative position has improved. From having the highest level of sulphur dioxide emissions in 1975, London ranked third after Berlin and Paris during the latter part of the 1980s.

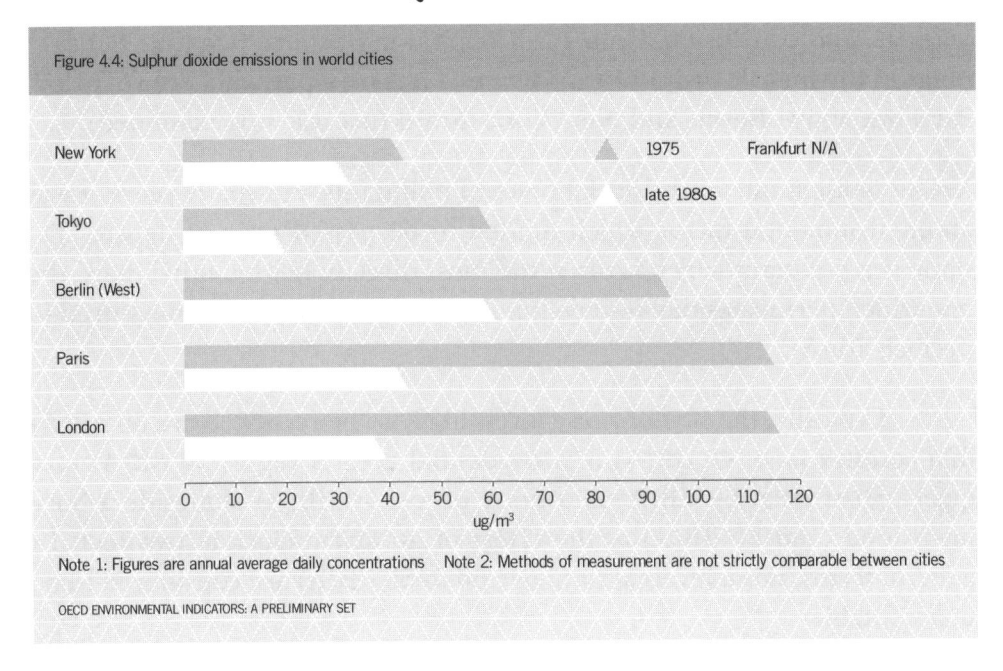

Figure 4.4: Sulphur dioxide emissions in world cities

City	1975	late 1980s
New York		
Tokyo		
Berlin (West)		
Paris		
London		
Frankfurt	N/A	N/A

x-axis: 0–120 µg/m³

Note 1: Figures are annual average daily concentrations   Note 2: Methods of measurement are not strictly comparable between cities

OECD ENVIRONMENTAL INDICATORS: A PRELIMINARY SET

Carbon dioxide emissions Comparative data for carbon dioxide emissions are not readily available for the world cities. Road transport is a significant contributor to carbon dioxide levels, particularly within the urban environment. For example, in Britain it is estimated that 25 per cent of total carbon dioxide emissions derive from road transport sources. Although on a per capita basis emission levels in Britain are low, other countries' emission levels have been in decline, while in this country the volume of carbon dioxide has been rising.

The problems associated with obtaining quantitative data measuring air pollution in cities, particularly on any comparative basis, is highlighted by the 1990 report of the Population Crisis Committee. The report examined air pollution in cities as part of a much wider review of urban living standards. Data problems forced the Committee to assess and rank air pollution conditions in the cities on the basis of a number of different criteria. The conclusion from the Committee's report was that London ranks in the middle order of world cities – it is on a par with Tokyo, below Paris but above Berlin and New York (Frankfurt was not examined).

Noise Noise is one of the dark horses of pollutants. For many years, it was an environmental factor which tended to be passed over in debate. Yet noise is a pollutant which is often the most directly felt by individuals, the one which permeates day-to-day life. Ambient noise is usually measured in decibels (dbA).

Typically, the sort of noise levels likely to be recorded are 30 dB(A) in a country lane; 40 dB(A) in a residential area at night; 50 dB(A) in a quiet urban area; 60 dB(A) in a noisy office; 70 dB(A) alongside a busy main road; and 80 dB(A) as the effect of an alarm clock at two feet. In general terms, noise levels at or above 60 to 65 dB(A) are considered to be unacceptable.

There are a variety of sources of noise which, taken together, can add to the stress of urban life – for example, people, traffic, radios, TVs, animals, aircraft and helicopters, industry, construction activity and so on. Of these, the prime offender for most people tends to be noise from traffic with aircraft noise a close second. Noise is an issue of increasing concern in urban areas. In Tokyo, over 50 per cent of pollution-related complaints brought to the Metropolitan Government concerned noise and vibration. In Paris, more than 90 per cent of the complaints reported to the city police departments nuisance bureau concerned noise-related issues.

We have been unable to identify any recognised comparative assessment of noise levels in world cities. If data from an OECD report are used, the suggestion is that a wide range between 5 to 30 per cent of the population in urban areas are regularly exposed to a noise level, principally from traffic, over 65 dB(A). The Population Crisis Committee attempted to obtain standardised data on ambient noise in cities for comparative purposes, but were unable to do so. Consequently, a more qualitative evaluation was used and cities were rated on a scale where a score of ten meant no noticeable ambient noise, while a score of one meant that noise levels represent a health hazard. The results of this assessment of cities' noise levels places Paris above London and New York in terms of "peace and quiet", but below Tokyo and Berlin – see Figure 4.5.

Litter   In recent years, it has become conventional to stigmatise London as dirty, particularly in relation to other cities. For example, the "Life in

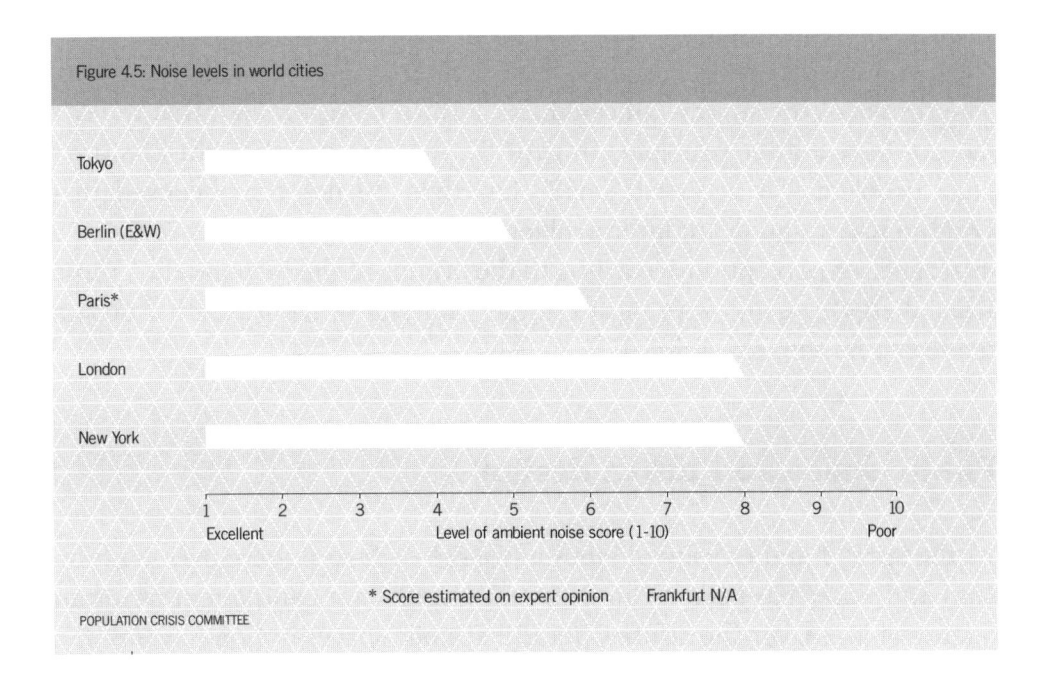

Figure 4.5: Noise levels in world cities

Tokyo	
Berlin (E&W)	
Paris*	
London	
New York	

Level of ambient noise score (1-10)
1 Excellent — 10 Poor

* Score estimated on expert opinion   Frankfurt N/A

POPULATION CRISIS COMMITTEE

London" Survey undertaken for London Weekend Television in August 1990 showed that 66 per cent of respondents felt that London was a "dirty place to live". But, by comparison, a survey of New York residents two months earlier for *Time Magazine* and CNN showed that 75 per cent of them agreed that their city was dirty. Moreover, even direct comparisons can be misleading. For example, expenditure statistics suggest that Paris spends twice as much on street cleaning as London. On that basis, it is argued that Paris is twice as clean as London. There is, however, no empirical evidence that the streets are actually cleaner, nor is there any suggestion within the studies that the expenditure information has been disaggregated to ensure that like comparisons are being made.

This is not to suggest that London does not have a litter problem; simply that it is probably no worse than that of most of the other world cities. A survey among overseas visitors to London during the summer of 1990, conducted for the London Tourist Board, sheds some light on this. The results of the survey indicated that a third of visitors felt that the city did not have a litter problem. In general, the majority thought London's litter problem was at worst 'small'; less than 20 per cent believed that London had a significant litter problem. Predictably, the survey revealed a difference of perception according to the origins of the respondent – those from West Germany were most critical, while those from North America tended to be the least critical.

Public space and urban design

As the spread and density of cities has increased, so public space both on land and water has become an ever more significant component of urban quality of life. Over the last few decades, public spaces in London with the exception of a few significant, often centrally located parks, have tended to be neglected and degraded. Yet the evidence increasingly emphasises the high value individuals place on access to public space and the appreciation they show for the urban fabric of the cities in which they live and work. This point was raised by the European Commission's 1990 Green Paper on the urban environment where it was highlighted that a "general increase in leisure time has made cities increasingly aware of the value and importance of such open spaces in or close to the city".

Public space and the urban fabric play a significant role in defining a community. Waterfronts – rivers and lakes, the pavements and streets, public squares, parks and greenery, woodlands and farmland, the historic buildings and the diversity of architectural styles all combine to establish a city's unique sense of place. There is, however, a trend for spaces to become less well used by the public, either because for security reasons they are closed by their owners, especially at night, or they are severed by traffic.

There are two particular aspects of this attribute which we can describe and, to some extent, assess. The first is the availability and distribution of what we have called "green space" in cities; the second is concerned with architectural development, built form and the city skyline.

Green Space

This is a combination of two concepts – the availability and quality of green space and the ease of access to it. The latter is almost impossible to quantify. One method of assessing the availability of green space is to compare the amount of parkland and other green areas with the floor area of office stock in the central area. These ratios are set out for world cities in Figure 4.6 on the next page.

Considered in terms of this ratio, only Berlin has a greater amount of park provision to office space than London. Indeed, London has a much better ratio when compared to Tokyo and Paris and also, to a lesser degree, ranks higher than Frankfurt and New York. Below we describe the green space areas in the central districts of the world cities.

Frankfurt Frankfurt has around 1,485 hectares of parkland and green spaces, of which nearly 10 per cent is in the central area of the city. The largest green space in the commercial area is the Grueneburg Park (including the Botanical Gardens and Palmengarten) towards the north of the West End (55 hectares). The core of the city, on the north bank of the

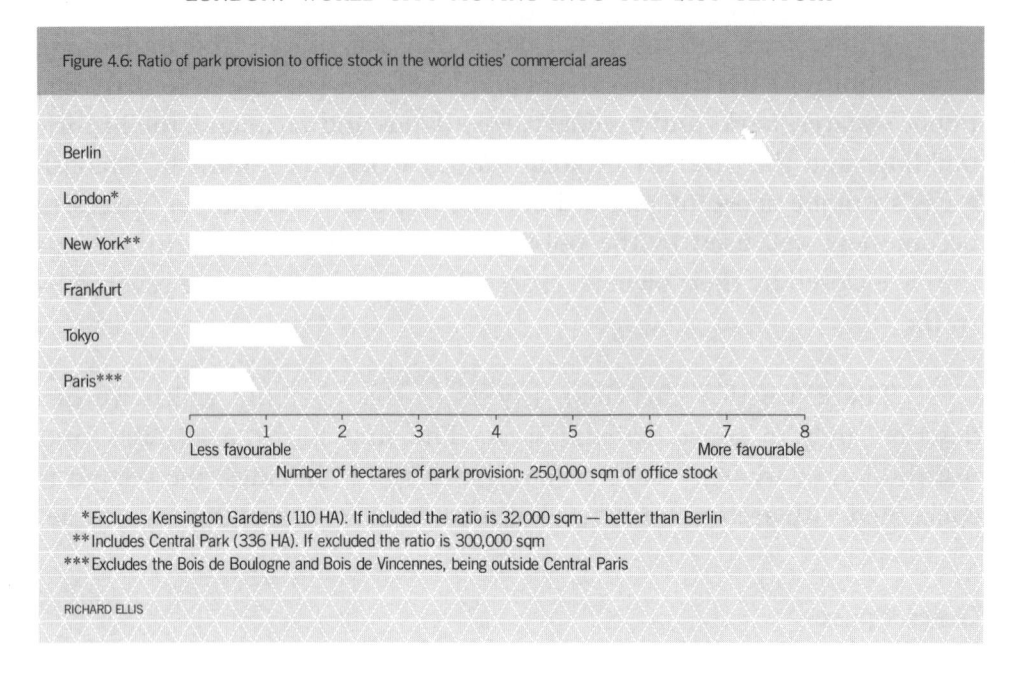

Figure 4.6: Ratio of park provision to office stock in the world cities' commercial areas

Berlin	▬▬▬▬▬▬▬
London*	▬▬▬▬▬▬
New York**	▬▬▬▬▬
Frankfurt	▬▬▬▬
Tokyo	▬▬
Paris***	▬

0 — Less favourable ... 8 — More favourable
Number of hectares of park provision: 250,000 sqm of office stock

*Excludes Kensington Gardens (110 HA). If included the ratio is 32,000 sqm — better than Berlin
**Includes Central Park (336 HA). If excluded the ratio is 300,000 sqm
***Excludes the Bois de Boulogne and Bois de Vincennes, being outside Central Paris

RICHARD ELLIS

Main, is enclosed by a semi-circular, 50 metre-wide ribbon of parkland known as the Wallanlagen. Further east, the Zoological Gardens and Ost-Park provide substantial areas of green space within easy reach of the city centre.

Berlin Over 10 per cent of land in former West Berlin (49 sq.km) was used for parks and recreational areas. The historical Tiergarten is one of the largest green spaces in the middle of the city (200 hectares), although many small parks are scattered throughout the commercial area. Prior to unification, one of the aims of the West Berlin Preparatory Land-Use Plan (1984) was to link these smaller green spaces to provide continuous green "corridors" running through the city. The Federal Garden Festival, due to be held in Berlin in 1995, should further this aim. It has recently been emphasised that green spaces in the city centre will be maintained and new spaces created, particularly now along the strip formally occupied by the Berlin wall. This creates a unique opportunity to strengthen further the network of green corridors.

Paris Most of the green open space in Paris is to the east and west of Paris either at the Bois de Boulogne, or the Bois de Vincennes. The central business district contains relatively little green space; within walking distance is the Parc le Monceau, le Jardin de Tuileries and the open space at the lower end of the Champs Elysees. There is in total around 139 acres of open green space within easy walking distance. People on the very western edge of this district are also within walking distance of the Bois de Boulogne. A major effect of height controls on all buildings in central Paris is to minimise the visual intrusion of buildings on open spaces – and Paris' strong architectural character we believe helps to unite buildings and open spaces into a special inter-relationship.

Tokyo Open "green space" provision within central Tokyo is severely constrained despite the efforts of the Tokyo Metropolitan Government. According to the latter, Tokyo has below the Japanese national average of park area per citizen.

Within the business district central wards (Minato-ku, Chuo-ka and Chiyoda-ku), the major open green space is the Imperial Palace (285 acres) However, this is not a public place; the only public park is Hibiya Park and Akasaka Palace (approximately 220 acres in total).

Recognising that Japan's cities are under-provided with green space, the Government, under the Urban Parks Law, set a national target to double the amount of green areas by enlarging the average park area to 6 square metres per citizen by the year 2000. The financial, social and other costs of such large-scale park creation are significant, as London's post-war experience demonstrated.

New York Park provision within Manhattan is dominated by the 840 acre Central Park. However, Central Park lies to the north of the conventional boundary of Manhattan's central business district (from the Battery in the south to 61st Street in the north). Excluding Central Park, there are 15 public parks in downtown Manhattan which total some 148 acres (with an average size of 9.8 acres); in midtown there are 10 public parks totalling 38 acres. Park provision is particularly low in the midtown area, but the fact that Central Park is immediately adjacent to midtown more than compensates for this apparent low provision.

Downtown's largest parks are at East River (56 acres) and Battery Park (23 acres). However, by excluding these parks, the average size of park provision is only 5 acres.

London Within London's central area, park provision is dominated by the Royal Parks. Provision is concentrated in the West End; the City of London has no major public parks. The principal parks in Central London comprise over 1,000 acres and include Hyde Park, Regents Park, Kensington Gardens, St James's Park and Green Park. Also important to the character of central London is the array of urban squares, some modern, some Victorian or Georgian – some, like Covent Garden, from even earlier periods. Each is different and the majority are protected by specific legislation.

Urban Design

The architectural development of a city and its overall quality of urban design, including its skyline, play a key role in the aesthetic appreciation of the environment in which we live and work. It also has an impact on the desirability or otherwise of one locale over another and, as a consequence, can play a key role in determining the prosperity not only of a city as a whole but of particular neighbourhoods within a city. If properly employed, conservation and planning restrictions can enhance the beauty of an area. In short, the prevalent shape and quality of the built form in a city has a significant effect on the quality of life in a metropolis and on the economic viability of the surrounding development. This section offers a descriptive overview of the characteristics of the built form in each of our world cities.

Frankfurt Frankfurt has earned a reputation for being a city of rather uninspiring office blocks. The construction of the 256 metre high Messeturm – Europe's tallest building – has done little to dispel this image. The city suffered extensive bomb damage during World War II and what might appear to be a relaxed attitude to building regulations resulted in a considerable escalation of the Frankfurt skyline. However, the location of the Messeturm in the Trade Fair area is indicative of more restrictive regulations pushing new developments westwards away from the traditional office districts of the main banking area (centred on the eastern end of the Mainzer Landstrasse) and the West End.

Many of the buildings in the banking area were constructed in the late 1950s, although new developments have emerged during the 1980s. The West End stock offers a mixture of residential and commercial accommodation, much of which dates from the 1960s. The average height of city centre tower blocks is approximately 80 metres – about 20 storeys.

Berlin During the last forty years, the development of West Berlin has been constrained by its enclosure by East Germany. Berlin's "island" nature deterred many firms from constructing or renting large premises in the city. As a result, although much of Berlin was destroyed in World War II, only a small number of high-rise buildings have been constructed and these are dispersed throughout the city rather than being a feature of any particular area. Examples in the former western sector include the Europa-Center, the Axel Springer Haus, Kochstrasse and the Steglitzer Kreisel (130 metres). At 96 metres, the International Trade Centre is the tallest building in what used to be East Berlin.

There is no dedicated office area in Berlin. Indeed most of the districts in former West Berlin include buildings which contain a mixture of office, retail and residential accommodation, many of which were constructed in the 1950s and 1960s and remain in their original condition. However, a number of buildings – including a concentration of office buildings around Ernst Reuter Platz – were erected during the construction boom of the late 1960s/early 1970s.

There are few physical features to affect major development in the city. Perhaps the major physical constraint is the large amount of forest, wooded area and lakeland to the west of the city in the districts of Reinickendorf, Spandau and Zehlendorf. Although this area, effectively a green belt, has been breached in the middle (Spandau Centre), it had previously been subject to strict conservation controls and it is likely that this will continue for the foreseeable future. But the development industry is inevitably casting its eyes at the potential in Berlin and the city, like other world cities, may find it difficult to resist proposed developments.

Paris The architecture of Paris has been characterised for at least a century by the "traditional" six-storey buildings created by Baron Haussmann. This mode of architecture dominates the city, including the central commercial district, and ensures steady, uniform height broken only by the Eiffel Tower, and in the south of the city by la Tour de Montparnasse (with 56 floors and at 229 metres the tallest office building in Paris). Heights of buildings are regulated in local plans, and vary by district. Buildings above the stated heights are not permitted.

There are very few natural physical factors likely to affect the development of Paris. This said, the river Seine can be perceived as a "border" to the west of the city. Consequently areas such as Neuilly, Boulogne Billancourt and Levallois-Perret which are inside the Seine – although outside the city – are more favoured than areas on the other side of the river. One man-made barrier has been the boulevard Peripherique which has effectively constrained the city. The strict preservation of the Bois de Boulogne has also effectively stopped development of some of the western side of the city.

The skyline formed by La Defense is completely different. Here, most, if not all, buildings are, as a matter of considered design, very tall and built in a variety of styles. The image of the area is dominated by the 36 floor Grande Arche de la Defense completed in 1989. Most office-based employment over the last ten years in Paris has occurred in this area and its growth has been enhanced by substantial new infrastructure provision.

Tokyo Tokyo's Central Business District is located on delta land formed by the Edogawa and Arakawa rivers. Because of the difficult sub-soil strata, the frequency of earthquake movement and absolute height controls imposed by the City administration, high-rise commercial development did not take place. Consequently, the skyline of Tokyo was, until the early 1970s, characterised by low-rise conformity and structure. An additional feature was the extensive urban sprawl of high density, wooden apartment homes surrounding the business district.

However, with modern engineering and building techniques and a relaxation of height control regulations in the central and the waterfront areas of Tokyo, the skyline is now being rapidly transformed into a "Manhattan" style. Disputes have arisen from neighbouring users of the proposed super-high rise buildings (defined as being over 100 metres). The Tokyo Metropolitan Government has now established the Tokyo Metropolitan ordinance for prevention and co-ordination of disputes arising from the construction of medium to high-rise buildings.

In recent years, the Tokyo government has divided Tokyo's central business district into blocks in which the lower or upper limits of the height of buildings are fixed. Three types of districts have now been established in which maximum building heights are fixed. The government has also created "specified blocks" within which floor area ratios and the height of buildings are stipulated. Presently, there are forty-nine such blocks covering 88 hectares.

By March 1989, the central business district had ten super high-rise buildings, with another ten or so planned. Outside the established business district, the New City Hall development at Shinjuku sub-centre, is also altering the skyline with eight super high-rise buildings. Shinjuku is well connected by new infrastructure to the old central business district.

Because of the planning restrictions surrounding the central business district, the only potential physical expansion of the area lies to the south in Tokyo Bay, where land is being reclaimed from the sea. The proposed development of the Tokyo Waterfront sub-centre is to have high-rise commercial development focused upon the Tokyo Teleport (due for completion 2001), and will reclaim land totalling some 448 hectares. Indeed there are proposals by the Ohbayashi Group to build a mixed use development more than 2,000 metres tall in the middle of Tokyo Bay.

New York Business activities in New York are centred in Manhattan. This has directly affected the city's urban form. Being surrounded by the Hudson and East rivers, Manhattan has had to accommodate market pressures for commercial development. The rapidly expanding population and commercial activity during the late nineteenth and early twentieth centuries, coupled with the limited amount of physical space in Manhattan, conspired to shape New York's now characteristic urban form. The development of the 'skyscraper' was also facilitated by the development of the high-speed elevator and new skeleton steel construction methods of building.

"Skyscrapers" were initially constructed in "downtown" New York, in the financial and banking sector based around Wall Street. However, a separate business district was also established in midtown, based upon head offices of the big new industrial combines. The result is the characteristic urban skyline of Manhattan: two distinctive zones of skyscrapers with downtown at the southern tip of Manhattan, now dominated by the World Trade Towers (1,350 ft high) and the midtown complex of such well-known buildings as the Empire State (1,250 ft high) and Citi-Corp (900ft).

The city's zoning controls have had a significant impact upon the New York skyline. For example, changes in the 1916 zoning laws (which regulated the height and volume of buildings in relation to the width of the streets), account for the "wedding cake" urban shape of the 1930's skyscrapers – being built in successive layers with setbacks at given heights.

In recent years, the physical expansion of downtown Manhattan has been made possible by the reclamation of waterfront land at Battery Park from spoil of excavated land from the World Trade Centre, which has its own zoning regulations, and by the provision of appropriate transport infrastructure.

London Historically, London's development can be considered as the merging of two distinct centres in two distinct locations. The City of London developed as a response to its port-related activities and as the lowest bridging point on the Thames which, in turn, evolved into a centre of commerce and finance. Up river, Westminster became the seat of Government from 1066. London has traditionally not developed from a "grand design" like Paris or Berlin, nor a rigid planned streetwork like New York.

This parallel/dual development of London has historically affected its urban form. Westminster remains the focal point for Government, although the adjacent West End has now attracted the headquarters functions of some UK and international manufacturing and service industries. However, unlike the City, the West End also has for the last two hundred years built up a tradition of being London's prime residential area and foremost international shopping, entertainment and cultural centre. From these town centres, London has grown outwards to create suburbs, initially within walking or coaching distance, later by railway, often centred on market towns like Uxbridge, Croydon and Romford.

The urban skyline in London continues to reflect this historic evolution of the capital and the building conditions and regulations which, until after the 1920s, made the church spires and the towers of Westminster Palace unusual features. Throughout London, and in Westminster in particular, building heights have been strictly controlled. The legislation which enforces conservation area and listed building controls ensures that the height of new developments are constrained. Since 1945 in the City, commercial and office development has been generally encouraged. As a result controls have been, in practice, more flexible in order to facilitate the provision of new office buildings to accommodate today's financial and commercial requirements. The principal means of building height control is based on a standard plot ratio maximum of 5:1. As a consequence, even in the office boom of the 1970s and 1980s broad floor plate buildings like Broadgate were more commercially viable than tower blocks.

In addition, throughout London building heights had also been controlled in order to preserve strategic views and the surroundings of landmarks such as St Pauls and the Houses of Parliament. The result of such constraints is that, today, London has relatively few high-rise buildings outside the City, with the exception of a number of point blocks in Victoria and the West End, beside the Thames and groups of high buildings along the Euston Road, around London Bridge Station and at some strategic centres like Croydon.

In East London, the skyline is now being dramatically transformed by the development of Canary Wharf, by Olympia and York, which now boasts the UK's highest building. This development represents, in effect, an extension of the central business district towards the east. In infrastructure terms, it is not, at present, well connected to the City and the West End, but construction is underway to remedy the situation in the 1990s. It is acknowledged that good infrastructure is essential to the success of the development if it is to contribute to redressing the wider East/West imbalance in London.

Personal Safety

An individual's safety in an urban environment, or the threat to that safety, is perceived as being associated with specific types of crime – murder, assault, robbery, sexual offences and theft. Such offences are, of course, a cause for considerable concern in their own right because of the damage they inflict on individuals. But, they also have adverse effects on the efficient operation of a city – they inhibit movement and create a climate of fear which discourages or restricts residence, mobility and social activity and heightens community tensions. For example, in 1989 the Quality of Life Group at Strathclyde University identified violent and non-violent crime as the most important dimensions in assessing urban quality of life. The results of our own survey reinforce this conclusion. However, as far as we are aware, personal safety rarely, if ever, features as part of any assessment of the urban quality of life.

Crime statistics provide an indication of the real threat to safety which individuals can expect in world cities. However, the manner in which crimes are categorised varies from city to city, as does the incidence of reporting and recording offences. Consequently, comparative data need to be treated with caution.

The Report of the Commissioner of Police of the Metropolis, June 1991, suggests that levels of safety in London are deteriorating. There have been marked increases in the incidence of violence against the person, robbery and sexual offences over the last decade. Indeed, figures have more than doubled. A 1989 report by London in Need pointed to the growing number of demands for assistance from victim support groups.

City comparisons of crime rates across national boundaries are particularly difficult to make. We have contrasted London statistics with those for other countries hosting world cities, adjusting the national figures for their city populations. This is a very crude estimating procedure. It suggests that Tokyo is extremely safe and that London is safer than the other cities. Despite the limitations of the estimates, the conclusions are broadly in line with those of the Population Crisis Committee. According to the latter, Tokyo, London and Paris were ranked significantly above New York and Berlin on public safety – London and Paris were ranked equal behind Tokyo.

CULTURAL PROVISION

The role of culture in enhancing the quality of life cannot easily be separated from its wealth creation and employment generation potential. We have deliberately assigned our most detailed examination of the cultural sector to the wealth creation chapter of this book because we wanted to align ourselves with those who assert that culture creates wealth rather than with those who perceive culture as a fortunate by-product of wealth creation. The aspect of cultural provision which we emphasise in this chapter is the access it affords the world city resident, worker and visitor to exercise his or her preference for fun, entertainment and intellectual stimulus.

This will be a rather qualitative and impressionistic assessment. We focus particularly on the relative contribution of each world city in terms of the standards of creativity and innovation, the availability of facilities which enable the cultural products to be consumed; and the activities – including promotion and sales – which facilitate public awareness of the products. We present our findings, from wide ranging discussions and interviews with about one hundred representatives of the cultural sector, by type of cultural provision.

Theatre

London's theatre infrastructure is large and comprehensive. In 1987/8, the metropolis had seventy-two venues – including the acknowledged world-standard centres at Covent Garden, the Albert Hall, the South Bank and the Barbican – capable of seating 59,000 theatre-goers every evening. London is home to the bulk of the UK's agents, impresarios and the headquarters of the majority of Britain's theatrical institutions. London's theatrical industry equals that of New York, and is significantly ahead of Paris, Frankfurt and Berlin. It is a current perception that what this sector lacks in innovation relative to New York, it makes up for in the profitable distribution of products to the United States and the rest of the world. Over the last 10 years especially, London has become the world leader in the production of worldwide distributed musicals. For example, *Cats* has now grossed more than £1.36bn worldwide, more than the largest grossing film, *ET*. This is a trend which began over thirty years ago with the staging of the hugely successful production of *My Fair Lady* and looks set to continue. There are indications that London's theatrical industry is beginning to overtake New York in these terms. According to a 1991 report in the Sunday Times, "over the last three years, the West End has had a boom period, with revenues soaring to £178 million and 11.3 million tickets sold ... while in New York this summer twenty-four of thirty-seven Broadway theatres were dark."

The visual arts

London has a tremendous artistic heritage and contains some of the world's finest museums and galleries. It also has a sophisticated auctioneering and arts marketing structure, although in recent years it has lost its lead to New York. London's commercial gallery network is strong, but its modern public galleries are less vigorous than their counterparts in New York and Germany, particularly in terms of commissions and acquisitions.

The strength of London's visual arts is in distribution, accessibility and marketing. Less impressive is the public access to and exposure to creativity in production. While there are a substantial number of artists at work in London – over three quarters of all visual artists in Britain according to Greater London Arts – it appears to be increasingly not regarded as a place where artists choose to settle. There is no acknowledged, permanently established artists' quarters to act as a focus for creativity and contact. Consequently, the sector is losing public visibility and the support that goes with it. By contrast, as a result of support schemes like the Artists in Scotland Project, Glasgow has significantly increased its status; by providing a shop window for Scottish artists and craft workers they are remaining in the city and using London agents. A decade ago they might have moved to the capital.

Film and audio-visual industries

Absolute pre-eminence in this sector is held by Los Angeles/Hollywood in the film and TV industries. Audio-visual products are reported to be the USA's second largest export after aerospace.

Of the world cities, New York is in the leading position in the audio-visual industry mainly because it hosts the financial and strategic headquarters of all the major US film studios. It is second only to LA in the production of film and TV. It can claim the Madison Avenue of advertising and marketing agencies. Its film and TV infrastructure is large, well organised and extremely experienced. The audio-visual sector in New York also has long established links with related fields in the arts and publishing, as well as lateral ties to the financial sectors and the East Coast business establishment. Overall, the global consumers' access to audio-visual culture is dominated by what Los Angeles and New York decide to produce.

London also wields considerable influence on a global scale. London's actors, musicians, playwrights and writers have made a major contribution to world culture, often capitalising on British history, real or imagined. London is home to the BBC (the largest broadcaster outside the USSR) and contains the most extensive film, TV and radio facilities in Western Europe, including the renowned World Service. In addition to the state broadcasting corporation, London is also the base of a cluster of independent television companies including Thames, London Weekend and Channel 4.

In contrast to New York, the industry in London has poor links with the financial and other commercial sectors. This, it can be argued, creates an unproductive dichotomy. The audio-visual sector is felt to have developed a disdain for financial disciplines and the financial sector is seen to be reluctant to take on the risks associated with the audio-visual business. The result is that British – and indeed world – audiences are not being given access to British products to the extent that isolated product successes such as *Chariots of Fire* or *A Fish called Wanda* suggest ought to be possible.

Lagging far behind New York and London, Paris is in the third division as regards the generation of audio-visual products. Nevertheless it both commands its home market and also oversees sales to and production for French-speaking Africa. This sector benefits from extremely well-funded audio-visual support programmes and media infrastructure. Over the years, the industry has established strong links with other cultural sectors such as fashion, music and the theatre. While the city has earned a reputation for its innovative development of media technology, the role of Paris in the global audio-visual industry is limited by the English-language domination in world markets.

Music

In relation to other world cities, London is surpassed only by New York in terms of the strength and influence of its music business (although once again Los Angeles plays an important role in this industry). Paris and Tokyo take third and fourth place respectively. London has high level facilities in all areas of the industry, including international standard venues. The metropolis also hosts the headquarters of most of the sector's influential institutions and companies. London undoubtedly dominates the European music recording business, its reputation encouraging producers to make records over here even though, for the most part, they can access comparable facilities at home.

Ever since the "Swinging Sixties" with the rise of the Beatles, the Rolling Stones and people like Mary Quant, London has been a world leader for setting popular trends in cultural areas. This reputation for generating new sub cultures especially in music has been largely maintained and strengthened by London being known as the A & R (talent scouting) capital of the world – with over 200 people employed by the music industry as scouts and thereby helping to project a string of new stars onto the world stage.

However, there is no room for complacency. For example, with the trend towards "world music", other cultures and languages are moving to the fore and Paris with its active encouragement of African music and strong links with Africa is becoming the centre of that increasingly important development. Additionally, as the major record companies, such as Sony, are headquartered outside of the UK, their loyalty towards British products should not be taken for granted, although the British music industry is still very strong, produces a disproportionately large number of stars and remains open to positive trends and influences from around the world.

Design

Although London has the largest design consulting sector in the world, its links with home-based industry are still relatively weak and under-developed. Consequently, many leading product designers work for Italian, Japanese or German companies rather than with resident producers. London has a world-class creative and technical infrastructure with excellent educational facilities, although complaints were made to us of underfunding and the consequent erosion of this capability. All the major international contract suppliers are based in London and the industry is well-served by a diversity of support facilities provided by model-makers, typesetters, printers and design engineers. There is a need to link international demand for designers trained in London with the funding requirements of the institutions that trained them.

Museums

London is unique in the richness of its museum provision and vies with Paris for the number one spot in the world. There are some three hundred or so museums and collections throughout the capital with many new projects underway. This provision is often taken for granted, but is one of the reasons why this capital city is famous throughout the world. It includes 39 national collections, 194 independent museums, 51 local authority museums and 12 others.

There is a tendency to consider museums as a single entity and the rich variety of local museum provision within London is not always perceived. Collections range from internationally important ones at the British Museum and the Victoria and Albert to nationally significant collections of old master paintings at Dulwich Picture Gallery to the local historical identity preserved by the newly opened Wandsworth Museum. In addition, museums such as the London Museum of Jewish Life actively researches the lives and history of the Jewish community in London while the Museum of Methodism celebrates the life and work of the founder of a very different religion. Historic buildings, banking, a 19th century operating theatre in a church attic, famous personalities, maritime and regimental history are all available within the boundaries of Greater London.

Museums play a wide range of functions that are not universally recognized and public support is proportionately lower than our European partner cities. Museums have the capacity to use a wide range of interpretive techniques to meet the needs of specific groups. The full educational potential of museums is only just being realised as museums respond to the challenge of the new national curriculum. In this connection, it is noteworthy that the recent London Museums Education Unit set up to take up the tremendous demand generated by the provisions of the national curriculum has had to be largely funded by charitable sources.

As with other arts activities, museums contribute to the regeneration of depressed areas by stressing the importance of historical context, contributing towards the renovation of historic buildings and creating a cultural ambience. These qualities are highly prized by businesses considering relocation and by house builders. Museums also provide an informal place to learn throughout people's lives, encouraging and contributing to life-long learning and personal development.

London museums' infrastructure was largely put in place over a hundred years ago and in many instances is in need of substantial repair. Many buildings were constructed for different uses than are now appropriate. The major new museums redevelopments, as both in the past and elsewhere in the world, have been largely financed by the private sector – the Toshiba Gallery at the Victoria and Albert, the Sainsbury Wing at the National Gallery, the Clore Wing at the Tate and Museum of the Moving Image (which received a large proportion of its funding from the Getty Foundation) – which demonstrates the significance these organisations attach to investing in these facilities in London.

The pressure on museums and galleries to generate their own funds and market themselves has meant major changes of emphasis in the management of museums and a greater readiness to respond to "customers" need. While this has and is making them more accessible to a wider population – and thus contributing to the quality of life of both residents and visitors – it is argued that scholarship and research – on which all major museums are founded – has suffered in the process. It is also argued that the emphasis on private rather than public funding has meant that London suffers in comparison to Paris where there have been a number of highly visible publicly funded prestige projects. However, this argument should not be allowed to obscure the richness and diversity of London's current museum and gallery provision nor that, in recent years, a number of major and highly regarded projects have been completed – most notably the Sainsbury wing at the National Gallery. Perhaps, more importantly, as in other areas of London life, the qualities we have are not being maximised in terms of their potential, and overall impact in the global stage.

Sports facilities

We have not undertaken a comparison of the provision of sports facilities for this study nor were comparative data readily available for the world cities. However, we are able to make some general remarks about the quality and level of provision in London compared with elsewhere in Europe.

The public facilities available for general use are well provided for in London compared with many other European cities. In 1990 there were about 150 sports halls, some 115 swimming pools and about 40 intensive use pitches (artificial and porous) – all of which with the possible exception of swimming pools are provided to a good quality standard. In terms of specialist facilities, London rates well against other European cities in terms of athletic tracks and golf courses (most of which are located in the Green Belt or Outer Metropolitan Area) but poorly on cycling tracks, indoor tennis centres and ice-skating.

In terms of competition venues, London is relatively poorly served for outdoor stadia and indoor arenas. London's sporting stadia such as Wembley, Wimbledon, Lords and Twickenham have become household names for world sport. However, several are in need of major refurbishment and some – such as White City – have disappeared altogether.

Crystal Palace is London's only post-1945 stadium development of any scale but is largely a training venue and its facilities and spectator capacity render it unsuitable for major events on the world stage.

Summary on relative cultural provision in London

London is clearly a world-class centre of culture. It has a wealth of museums and galleries, internationally renowned theatre, opera and ballet companies, major symphony orchestras, an unsurpassed concentration of theatre in the West End as well as an internationally respected training infrastructure for the arts. London is also both a showcase and seed-bed for popular culture; the natural birthplace of international events like BandAid and trends which shape the course of popular music. Over the last few years, London has once again become a major centre for jazz, with nightclubs mushrooming throughout the city. London remains an important centre of radio, television and the media.

However, as with other aspects of London's quality of life, we discern a complacency and a tendency to take the advantages too much for granted rather than to build on them, to experiment and to have an eye for the long term. Unlike Paris, and with stronger advantages, London is making no concerted effort towards assessing its cultural attributes and promoting them for the 1990s.

The way in which arts and culture are projected in London limits the nature and extent of audience participation. This was one of the main conclusions to emerge from a wide ranging quantitative and qualitative study into peoples attitudes to, and participation in, arts events in the city. The study, undertaken for Greater London Arts (GLA) in 1989, showed that while participation in the arts is extensive, there exists a significant latent demand, which is not being translated into real demand in terms of attendance. To a large extent, this was because respondents felt that arts activities and events were "too exclusive" and "old fashioned". There was also a strong perception that the arts were too "high brow" and consequently respondents would be made to feel unwelcome.

While the evidence suggests that these perceptual issues are important and need to be overcome if London is to make greater use of its arts and cultural facilities, the GLA study also revealed a number of more practical barriers to arts participation. These related to the high cost of the arts events; the cost and lack of access to convenient pubic transport to many venues; and fears for personal safety, particularly when travelling to and from some events. The cultural sector can go some way to mitigate these barriers. In the final analysis to improve this element of quality of life will require the improvement of other key components in the city's infrastructure.

Concluding Observations

According to the London-based firms and other organisations in our survey, London's position was rated inferior to that of the other world cities on two of the four key quality of life attributes – namely, intra-city mobility and a clean and pleasant environment. The response from foreign-based organisations was generally more positive about London's position. However, the view of foreign-based organisations of their own cities was more favourable than London's view of itself with the major exception of London's ability to provide a strong, well-balanced cultural dimension – see Figure 4.7.

This generally poor perception of London was reiterated in our survey of London Forum members. Once again, apart from a favourable assessment of cultural provision, London was seen as providing a poor quality of life across the spectrum of attributes. Indeed, London Forum members considered quality of life and other environmental factors as constituting one of London's principal weaknesses – see Figure 4.8.

Our conclusions here are not new. The general message which emerged from a survey conducted for the *Evening Standard Magazine* in 1989 and London Weekend Television in 1990 suggested that the quality of life in general terms was perceived as poor and deteriorating. In fact, respondents felt so strongly about the situation in the city that in both

QUALITY OF LIFE

Figure 4.7: London's ratings on quality of life attributes

Intra-city mobility
Clean, safe pleasant environment
Creative centre
Cultural centre

1 2 3 4 5 6 7 8 9 10
Poor   Excellent

▲ London's rating by London businesses
▲ London's rating by all businesses
△ Overseas cities rating by overseas businesses

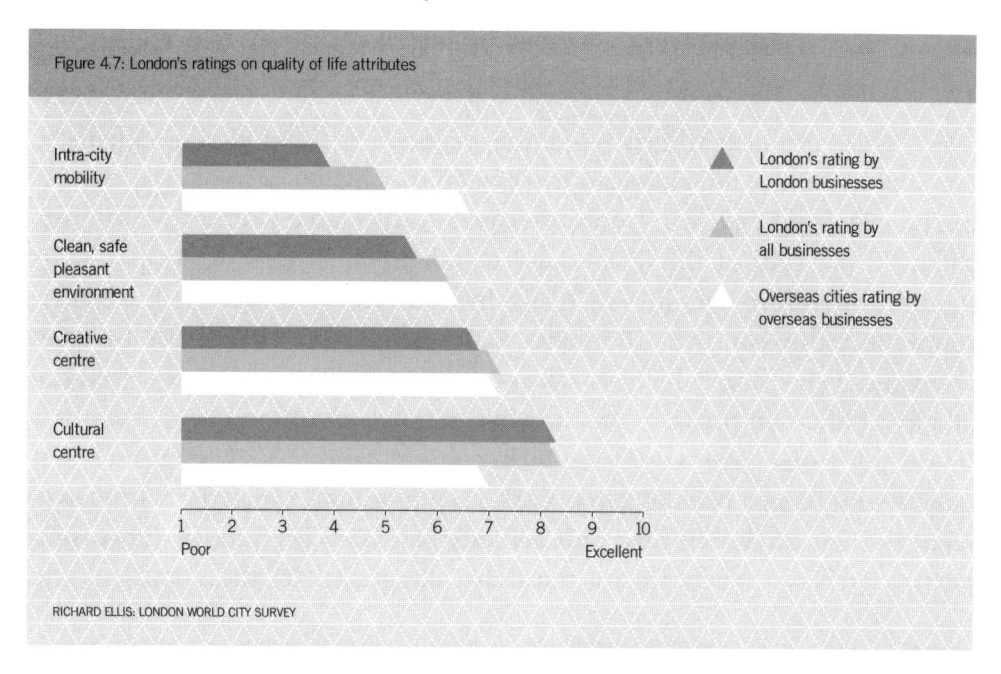

RICHARD ELLIS: LONDON WORLD CITY SURVEY

Figure 4.8: London's ratings on quality of life attributes

Access to safe reliable transport
Air pollution
Crime against person
Culture

1   2   3
Very Poor   Very Good

△ London Civic and Amenity Societies

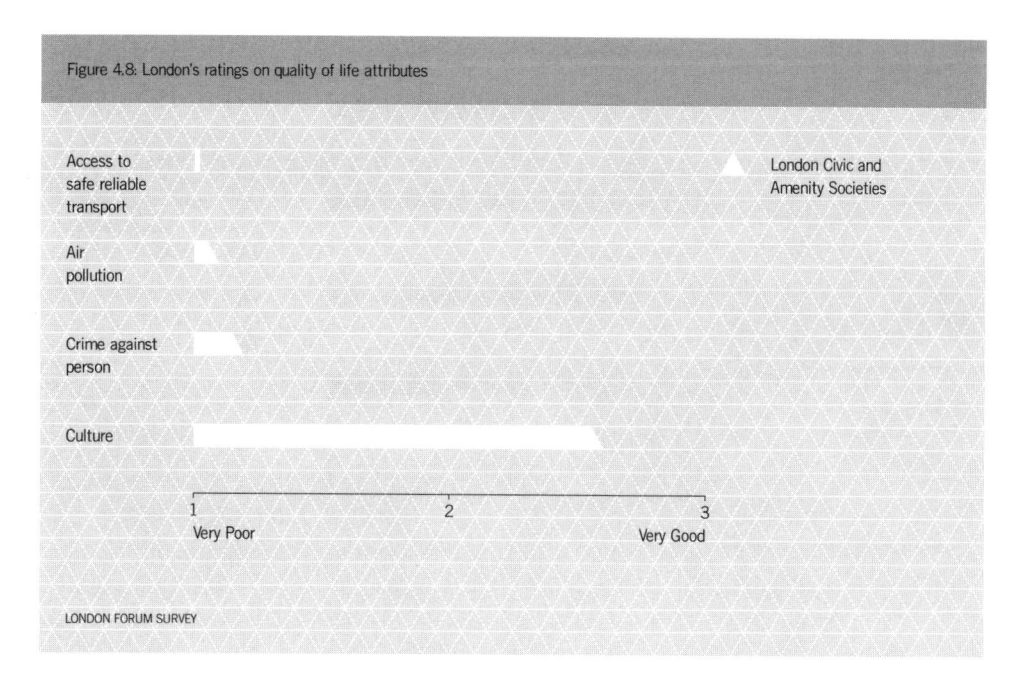

LONDON FORUM SURVEY

surveys nearly 50 per cent of them indicated that they had considered moving away.

Over the next fifteen years, the majority of London respondents to our survey did not anticipate an increase in the quality of life in the city. As can be seen from Figure 4.9, only 20 per cent expected it to improve, whereas about 40 per cent of the Tokyo and mainland European city respondents thought an improvement was likely in their cities. As far as London is concerned, this confirms the views expressed in the survey for London Weekend Television, which also showed that only 20 per cent expected the quality of life to improve in the next five to ten years, 49 per cent thought it would get worse. We would see little comfort in our survey finding that only about 10 per cent of New York respondents expected an improvement in their quality of life. This actually paints an even more depressing picture of New York's future than that suggested by the results of the

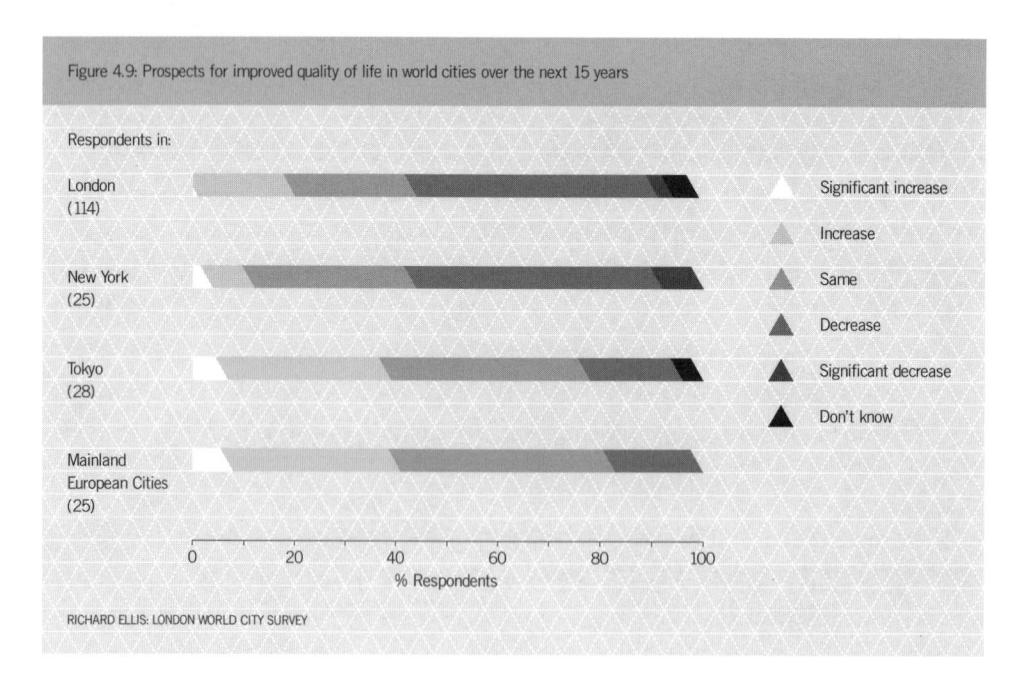

Figure 4.9: Prospects for improved quality of life in world cities over the next 15 years

RICHARD ELLIS: LONDON WORLD CITY SURVEY

Time/CNN survey undertaken in 1990, where 23 per cent thought the quality of life in that city would improve; 45 per cent believed it would get worse.

We draw two conclusions from our assessment of London's relative position on the quality of life. They should by now be familiar, because they have featured in each chapter so far. First, London has advantages which are not being built on sufficiently and, at worst, are being allowed to erode. Second, Londoners' perception of London's prospects is generally not optimistic and more pessimistic than other respondents' views of the prospects for their own city (except New York). We have in our capital all the necessary ingredients of a self-fulfilling prognosis for relative decline. London must find a way to make its perception of itself and by others more fairly reflect its relative strengths compared with other world cities. This should not be an exercise in self-congratulation – although a little bit more of this would be fitting – but a genuine audit of where London can be proud of the quality of life it offers and where action is needed.

We have not in this study undertaken such an audit. But we are persuaded from our review of readily available evidence and our survey work that London's relative strengths, particularly in open and green space, cultural provision and personal safety, deserve to be enhanced and promoted. The relative weaknesses appear to be in transport related pollution and noise. Since we also concluded in the previous two chapters that improved intra-city mobility would contribute significantly to London's wealth creation and job generation for its residents, we make no apology for adding our voices to the growing chorus for more robust and co-ordinated strategic thinking and funding of public transport and traffic management within London.

SUMMARY

- ☐ For those living and working in a busy world city, stress will be a constant companion. Beyond certain limits and in those aspects of life over which the individual has little control, stress can cease to be a stimulant to creativity and innovation. It therefore must be managed.

- Our survey respondents identified the key quality of life attributes in a world city to be a clean and safe environment, safe and reliable public transport, low levels of crime against the person and a diversity of high quality cultural provision. We have focused in this chapter on environmental quality, access to public space and the design of the built form, personal safety and cultural provision.

- By comparison with other world cities, London's environmental quality is not as bad as often suggested in survey results. It ranks in the middle order of world cities on air pollution, above Berlin and New York and on a par with Tokyo. Less than 20 per cent of overseas visitors thought London had a significant litter problem. But, on ambient noise levels, London and New York were rated to be noisier than the other world cities.

- Only Berlin has a greater amount of park provision relative to office space than London which rates much better than Tokyo or Paris on this measure. London has relatively few high-rise buildings outside the City with the significant and recent exception of East London developments. New York and Tokyo are renowned for their high-rise sky-lines; Frankfurt has a reputation for uninspiring office blocks; and Paris is characterised by traditional six-storey buildings except for La Defense with its very high buildings designed in a variety of styles.

- There have been marked increases in the incidence in London of violence against the person, robbery and sexual offences over the last decade. But in terms of world city comparisons, London and Paris tend to be ranked equally on public safety and only behind Tokyo.

- London is a world-class centre of culture only surpassed by New York. It has a wealth of museums and galleries, internationally renowned theatre, opera and ballet companies, major symphony orchestras and an internationally respected training infrastructure in the arts. However, unlike Paris and with stronger advantages, London appears to be making little concerted effort to assess its cultural attributes and promote them for the 21st century.

QUALITY OF LIFE

☐ According to our survey respondents, London was rated more highly than other world cities on its cultural attributes but less favourably on the cleanliness and safety of the environment and on access to safe and reliable transport. Less than 20 per cent of London respondents anticipated an improvement in its quality of life over the next fifteen years – only New York respondents were as pessimistic.

☐ London must find a way to restore its perception of itself and by others more fairly to reflect its relative strengths. This would require a city-wide audit to identify where London can be proud of its quality of life and where action is needed.

THE LONDON UNDERGROUND
SYSTEM REMAINS IN A POOR STATE
EVEN NOW, WITH WORK REQUIRED IN THE
DRAINS, THE PERMANENT WAY, THE SIGNALLING SYSTEM,
THE STATION INFRASTRUCTURE AND THE ROLLING STOCK — THE
DEBATE MUST BE CONCENTRATED ON THE MEANS BY WHICH
RESOURCES CAN BE FOUND TO GIVE LONDON THE
TRANSPORT SYSTEM IT NEEDS — IT'S A
CRITICISM OF ALL GOVERNMENTS
FOR THIRTY YEARS.

Wilfred Newton, May 1991

British Telecom Earth Satellite/Station
LONDON DOCKLANDS DEVELOPMENT CORPORATION

5

ENABLING INFRASTRUCTURE

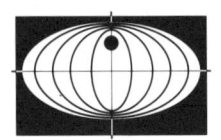

We have identified and analysed the parts played by wealth creation, jobs and income and a high quality of life in the development of a successful world city. Yet these key attributes do not exist in a vacuum. Their performance and potential are enhanced or inhibited by a second set of factors which we describe as a city's enabling infrastructure. This relates to and interacts with each of the key attributes in somewhat different ways, but its components remain the same. The elements we have identified as comprising the enabling infrastructure are the physical fabric of the city including transport, communications, and land-use – which includes both commercial property and housing; and the social and economic infrastructure, including education and training.

THE INFRASTRUCTURE COMPONENTS

The above components of the enabling infrastructure were identified from our analysis and by our survey results. First of all, we summarise these findings.

In our discussion of wealth creation, we identified the need for a large pool of labour on which business can draw. This, in turn, requires an efficient transport system. The significance of transport to a world city's success was emphasised throughout our survey – more than half of the respondents considered both national and international transport networks to be "critical" to a city's operation, while more than a third also pointed to the significance of "fast and easy mobility within the city" in enhancing wealth creation prospects.

Our examination of jobs and income brought to light the punitive effects of labour mismatches in a city's labour supply and on its ability to respond to the changing requirements of a global market. In other words, it is essential to have the right people, with the right skills, in the right place at the right time. Thus the city's capacity to educate, train and retrain the workforce emerged as an important attribute of a successful world city. This conclusion was confirmed by the majority of respondents to our survey. In addition, most of the respondents believed that it was important for a city to have a large stock of suitable housing, while our own analysis also pointed to the value of affordable housing close to centres of employment.

Finally, in the analysis of the attractions for businesses of one world city over another, we identified the availability of well placed, affordable office space and world-class communications networks as crucial to choice. Once again, these findings were strongly supported by our surveys in which more than 50 per cent of respondents deemed state-of-the-art communications critical to the effectiveness of a world city. The majority also put high quality office accommodation near the top of their list of locational requirements.

In the sections which follow we will examine in detail how the world cities compare in the provision of each of the components of the enabling infrastructure.

Transport Systems

An efficient transport system is crucial to the success of a world city. Over half our survey's French and German respondents considered improving transport the single most important way of enhancing the competitiveness of their cities. More than two-thirds of the London sample felt the same way.

Over the last two decades, all world cities have seen an escalation in the demand for transportation, the increase in private car use probably putting the greatest strain on infrastructure, resources and the environment. After twenty years in which population trends took people away from city centres, the economic boom of the 1980s brought them back – this time as commuters with demands for safe and efficient transport. For example, on an average working day in London, there are almost 25 million passenger journeys made by wheeled transport and on foot. Whatever the world city, the transport problems can be characterised in more or less the same way. The distinctions are usually a matter of degree.

Employment tends to be focused in a central business district and most of the trips to this area are made by public transport. Although only a minority of journeys tend to be by car, travel demand to the centre is sufficiently high to ensure that this ineffective use of road space leads to congestion, high levels of pollution and economic inefficiencies. The significance of these issues was highlighted by a 1989 task force report for the Confederation of British Industry which examined the costs to business of transport congestion in London. The Chairman of the task force, Stephen Hayklan, argued that "an immense cost is placed on business and the nation through the dilapidation and inadequacy of the capital's transport system". The estimated costs involved were put at £15bn, of which almost two thirds related to waste in London and the South-East of the country. More particularly, the report suggested that congestion in London adds about 20 per cent to transport costs overall. It also went further, indicating that congestion "... leads to individual frustration, time wasted, poor attitudes at the start of the workday, having to work longer hours at the end of the day, and finally to degradation of social activities and disruption of the family environment." This, it was argued, results in poor individual and organisational productivity the cost of which to industry could be "hundreds of millions or billions of pounds".

LONDON: WORLD CITY MOVING INTO THE 21ST CENTURY

During the 1950s, 1960s and 1970s, many cities saw a migration of employment and population away from the city centre to the economic hinterland and beyond. In most cities, this resulted from a decline in the urban fabric – in London's case it was a positive result of the post-war planning of new towns and town enlargements. As a consequence, London's growth was diverted beyond the Green Belt into the South-East region. This trend increased the demand for orbital and longer distance radial movement which was met by the construction of new motorway rings. To a greater or lesser degree, the mass transportation systems within the world cities were allowed to fall into decline as some users switched to travel by car as the preferred mode. As the cities emptied, the buses and tramways tended to be the first casualties of neglect, the lack of demand for inner city rail travel to some extent offset by an increase in longer distance travel. The metro systems also suffered a decline in patronage during this period.

In subsequent economic booms – and, in London, particularly that of the 1980s – a widespread return of employment to city centres, ensured that under-financed and poorly maintained public transport systems buckled beneath the strain of their own renaissance. Constrained by this situation, the implications of a seemingly unending demand for car use became all too clear with its detrimental effects on the efficiency of the road system and quality of life.

The problems may be more or less the same in all the world cities, but a wide variety of solutions have been applied and considered. In our analysis, we identified five attributes which seemed critical to the creation and survival of a world-class urban transport system.

The first concerns the role of *government*. A world city needs a policy-making process – whether at central, regional or city levels – which allows for strategic integrated transport planning and effective policy implementation. An essential part of this function must be to secure stable, long-term funding for the transport system over the very long timeframes which such work requires. The key is consistency of funding.

ENABLING INFRASTRUCTURE

It is ineffectual and uneconomic to consider particular forms of transportation in isolation. Thus a world city will require an efficient, high quality, safe and *integrated mass transit system*. It is crucial that there be a high provision of interchange between the various forms of public transport. The public system must be capable of providing a real alternative in both qualitative and quantitative terms to the private car.

Transport in a world city must be supported by a *fares system* which actively encourages people to use public transport. The system must be flexible. It must enable passengers to mix and match the various forms of transportation to create their own routes. Decisions about fare levels and subsidies must relate to the overall economic efficiency of the city as a whole, rather than the short-term financial requirements of individual transport components.

However well-developed the other forms of public transport, for the foreseeable future efficient *highway networks* will continue to be important to the wealth creation prospects of a world city. There must be a sophisticated balance established between supply and demand. Thus the highway network must be improved to meet demand, especially for freight, essential services and public transport without the network becoming congested by car-borne trips which could be better made by public transport. Demand must therefore be managed to ensure that journeys which could be made more efficiently by other forms of transport are not undertaken by car.

Environmental issues are the final attribute to be considered in the development of a world city's transport system. A successful world city will need to take affirmative action to protect and improve the quality of life, particularly in respect of the adverse environmental impacts of traffic. The environmental agenda is central to the quality of life in a world city and is thus discussed in Chapter 4.

So much for the ideal. The sections which follow assess the performance of our world cities in the areas outlined above.

Government London has never had a single body responsible for the overall planning of its transport services. In the other cities, while the detailed planning of particular forms of transport may be tackled by individual providers, such responsibilities normally operate within the context of a wide-ranging policy directed by a central agency.

The integrated approach is perhaps most developed in Paris which has produced a regional masterplan to integrate all the city's various forms of transport. The approach in London is something close to an inversion of the Paris strategy. London's Borough-level planning inevitably reflects a rather parochial view of transportation with the emphasis on local rather than regional issues. The continuing lack of a coordinated approach to transport in the broadest terms must be regarded as detrimental to London's long-term prospects. What other world city would design a major extension to its largest airport without agreeing its proper mass transport links? Or initiate the most substantial office development in Europe without a proper tubeline or roads to service it as it opens? In both of these cases, the professional strategic planners have resolutely given advice which has been ignored by the political decision makers.

Our sample of world cities reveals the variety of ways in which transport services can be funded. In Tokyo, the majority of costs on the EIDAN services are met by the users, who pay 90 per cent of their travel costs, with only 10 per cent subsidy from central funds. Privatised services are fully funded by the users. In New York, MTA services are cross-subsidised by road users, via bridge and tunnel tolls, and from an explicit federal fuel tax which subsidises urban mass transit. In Paris, subsidy is used as an explicit policy tool to encourage the use of public transport. Passengers meet about one third of the cost of travel, the rest is subsidised by the state and by explicit taxes on businesses in the Paris region. For the journey to work the subsidy is taken one stage further, with *employers* required to meet 50 per cent of their employees travel costs.

London's transport services are government subsidised, with stringent spending limits established for both London Regional Transport and

British Rail. The level of support for London Regional Transport has risen from £314 million in 1989/90 to £709 million in 1991/92. Part of this is to be spent on new infrastructure. The London Boroughs also play a small role in funding specific local services which are considered socially desirable to their area. Loans can also be raised from the private sector to fund specific new projects. However, in most cases the high risk, low profitability and very long timeframes have ensured that, since the last war, private funding has been less than eager to become involved in such schemes. As regards private sector funding, it is the taxi business and tourist and private coach trade which has been of significance.

Integrated Mass Transport The typical world city is served by four modes of mass transport. Conventional rail links the hinterland to the city (and also carries inter-city/international links); the metro light rail systems serve the city centre and the bus system employs the highway network. In some cities, bus services are supplemented by tramways or light rail. Some tram/light rail systems are well established, as in Frankfurt and Berlin, while others are still in the early stages of re-creation, as in Paris and London. Finally, it is important not to forget journeys by cycle or on foot. About a third of all journeys in London were made by these two means according to evidence from the early 1980s.

Increased demand for travel has forced operators and planners to focus on developing a high degree of coordination between modes of transport in an effort to make more efficient use of limited resources. In addition, new cross-centre links have been developed in a number of cities so that a wider range of journeys can be made without the need to transfer.

In cities like Tokyo and Paris, which are encouraging certain types of economic activity away from the centre, new orbital links are being developed to improve accessibility to the outer areas. Paris, Tokyo, Frankfurt and London are all pursuing proposals to increase network public transport capacity in and to their central business districts. London is proposing significant improvements. New metro lines will provide relief on the most congested parts of the network, and the expansion of Crossrail and Thameslink services will reduce the need to change to reach or cross the centre. British Rail also plans to increase central London services capacity by 15 to 20 per cent.

A unique feature of the development of the mass transit system in Paris has been the effort to create a more positive image for the metro and bus services. Considerable resources have been committed not just to new and better managed trains, but also to redesigning stations, enhancing security and even promoting live artistic performances to enliven its primary function as a transport system. By comparison, the image of the London system is poor. Limited resources and the consequences of safety requirements have led to a substantial decline in the appearance and general environment of the system. London's particular problem is not just its inadequate public transport reliability, but also poor travelling environment.

In many world cities bus services are being integrated more effectively with other modes of transport. Buses provide feeder links to rail systems and services where demand is insufficient to justify a fixed link. Where traffic levels delay bus services, priority measures (such as bus lanes) mitigate against the worst effects of traffic congestion. In London, the bus services are now more fully integrated with the rail network. Some bus routes parallel rail services, offering the option of using buses to help ease the strain of the increasing demand for rail transport. Priority for buses is provided by dedicated bus lanes, but on a site by site, rather than on a network basis, and only where to do so does not reduce road capacity.

Fares The appeal of public transport services is greatly reduced if users are required to pay for each part of a complex trip separately. Amongst the world cities, Paris and London have recognised the benefit of simplified fares. Both are adopting a simple multi-mode zonal fares system in which the user makes a single payment for a point to point journey and can select their most convenient route, using whatever combination of services they deem to be suitable. This encourages users to perceive the transport system as a whole rather than as discrete components.

The efficiency of the system in London and Paris is further enhanced by the use of period travel cards which allow unrestricted travel within specified zones. In London this system has been extended, so that rail travellers from beyond the region are able to combine their rail journey and zonal travel within the London region on a single ticket. Card holders can make extra journeys at no additional cost, making public transport significantly more attractive than the kind of flat fare system which operates in New York and Berlin. Indeed, the New York subway system, where the traveller has first to obtain a token, places the same unit cost on every journey and discourages the short distance traveller.

Highways Network World city highways networks have evolved from the paths and roads for pedestrian and wheeled vehicles which, before the motor age, serviced the access requirements of the cities. These days, roads are almost entirely given over to the mass movement of motorised traffic. Other demands for street space for pedestrians or cyclists have been excluded or heavily marginalised. In its most extreme form, Tokyo's expressway system has developed solely to meet the demand for vehicular movement. Most other cities have developed a more or less restricted network of urban motorways, relying more on relatively small scale improvements at the most congested points.

London has a limited network of high quality roads, comprising the main radial routes and the fringe orbital M25. Earlier plans for a series of concentric motorway boxes round London were abandoned because the economic and environmental cost proved politically unacceptable. More recently, studies of the traffic problems in parts of London failed to identify any acceptable major network improvements which would provide significant capacity gains without unacceptable environmental costs. Both the Greater London Council (now defunct) and LPAC's proposed strategies concluded that the only sustainable transport policy for London would have to continue to improve public transport combined with restriction of the use of private cars, particularly at the busiest times and in the most congested areas.

Both Tokyo and Paris have significant plans to improve their highways network. In Tokyo, increased demand has encouraged the development of plans to increase substantially the capacity of the existing expressway system. There are also plans to build new road links to help enable the development of the new de-centralised centres.

London has limited proposals for network improvements – for example, on the orbital North Circular Road – but these are very much directed towards meeting localised problems. The other major schemes proposed in London are the road improvements under construction serying East London and the Docklands. However, apart from the East London River Crossing and proposals to widen the M25, these are on a much smaller scale.

All world cities suffer from unacceptably high levels of traffic congestion and each has or is in the process of developing policies to discourage private car use and even ownership. However, as yet, none of the cities has taken any active steps to curb the relentless demands for the expansion of use of the private car, although in Japan a car may not be bought unless an off-street parking space is available. Paris, which has an unambiguous policy of promoting public transport, has made a policy decision *explicitly not* to condemn car use or ownership.

In London, the lack of a co-ordinated policy approach is exemplified by a national taxation system which, even after the 1991 reforms, still perpetuates the company car system but fails to encourage companies to subsidise public transport. At the same time, the stated government policy is to discourage car use in London.

As we have seen, while all the world cities show similar transport problems, each has adopted a different approach to dealing with them, based on balancing local perceptions and needs against available resources and political decision-making will. In an effort to determine the strengths and weaknesses of these systems, they were assessed against each of the attributes which we have described in the course of this section.

ENABLING INFRASTRUCTURE

As the assessment by The MVA Consultancy in Figure 5.1 demonstrates, in terms of current and proposed transport arrangements, London's relative position on these attributes lies below Paris and Frankfurt on the one hand and above Tokyo and New York on the other. Congestion and system constraints on the mass transport network appear to be less problematic in Paris and Frankfurt. Congestion on the road network is a problem in all world cities (the Population Crisis Committee ranked New York, Paris and London on a par and below Tokyo and Berlin on the measure of rush hour traffic flow). As a result, transport related pollution and noise are also problems for all the cities. Amongst our sample, Paris alone has a programme of action to reduce the noise impact of traffic on existing roads – only New York has a similar programme but that is directed at reducing subway noise. New York, Berlin and Tokyo lack an integrated fares system for mass transit.

Figure 5.1: Prospects for effective transport provision

	MASS TRANSIT	FARES SYSTEM	ENVIRONMENT PROTECTION	HIGHWAY NETWORK	STRONG & EFFECTIVE PLANNING CONTROL
London	2	5	3	2	1
Paris	5	5	4	3	4
Frankfurt	5	4	N/A	3	3
New York	1	1	1	1	1
Tokyo	3	1	2	3	4

Excellent provision = 5   Poor provision = 1   Note: The re-unification of Germany and subsequently East and West Berlin means that, at the present time, prospects for Berlin remain unknown.

THE MVA CONSULTANCY

The strength and effectiveness of the transport planning regime is lowest in London and New York and highest in Frankfurt perhaps because it is the smallest city in comparison.

INTERNATIONAL TRANSPORT LINKS

Airport Facilities

In a 1989 survey by Coopers & Lybrand Deloitte, London's Heathrow ranked ahead of all the other world city airports in terms of international passenger throughput (see Figure 5.2). It was rated second on air transport movements to New York's JFK and fourth on cargo throughput (in tonnes) where Tokyo's Narita airport ranked first. London is now reaping both the negative and positive consequences of being the premier international air services hub in Europe and perhaps the world. London's capacity problems are shared by New York and Tokyo. By contrast, the other European world cities are far less constrained.

London's airport capacity constraint is likely to be more significant if, as many expect, the world's air services network develops further on the basis of a limited number of "worldports" – that is, existing major airports, with good infrastructure, offering frequent transfer connections to a wide range of destinations. Even if this concept does not transfer as readily from the US as some have thought, the London network may still lose its comparative advantage in high density air service routes as other airports grow.

The results of our survey indicate that London is perceived as offering poor international transport facilities. Since this perception clearly has little to do with the actual volume of flights or variety of destinations, it may well be a function of the perception of the airports themselves and/or poor intra-city mobility. Such impressions may well be dispelled by future developments, such as the continuing redevelopment of new airport terminals and of the proposed Heathrow Express which could initially carry passengers to Paddington in sixteen minutes

ENABLING INFRASTRUCTURE

Figure 5.2: Airport capacity in world cities

		1989 RANKINGS ON:		
		PASSENGERS ('000)	AIR TRANSPORT MOVEMENTS	CARGO (TONNES)
LONDON	Heathrow	1	2	4
	Gatwick	7	8	9
PARIS	Orly	5	7	8
	Charles de Gaulle	9	6	5
FRANKFURT		4	5	3
BERLIN	Schonefeld	12	12	11*
	Tegal	11	11	11*
NEW YORK	J F Kennedy	3	1	2
	Le Guardia	6	4	10
	Newark	7	3	7
TOYKO	Haneda	2	9	6
	Narita	10	10	1

*Joint ranking

COOPERS & LYBRAND DELOITTE

and has the potential to link into the planned Crossrail and access the heart of the city by 1999.

International rail facilities

Continental European cities have long benefitted from a comprehensive network of international rail services. The development of a high-speed rail network within Europe is leading to the renaissance of rail travel as an important mode of business travel. London, although the centre of the British Inter-City network, has been excluded from the European network until recently by its geographical position. With the opening of the Channel Tunnel all this will change. For the first time, direct rail services between London and major European cities will be possible with, for example, a city centre to city centre service between London and Paris in three hours.

The benefits of high speed rail travel for London will not be fully realised until the planned new link to London from the Channel Tunnel is operational, but of all the European cities London has the potential to gain the greatest benefit from the Tunnel because of the new dimension in travel which it affords and the opportunity of being integrated into the new European High Speed Rail Network.

WATERWAYS AND WATERFRONTS

It is not a matter of chance that all the five world cities we are comparing are ports – three on the sea or estuaries – London, New York and Tokyo, three on major rivers – Berlin, Frankfurt and Paris. Their sites were fixed by the availability of water-based transport, which, though it has become less important since the growth of road and then air transport, is still a major part of each city's infrastructure – both for local and national, and for international trade.

The Statten Island Ferries, the Parisian Bateaux Mouches, the London river boats, all form part of the tourist infrastructure – and no doubt soon Berliners will, once again, be going on a Spree on their days off. The growing demand for berths for cruise ships means that once again large ships can be seen close to the centre of London.

Since the war, waterborne traffic has significantly changed, with the loss of international passenger traffic and much high value low weight freight to the air. City centre docks, wharves and jetties have become redundant and, with their associated industries and supporting facilities, have been redeveloped for other uses – most significantly in London's Docklands, New York's waterfront and now Tokyo. But pressure from such redevelopment has meant that the essential infrastructure to allow the important import of fuel, aggregates and minerals, as well as export of waste, is being put at risk. There is a requirement for new investment for specialist cargos and for cruise ships. In addition, there is a need to maintain and take up opportunities for other passenger traffic, like London's riverbus from the central area to Docklands.

The sea and major rivers form part of the geography of all the world cities. They are important not just as highways for boats and shipping, but as part of the environment, ecology and open space network of all cities. They also contribute to the special quality of them all. Tower Bridge and the Palace of Westminster in London, the New York Skyline from the sea, the Louvre, Quai d'Orsay and Notre Dame in Paris are all important elements in the image of each city. All these cities are now revising their policies for their waterfronts – some having made major mistakes in the past are now attempting to redress them. What is clear is that the waterways and waterfronts, and their future use are of such importance as to require both special policies and care in their implementation.

COMMUNICATIONS

Until recently, telecommunications have been somewhat neglected in any discussion about urban infrastructure, the rapid pace of change ensuring that the subject is seen as the preserve of technocrats. However, there is now a growing awareness that a well-developed telecommunications infrastructure can make a positive contribution to the expansion of business and the development of employment prospects. This recognition is reflected in the results of our survey in which more than 80 per cent of respondents suggested that state-of-the-art telecommunications were critical to the success of a world city.

Although these days telecommunications play an important role in almost any business, they are of particular value to the knowledge- and information-based industries of the soft economy. Given the intensely competitive characteristics of this sector, many businesses have come to regard telecommunications as an essential strategic tool capable of providing them with an edge in increasingly aggressive markets.

The convergence of sophisticated network capabilities and advanced computer technology has revolutionised the way businesses operate and led many firms to increase their reliance on advanced telecommunications. For example, headquarters functions are facilitated by the rapid data exchange of management information between local, regional and international operations. Retail outlets rely on telecommunications networks for everything from credit checks to stock purchase on an international basis. For example, Marks and Spencer's headquarters in London know as it happens how their businesses in Canada and France are doing.

Advanced telecommunications facilities have revolutionised the development of business services, publishing, the media and transportation. They have also played a key role in the rise of the financial services sector. For a world city like London to sustain and enhance the competitiveness of this sector, it must continue to provide reliable, state-of-the-art telecommunications with adequate capacity to serve the escalating communications demands of the media, airlines, the cultural services, banks, brokerage houses and insurance companies which exchange and process enormous volumes of data twenty-four hours a day. As in other sectors of the economy, investment in telecommunications is essential to maintain and strengthen competitive advantages.

Sometimes innovation in the financial sector is driven by technological advance. While such developments can significantly decrease the cost of transactions, this must be set against the often extremely high cost of capital equipment. For example, over a seven year period (1981–7), US commercial banks more than doubled their annual spending on information technology; New York's largest financial institutions regularly spend over $200 million a year keeping their systems up to scratch. Furthermore, the pace of technological advance makes it difficult to judge the viability of such investment, since equipment often becomes obsolete faster than anticipated.

Since 1981, London has enjoyed a comparative advantage over its European rivals in telecommunications as a consequence of liberalisation of the regulatory regime. It appears not so much to be the cost of telecommunications as the basic quality of provision and the innovative potential in supply which influences locational decisions. For example, in the mid-1980s a major international airline moved its reservation computer system to London from elsewhere in Europe because it could no longer satisfy its telecommunication requirements there. London was also fortunate that it was able to utilise redundant pipelines formally used for hydraulic power to provide routes for glass fibre telecommunications links without severe disruption of the urban fabric. The telecommunications restructuring process in London has so far only been matched in New York and Tokyo.

There are two major developments which to a large extent serve as a measure of the status of a world city's telecommunications infrastructure. These relate to optical fibre transmission capability and deployment levels of advanced digital switches. The first is significant because it enhances the speed, volume and reliability of data transmission, while the latter enables the flexible customisation of systems to meet the specific demands of particular types of business. In terms of optical fibre deployment, according to 1989 figures, London and New York lead the world, with 400 and 470 offices respectively served by fibre optics as compared to only 110 buildings in Tokyo. However, all three cities have announced their intention to serve all major office buildings with fibre optics by 1992. In 1989, the percentage of major offices with digital switches put New York in the lead (83 per cent), followed by London (65 per cent) and Tokyo (32 per cent), but once again the levels of investment announced by all three contenders suggests that this running order may change.

The level of infrastructure provision is not the only factor associated with the efficient and effective functioning of a city's telecommunications system. There are a number of other factors which comprise the overall telecommunications environment. Consideration also needs to be given to: the cost of telecommunications services; the responsiveness of service providers in taking advantage of modern technologies; the level of investment; and the presence of a favourable regulatory environment. When all of these other factors are taken into account, our reading of the evidence shows the overall telecommunications environment in each of the comparator cities is good. In comparative terms, Tokyo appears to have an advantage over the other cities but is closely followed by London, New York and Paris; the differences between the latter three being marginal.

LAND USE

Land use is a term used to refer to existing and planned development of any kind. It ranges from business, retailing, industrial or warehousing, through housing and other facilities such as schools and hospitals, to buildings for the arts, culture, entertainment and sport. In our study we have concentrated on the key areas of commercial business development and housing.

Commercial property

This section notes how the commercial property market operates in world cities and focuses on the three main components of that market – the existing stock of modern office accommodation, the degree of choice available in that accommodation and the occupational costs in each city. Urban planning issues relating to commercial development are discussed in Chapter 6.

ENABLING INFRASTRUCTURE

Like any other market, the office sector is shaped by supply and demand, with the occupiers on one side of the equation, and a combination of developers, investors and owners on the other. Each side will have a different set of expectations which have to be met for the market to operate successfully.

On the supply side, developers seek to achieve the specifications set by their clients and to do so in the appropriate location. They look for consistency of regional planning directives to provide a firm framework in which plans can be developed with a high degree of confidence. The developers can then expect to secure levels of rent which will justify the construction of buildings to the standard and specifications required by their clients, while investors can expect to secure an adequate return on their investment through rental and capital growth.

On the demand side, the most important consideration to occupiers relates to the choice and range of office accommodation in terms of location, building quality and price. This includes the provision of accommodation ranging from high specification, high profile offices to the availability of inexpensive space for new or small businesses.

Office costs are only one element in an account which international businesses need to draw up to work out the "profitability" of operating in different world cities. While office costs may be a significant consideration in some firms' locational decision making processes, they are set beside other criteria which are less amenable to quantification. For example, it is very difficult to put a value on 300 years of historic association when dealing with the insurance market or on the use of English as the lingua franca of both business and domestic exchange.

In the sections which follow we provide a brief overview of the office stock on offer in each city. Our assessment is summarised in Figure 5.3, page 150.

Frankfurt The office stock of Frankfurt is estimated at approximately 8 million square metres. Vacancy rates in the centre of the city were low during the latter half of the 1980s, and currently stand at 1.5 to 2 per cent. Over 80 per cent of Frankfurt's buildings were destroyed in the Second World War, with the majority of the city centre demolished in 1944. The city was rapidly rebuilt, but the architecture is considered by many to be rather bleak. The old financial district of the city is now some 35 years old and the buildings in the West End 20 to 25 years old. The new banking district has modern offices of up to 10 years old.

According to statistics produced by the Hessisches Statistisches Landesamt, some 980,000 square metres of new stock (12 per cent) was built during the years 1983–1989. Frankfurt is a city of tower blocks, the most recent being the Messe Turm building, located at the Exhibition area to the west of the city centre. The total development size is around 60,000 square metres. Another major development is the Westend Carree which boasts a total of 35,000 square metres of accommodation. Most of the major developments currently underway are outside the city centre in suburban or decentralised locations. Many of the major schemes proposed in more central locations continue to have planning difficulties, although the pipeline is potentially large. An example is the proposed Campanile development adjacent to the railway station, comprising some 56,000 square metres, which has been delayed by planning objections.

Berlin The office stock of West Berlin is estimated at approximately 6.5 million square metres and is in extremely short supply. The current vacancy rate is less than 1 per cent. According to the Berlin Development Corporation, there is presently 9 million square metres of office space in Berlin as a whole and it is estimated that 19 million square metres will be needed by 1995.

There is no dedicated office district in West Berlin, although favoured office locations include Charlottenburg, Tiergarten and Schoeneberg, with emphasis on Kurfuerstendamm, Tauentzienstrasse and adjacent streets. One of the few modern office buildings in the east is the Internationales Handelszentrum. In general, in the west, most districts and buildings contain a mix of office, retail and residential accommodation.

Much of West Berlin was destroyed during the Second World War, reconstruction taking place in the late 1950s, throughout the 1960s and early 1970s. The late 1960s saw a boom in construction which was fuelled by tax incentives. However, once these were withdrawn the pace of development declined and throughout the 1980s construction was principally devoted to owner occupation.

Between 1971 and 1979, approximately 800,000 square metres of office space was built in West Berlin (over 70 per cent between 1971 and 1974), and only 380,000 square metres between 1980 and 1989. There have been few high-rise buildings developed, and these are dispersed across the city. An overall strategy for the redevelopment of a reunited Berlin is currently being prepared. A number of significant office schemes are proposed. Among these will be the redevelopment of the Potsdamer Platz, the old heart of Berlin which fell into disuse with the division of the city. Daimler-Benz has already purchased a plot in the area. There are also plans for a World Trade Centre, comprising some 50,000 square metres as well as an East-West Trade Centre at Moritzplatz. At the western end of the Kurfuerstendamm, Halenseebruecke is generally regarded as a site for development and the area is capable of supporting up to 60,000 square metres of office and residential space, although the project will not be completed until the mid-1990s. Other significant schemes include the proposal to redevelop the bus station at Messegelaende, producing up to 60,000 square metres of office space; the development of up to 80,000 square metres at the Dienstleistungszentrum Alt-Moabit; and a number of potential sites in the eastern part of the city.

Paris The Central Business District can be broadly defined as an area containing the 8th, 1st and 2nd arrondissements, plus parts of the 16th, 17th and 9th. Other central office locations include the area close to the French Parliament, the areas around the Gares Montparnasse and Austerlitz and the Gare de Lyon and Quai de Bercy. Planning restrictions aimed at conserving the traditional, historic atmosphere of central Paris are stringent, despite some relaxation in the 1980s. Consequently, much of the stock is in period buildings. Where new development is permitted, building usually has to conform to existing plot sizes, and thus is not always suited to modern business needs.

Outside the central area, a notable example of new office development is the new Ministry of Finance building at Quai de Bercy. We estimate that only 15 per cent of the stock of central Paris has been built during the past 15 years, compared with around 45 per cent in the Paris region. Significant office locations outside Paris include Neuilly-sur-Seine, Levallois-Perret, Boulogne-Billancourt, Nanterre, Rueil-Malmaison, St. Cloud, Sevres, Meudon and Issy-les-Moulineaux.

The major office concentration outside central Paris, however, is at La Defense, which has been built in three main "tranches" – 1963 to 1972 (9 per cent), 1974 to 1978 (22 per cent) and 1980 onwards (the remainder). Continuing restrictions on office development in the central business district will prevent any major office developments in the area, although a number of former national headquarter buildings in well located positions (Shell, Pechiney, Philips) are now coming up for refurbishment. Outside the CBD, but still within Paris, a 55,000 square metre scheme is under construction over the railway tracks adjacent to the Gare Montparnasse. This project will be completed in the next year or so. Other schemes are proposed at the Gare d'Austerlitz, Porte Maillot and Porte de St. Cloud. Around 220,000 square metres is underway at La Defense, with potential in the medium term for an additional 700,000 square metres. Some of the first generation of buildings are now coming up for redevelopment. In addition, the pipeline of new development within the Paris Region outside the areas referred to above is extensive.

Tokyo The office stock of the three central wards of Tokyo is estimated at 15.3 million square metres. Current vacancy rates in the main business districts are very low (less than 1 per cent), although this level increases with the distance from the centre. Historically, earthquake-related regulations restricted high-rise developments, but this is changing with the improvement of building techniques. Ownership patterns inhibit development in the centre of Tokyo, and it is rare for properties to change hands.

At Shinjuku, some 4 miles west of the traditional area of Marunouchi, a new high-rise office area has been developing since the late 1970s. It has been estimated that, during the first half of the 1980s, around 460,000 square metres was built. Between 1987 and 1989, net addition to stock was estimated at 650,000 square metres.

Although there is limited opportunity for expanding the office stock in Central Tokyo, a number of major proposals exist for waterfront schemes.

New York The majority of office space in New York is in Midtown (15 million square metres as compared to Downtown space of 7.5 million square metres). The vacancy rate is high in both Midtown (16.1 per cent) and Downtown (15.9 per cent) and both areas are characterised by large, high-rise buildings. As an example, of the twenty-one buildings completed between 1989 and 1990, twelve were above 50,000 square metres in size, and three above 100,000 square metres. Some 4.6 million square metres were completed between 1983 and 1990, an average of 575,000 square metres per annum. With current vacancy rates at around 16 per cent, this points to a strong supply of modern space.

Of late, Midtown West has attracted a number of large tenants looking for large blocks of new, efficient, technologically advanced office space, generally not available in Midtown East. A lower level of development activity – brought about by greater funding difficulties and a depressed market – means that relatively less amounts of space will be completed during 1991 and 1992. Several projects are now on hold. As at mid-1990, the development pipeline for Midtown New York 1991 to 1994 stood at around 500,000 square metres, of which less than 100,000 square metres was expected to be completed in 1991. Of five Downtown buildings proposed for development at the beginning of 1990 totalling 630,000 square metres, only one (37,000 square metres) is now likely to be built in the immediate future.

London Central London's office space is defined for the purpose of this section as being located mainly in the West End (7.0 million square metres), the City as defined by Richard Ellis (4.3 million square metres) and Holborn (1.7 million square metres) with another 1.1 million square metres in other areas. This makes a grand total of 14.1 million square metres of office space in Central London. The potential for the Docklands development is estimated at a further 2 million square metres by the mid-1990s. There is, in addition, a further 4 million square metres elsewhere in London.

Vacancy rates are high in the City area (14 per cent), followed by the West End (8 per cent) and Holborn (6.5 per cent), making an average for Central London of about 10 per cent at the end of 1990.

Including owner-occupied schemes, approximately 1.2 million square metres of office space (28.6 per cent of the stock) was completed in the City area between 1985 and 1990 (this figure includes new developments, development with some refurbishment and development behind retained facades, but excludes simple refurbishment). In the West End, only 0.4 million square metres of larger schemes over 1,000 square metres (less than 6 per cent of the stock) was developed between 1985 and 1990. According to 1986 figures provided by Westminster City Council (which largely corresponds to the West End area), the age profile of office buildings (by floorspace) in Westminster shows 66.5 per cent as pre-1945, 14.7 per cent built between 1945 and 1964, 12 per cent built during the period 1964 and 1970 and 6.8 per cent built post-1970. While much has undergone substantial refurbishment, it is clear that a large proportion of the West End stock is not of the same modern standard as, for example, that in the City or Docklands.

Between 1985 and 1990, a total of thirty buildings above 10,000 square metres were newly developed in the City area but only six in the West End. Westminster City Council figures suggest that around 23 per cent of the West End floorspace is in units above 10,000 square metres, and almost 62 per cent in units below 5,000 square metres. A comparatively large proportion of the stock in the West End is in mixed use buildings. In the City area, approximately 760,000 square metres (including refurbishment) was under construction at the end of 1990, with a further 320,000 square metres in the West End. In total, in our Central London market definition we estimate that around 1.3 million square metres was under construction at that date. Proposals for major office schemes currently exist in LPAC's special policy areas at Paddington (0.39 million square metres in three schemes), and Kings Cross (0.5 million square metres), but neither has full planning permission, although the scheme at Paddington is agreed in principle. If all schemes currently proposed for Docklands go ahead, in addition to those already completed and under construction, the total office stock there will reach some 2 million square metres by the mid-1990s.

Stock creation, choice and price

Having outlined the characteristics of the commercial property markets in each of the world cities, we are now able to draw some comparisons. Figure 5.3 on the next page is a snapshot of the commercial property market at the end of 1990. It provides a comparative overview of office stock creation, choice and cost in each of the world cities.

New York has the largest office stock amongst the world cities and, over the last decade, has added a great deal of modern accommodation to augment existing stock. The vacancy rate is currently high. Although, in international terms, the price of New York office space is relatively low, in national terms costs remain high and often lie at the heart of relocation decisions.

In Paris, development restrictions in the centre of the city have led to limited creation of new space and low vacancy rates. However, the pressure has been somewhat alleviated by the creation of La Defense development. In terms of occupation costs, Paris CBD ranks in the middle of the world cities covered by this study — after London its costs are the highest in Europe and the differential with London is closing.

Land-ownership patterns and space restrictions have inhibited any major redevelopment of the most sought after areas of Tokyo, which goes

LONDON: WORLD CITY MOVING INTO THE 21ST CENTURY

Figure 5.3: Office stock: creation, choice and cost

		ADDITION	CHOICE	COST INDEX END 1990 (CITY OF LONDON = 100)
LONDON	City	▲▲▲	▲▲▲	100
	West End	▲	▲	114
	Docklands	▲▲▲	▲▲▲	N/A
PARIS	Central Business District	▲	▲	64
	La Defense	▲▲▲	▲▲	N/A
FRANKFURT		▲▲	▲	44
BERLIN		▲	▲	32
NEW YORK		▲▲▲	▲▲▲	38
TOKYO		▲▲	▲	135

Addition to stock of modern accommodation
Choice of available accommodation

▲   ▲▲   ▲▲▲
Low   Medium   High

RICHARD ELLIS

some way towards explaining why costs in the main CBD are far and away the highest in the world. Outside the business district, office space is in greater supply and there has been major office development in the Shinjuku region.

During the early 1980s, supply of and demand for office space in Frankfurt was well balanced until the rapid development of the financial service sector in the last five years increased demand and drove up rents. However, despite the recent rent rises, in international terms Frankfurt's commercial property remains relatively cheap and, although vacancy rates are currently low, the new developments outlined above should improve supply in the near future.

Berlin has only assumed significance as an office market since the fall of the Wall at the end of 1989. As a consequence, office stock tends to be sub-standard although vacancy rates are low. At present, office space is in extremely short supply, although the development of East Berlin should change the situation markedly by the year 2000.

Our comparison makes it clear that London has added more stock of modern office accommodation and is currently offering a greater choice of such accommodation in the City and Docklands than Frankfurt, Berlin, the Tokyo central business district (CBD) and the Paris CBD. Nevertheless, the costs of office accommodation in London, although presently falling, are higher than in any other world city except Tokyo (CBD) and parts of Paris.

There can be no doubt that London has been successful in regenerating and creating office stock. There is now a very substantial supply in Central London of vacant offices and potential office schemes in the development pipeline. LPAC has quantified this and will publish its results in its December 1991 Annual Review. This will confirm a significant excess of supply over demand.

The Central London office market is a key part of London's role as a world city. It must be seen as part of the broader London-wide and regional provision. Over the last decade a substantial new supply of offices has been created, particularly in the City and adjacent areas including Docklands. In the West End, however, office development has been set in the context of the needs of other important Central London activities and policies for mixed uses and the national policies for listed buildings and conservation.

It seems likely that until the stock of modern, high quality, yet relatively inexpensive office accommodation in areas adjacent to Central London, including in Docklands, comes to be accepted as an integral part of the Central London office market, other essential activities and conservation areas in Central London will continue to be kept under pressure for office development. However, given that 5,500 office jobs will move to Docklands in 1991 this acceptance may arrive faster than some commentators believe.

Housing

There are three main ways in which the housing market directly affects urban development especially through its influence on the labour market – through the prices that people have to pay for their housing; the ease of access for new entrants into the housing market; and the quantity, quality and location of housing investments. To a significant extent, especially in European countries, these are affected more by central government than by local government policies.

Prices Contrary to general belief, house prices in London are, on average, as low or lower than those to be found in other world cities – see Figure 5.4. Moreover, the ratio of these prices to those found in other parts of the country is also amongst the lowest. Only Frankfurt, which does not hold anything like the same dominant position in the German economy, appears to have a lower ratio than London.

Once incomes are taken into account the position appears to be only slightly less favourable. Figure 5.5 presents some material collated by the World Bank on price/income ratios which suggests that only Frankfurt and

ENABLING INFRASTRUCTURE

Figure 5.4: World city house prices

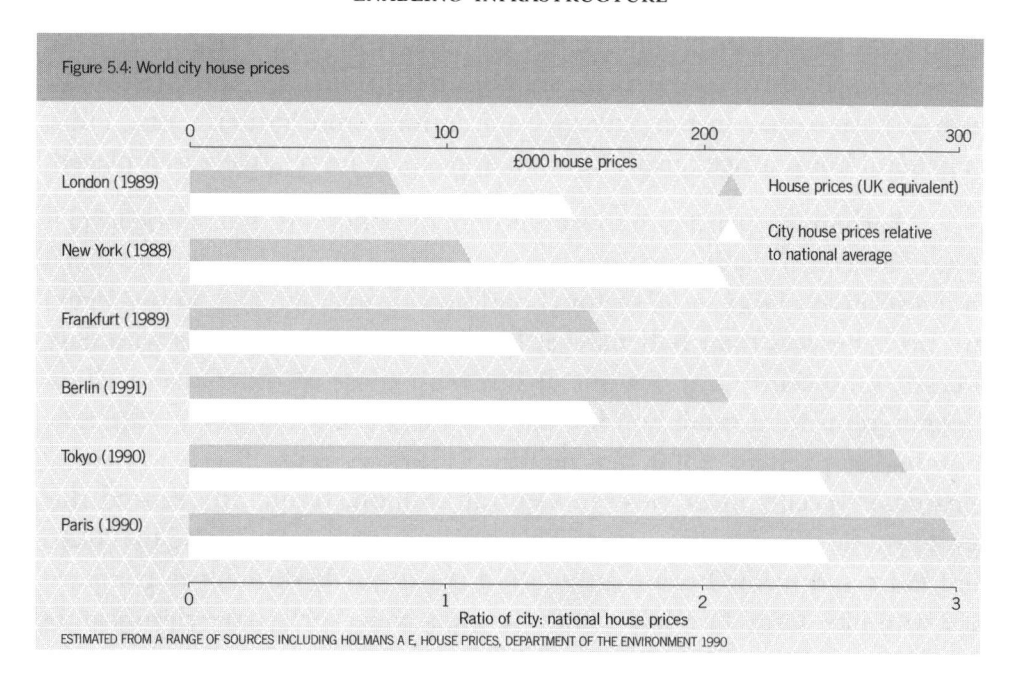

ESTIMATED FROM A RANGE OF SOURCES INCLUDING HOLMANS A E, HOUSE PRICES, DEPARTMENT OF THE ENVIRONMENT 1990

Figure 5.5: House price/income ratios in major countries and cities

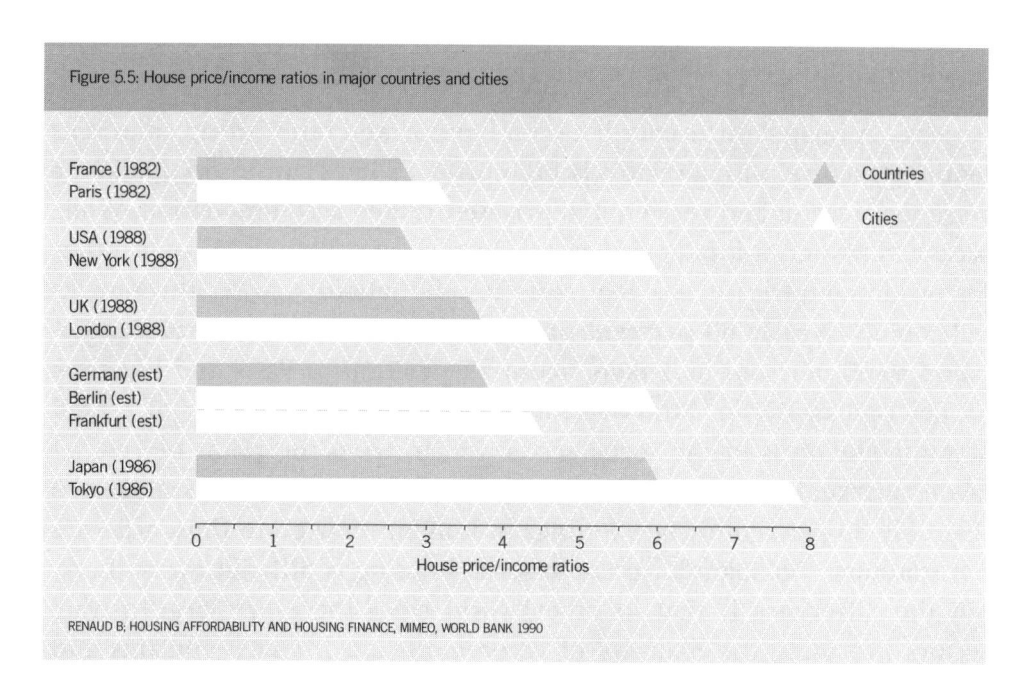

RENAUD B; HOUSING AFFORDABILITY AND HOUSING FINANCE, MIMEO, WORLD BANK 1990

Paris have lower ratios – and most commentators would argue that the figures for Paris, in particular, significantly understate the price most people have to pay in that city given premiums and hidden costs. Thus, in general house price terms, London appears to be relatively well placed.

Perhaps surprising to those who live in London is that at one level it is not particularly badly served, even with respect to rented housing. Rents in the relatively large *social* sector (London-wide average £28.50 per week) are probably less than half market levels while prices in areas with easy access to the centre are not out of line with those in other major cities. Overall, rents for a small London flat – again in the social sector – are now running at perhaps £300 per month. However, rents for new private tenants, especially in or close to Central London, frequently exceed this level by a factor of two or more. This appears to be comparable to Tokyo and Paris and below Berlin, although it is extremely difficult to compare like with like. Only Frankfurt, and perhaps New York, have significantly lower rents. What differs markedly, however, in London are the lower number and range of properties available in the "easy access" sector and the lower incomes of many households being asked to pay these rents (moderated by the housing benefit regime).

Access A related difference between London and other world cities is its tenure structure, with a relatively high proportion of owner-occupation, a large social sector and very limited privately rented accommodation. While access to owner-occupation is certainly easier in Britain than in other European countries it has real costs for the labour market through its inflexibility. Nearly 60 per cent of Londoners are owner-occupiers compared to 50 per cent in Tokyo, about 25 per cent in Paris and less than 15 per cent in Berlin. Moreover, in London the vast majority of rented accommodation is in the social sector which, from the point of view of labour market flexibility, is notoriously inaccessible. Indeed it is suggested that only 30 per cent of new lettings in London now go to those who are not statutory "homeless". Access to social housing is difficult everywhere, but the difference is that in other world cities there are large private sectors providing the majority of accommodation for new entrants and often for lower income employed households as well. In Tokyo that proportion is over 30 per cent, in Paris it is over 40 per cent. In New York, the proportion is even higher, while the social sector is very limited and offers little to those in employment.

In all the major cities affordability of rented housing has historically been achieved through rent controls. These help those in accommodation but restrict private supply. The controls are being dismantled in all the world cities, except perhaps New York. In Europe the problem of escalating rents has been addressed by large scale subsidies to the full range of landlords, not just to local authorities, as has historically been the case in Britain. In France, there has also been an effective tax (the 1 per cent tax) on employers, the proceeds of which have been directed at additional housing provision. In more market-orientated economies such as New York and Tokyo, ensuring poorer employed households are housed sufficiently near their work to make the labour market operate satisfactorily has always been a major problem. In New York, the response has been overcrowding, unacceptably high rent to income ratios, homelessness (even among some employed households), and decentralisation of employment. In Tokyo, housing standards remain low, rents are high and people have very long journeys to work. Employers in the formal sector attempt to play an active role in ensuring that housing is available for their employees, but this has not made a significant impact on the overall problem. As London moves towards greater private provision and higher rents in the social sector these types of problems can be expected to emerge more strongly.

Affecting 2,000 to 5,000 people, homelessness, sleeping on the streets, the most extreme sign of the housing access problem, has become very visible in London over the last few years. It is a function not only of the general cost and availability of housing, but also of the government's "Care in the Community" policies and the restriction of housing benefit available to young people. The problem is not confined to London. It is also apparent in many other major cities, notably New York, Paris and Berlin. The problem of homeless families has significant implications for the labour market both directly and indirectly. Quite understandably, such households are housed by the social sector as a matter of urgency on social grounds. Moreover, the overall inertia and inflexibility in housing management mean that many properties in inner London which could be vacated – for example, by retired people who would like to move out – do not become available to the low-paid workers essential to the support of the central London economy. As a result access to social housing based on employment requirements is highly restricted. A similar situation prevails in both Paris and Berlin and involves an implicit restriction on the allocation of scarce housing resources.

New building In all world cities, the majority of investment in additional housing is provided outside the city centre. In the private sector, this investment mainly accommodates middle income employees. However, in London there has been a significant programme of new housing development in Docklands providing a wide range and choice of housing for all income groups, with the advantages of relatively easy access to the city and to employment in Docklands itself. Although significant in new building terms, this programme is minor in terms of the total stock.

Where London differs from other world cities is that, first, it is physically very large. Second, the surrounding South-East region is a relatively high income area. Third, London has imposed a stringent Green Belt policy which restricts development over a very wide area around the urban fringe. Finally London has carried out a massive slum clearance programme which has removed a large part of the older dwelling stock which, in principle, could have been renovated to provide private accommodation closer to the central area. Other major cities have one or more of these attributes. None have all four.

In this context, Paris is perhaps the best comparison. The central area of the city has been conserved, but there is no green belt. In addition, there are significant positive planning powers by which local objections can be overruled to enable central government policy to be implemented. As a result, large scale provision – albeit often unattractive and with increasing social problems – has been possible at some distance from the centre with new settlements supported by the development of transport infrastructure.

Finally, if London is to compete with other cities, developing a reasonable quality rented sector with easy access for employed households is a major priority. All the other cities have largely deregulated private markets and tax systems which do not discourage landlords. However, the majority of policies by which such a market can be achieved are nationally based. With respect to deregulation, significant changes have been put in place in Britain over the last few years and there are slight signs that landlords are preparing to respond. However, the taxation system remains highly distorted making private renting uneconomic in many circumstances, while the return required is adversely affected by the "political risk" of reregulation. The most obvious role for local policies is with respect to the planning system – through enabling the conversion of the existing stock, both of dwellings and property in other uses, into suitable units to rent to lower income households. Again this process is observable in all the major cities, except perhaps Central Paris.

Further, some commentators suggest that London needs more economically active people in the public and voluntary sector housing stock. The access to these types of housing need to be addressed as well as the training issues that are dealt with next. This might have the side-benefit of reducing the worries expressed in surveys about crime which are paralleled in New York and elsewhere.

EDUCATION AND TRAINING

The supply of skills to the labour markets of world cities is provided by those people working or seeking work in the cities. They will have acquired their skills in a mix of educational institutions, training facilities and companies or other employing organisations based in the city, elsewhere in the country or even abroad. The national education and training infrastructure is therefore essential to the supply of skills to the world city. However, the extent to which the city reflects or contains more of the national system's strengths or weaknesses will play an important role in determining both the city's competitiveness in global terms and as a location for international business.

Michael Porter in his recent analysis of "The Competitive Advantage of Nations" (1990) provides a useful framework for assessing the education and training infrastructure's role in sustaining a nation's competitive advantage. He concluded that "advanced" and "specialist" skills provided a stronger base for sustainable competitive advantage than skills which could be defined as "basic" or "generalised". This was simply because the latter are more easily replicable elsewhere. For this reason – the ready transferability of the skills – the private sector was less likely to be interested in risking their investment in such skills. However, advanced and specialist skills were both more integral to competitive advantage and less easily transferable and therefore private sector investment in such skills was more necessary, desirable and likely.

It is these ideas and the paucity of data for inter-city comparisons which have guided our approach to the comparative assessment in this section. We will concentrate on international comparisons of education and training, particularly of an advanced and specialist kind. Data limitations will constrain what can be reported. We will then consider whether London has any marked deficiencies or strengths relative to the national picture.

International comparisons

Participation rates in education and training for those aged between 16 and 18 years old are lower in the UK than in any other country hosting a world city, according to estimates published by the Department of Science and Education. The differential is even more marked for full-time participation rates – on one definition, 33 per cent in the UK in 1986 compared with 47 per cent in Germany, 66 per cent in France, 77 per cent in Japan and 79 per cent in the USA (see Figure 5.6).

Figure 5.6: National participation in education and training

% of 16-18 years olds in education and training; 1986

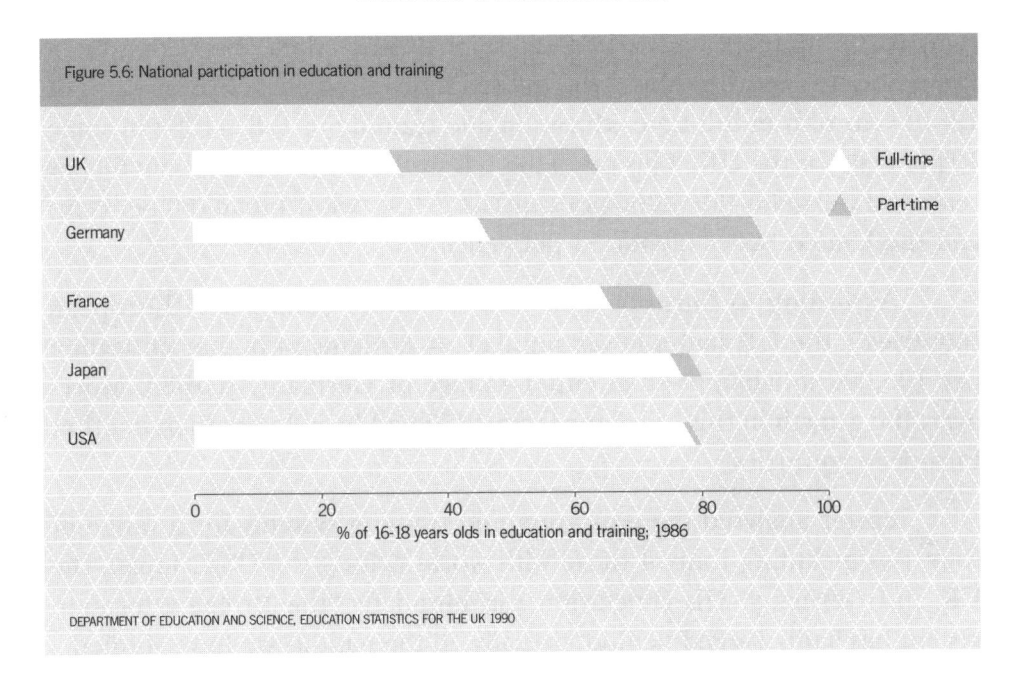

DEPARTMENT OF EDUCATION AND SCIENCE, EDUCATION STATISTICS FOR THE UK 1990

Training has been a source of concern in the UK for many years. Recently, the comparative advantage enjoyed by some other European countries is thought to have increased. In particular, France has made strong efforts to raise the standards of youth vocational training to match those of Germany. Currently, about 82,000 French students a year achieve the A level standard BTec (Technical Baccalaureate) compared with 25,000 passing the equivalent in Britain. About 120,000 workers in Germany attain engineering and technology craft qualifications each year, against 35,000 in Britain.

International comparisons of participation in higher education are even more fraught with definitional problems. Nevertheless, OECD figures suggest that the UK is on a par with France and Germany but below the USA and Japan. However, this comparison is based, of necessity, on some estimating procedures – especially for Germany. And the UK figure in the comparison appears high when set against other data. For example, a Royal Society report in May 1991 quoted figures for participation rates of 18–19 year olds in full-time education and training in 1987–1988 of some 19 per cent for the UK. This rated the UK well below France (about 60 per cent) and Germany (about 65 per cent) as well as below Japan (50 per cent) and the United States (about 55 per cent).

According to Eurostat data – by its nature confined to European countries – the UK had a lower number of students in higher education per 100,000 inhabitants than either France or Germany in 1985. Moreover, the growth in this indicator from 1970 had been lower than in other European countries.

Porter analysed the education and training systems for a range of countries including four of those with world cities – the USA, Japan, the UK and Germany. His conclusion was emphatic "the British education system has badly lagged behind virtually all the nations we have studied". We summarise below his key observations on each country's system.

USA US Government investment in education was substantial and continuous in the decades following the Second World War. In the 1960s, educational standards were high and provision was of high quality. One illustration of the perception of this was the large number of foreign students who sought university education in the US. Higher education was opened up to more US citizens by sustained government investment in both private and public colleges and universities. Cultural attitudes played an important role too: parents worked hard to put their children through college. At the other end of the ability spectrum, the US now faces workforce literacy and basic skills problems often worse than those of the UK.

The standard of education of the average student is a major problem. The improvement in human resources in other countries has set a rising standard for the US and other leading nations to meet to maintain competitiveness. Teaching is not highly respected as a profession and both pay and competence need to be improved, alongside prestige. The lack of national standards for education in the US, where local and state governments are the major providers, is thought to be a distinct disadvantage, given moves in other countries in this direction (for example, the UK national curriculum). However, the size and flexibility of the private sector as an education and training provider in New York and the rest of the US is sometimes considered a significant plus point.

Japan The cultural influences upon education and training are extremely important in Japan. There is a long tradition of respect for education. Students are generally disciplined, hard-working and ready to cooperate in a group. Up to university entry level, the education system is fiercely competitive and many commentators (including some Japanese) consider that this stifles creativity. But the end result is a literate, educated and increasingly skilled human resource base, well grounded in mathematics and science.

One factor that is perhaps unique about Japan is the companies' role in continuing education and training provision. Larger firms educate and train their managers and workers in-house, even up to post-doctorate level. Knowledge creation takes place to a greater extent in companies than in other institutions. In-house training is rigorous and continuous. Managers must pass tests in order to progress. It could be argued that one consequence is that university research is more limited and that links between companies and education institutions are not as well developed as in other countries.

Germany The German public education system is of high quality (public education, after all, began in Germany). It possesses excellent universities and well-regarded technical colleges. Higher education is of a uniform high standard. Education is the responsibility of the State Government (Länder) in Germany and provision is closely linked to the needs of local industry.

Germany has a distinctive apprenticeship system, sponsored by the Länder, whereby trainees spend half of their week at work and half at college. This produces skilled workers in specialised fields who also possess a theoretical base from which to enhance their skills. In addition scientific and technical skills are generally well regarded. An academic career in these areas is much more prestigious than in the US or the UK.

United Kingdom The UK possesses a very individualistic higher education system which fosters a spirit of independent thinking for at least the top tier of its students (though Britain's greatest inventors were often not university educated). In scientific and technical fields, the UK has long suffered from a brain drain because research conditions abroad are regarded to be more favourable, though several research-based companies (for example, pharmaceuticals firms) have located in the UK to take advantage of its low cost supply of skilled personnel. Access to the highest quality education is limited to a relatively small proportion of the relevant age group. The proportion of students going on to higher education is smaller than in most other advanced nations and the absolute number studying in technical fields is also relatively low. Engineering is looked down on as applied rather than pure science and no national certification exists for the title "engineer". Like the US, a key problem in the UK is the teaching of the average student. The UK workforce lags behind other advanced countries in educational and training endowments and UK managers are less likely to be college educated than their counterparts in other leading nations.

UK companies have failed to respond to a weak education system by investing in in-house training. Expenditure on training was 0.15 per cent of the turnover in the UK in 1980, compared with 2 per cent in Germany and 3 per cent in Japan. More recent figures published by the Training Agency in 1989 suggested that British employers spent 0.3 per cent of turnover on training. According to the same source, London ranked well down, if not lowest, amongst British regions in terms of days training per employee, the proportion of employees receiving training and days training per trainee. The relatively new Training and Enterprise Councils (of which some of the latest to begin their contracts were in London) have still to prove their ability to meet market demand and extend the provision of high quality training throughout the workforce in their area. Well developed links between the needs of industry and the provision of education and training have yet to be established on a wide scale. The August 1991 OECD Economic Survey on the UK stated that:

> A big handicap facing UK recovery is poor levels of skills and education compared with many other industrialised nations. The UK continue to suffer the effects of vocational and training programmes being relatively underdeveloped *and directed at immediate job creation rather than the acquisition of basic skills*". A priority, the study said, "is to increase the number of school-leavers with formal qualifications.

London compared with the UK

On the evidence of international comparisons the UK education and training system is poor. How does London compare with national performance?

Participation rates in education and training for post-16-year-olds are much the same in Greater London as elsewhere in the country. Indeed, the proportion staying on at school is higher in Greater London. But these figures mask significant differences within London, with inner London participation rates being much lower than the national average.

Examination achievements in Greater London were similarly much the same as elsewhere in the country. However, London had the highest proportion of students with no graded results amongst the regions of the UK – 10 per cent compared with the national average of 7.5 per cent. These figures again mask significant differences between inner and outer London educational achievements.

Training provision in London appears much weaker than elsewhere in the country. Only 2.5 per cent of 16-year-olds in London went on the Youth Training Scheme in 1988–1989 compared with 13 per cent nationally. This is because of traditionally lower levels of unemployment in London and because the Scheme's pay rates tend to be too low to attract young people living in London. London's implementation of the national training system is relatively poor. Less than 1 per cent of its labour force takes part in any form of work-related government training – half the national average – and training rates in company apprenticeships are much lower in London. Finally, the establishment of the Training and Enterprise Councils has been much slower in London than elsewhere in the country, in part because of problems in agreeing geographical demarcations between them.

The implications of London's relative position on education and training within the UK is that a higher proportion of school leavers (at 16 years of age) enter employment directly – over 21 per cent compared with the national average of 18.5 per cent – and when they do they are less likely to receive training. Moreover, there are significant differences within London. Participation rates, educational achievements, levels of education and participation in further and higher education are much lower in inner London and particularly in east and parts of south-east London.

Finally, a 1988 Department of Employment document concluded that London employers will be facing a quite different labour market in the future. The diminishing supply of workers needs to be seen in the context of a labour market that is resilient and flexible in very many respects. The London pool of skills and capabilities is substantial. However, the need for training will be increased by the demograpic changes which will cause increased competition for young people and an ageing workforce. There will also be further shifts from manual to non-manual and from skill to knowledge-based work and increased use of new technologies. In this situation the training needs of small companies were seen to be of particular importance.

London suffers relative to most other world cities from being part of a British system of education and training which lags behind that of the other countries. The USA, Japan, Germany and France have a greater volume of vocational training and education, reflecting higher investment in human capital formation by employers, employees and the state.

Moreover, there are aspects of education and training in London – and certainly within inner London – which are weaker than the national performance. The consequences are that London is likely to have exacerbated skills shortages and a workforce that tends to be less flexible and skilled than in other world cities. This was the view that emerged from our survey. It was also the view of the consultants working on this aspect of the study that the education and training systems of competitor world cities tended to be stronger than those of their nation states. They tend to benefit from coordinated city and regional monitoring and planning regimes in which employers were usually involved.

Finally, we make the observation that the pattern of weakness in London's education and training provision is very likely to perpetuate the urban polarisation between the "insiders" and the "outsiders" described in Chapter 3. Education and training can provide one mechanism to open up job and income opportunities for the disadvantaged. Yet in London education and training seem not to be realising these opportunities to the fullest possible extent.

Concluding observations

The evidence of this chapter is that London has two key weaknesses in its enabling infrastructure compared with other world cities – in transport, especially safe and reliable intra-city mobility, and in education and training. It has strengths in the availability of high quality office property and in segments of its housing provision, although there are important issues to be addressed with regard to housing for lower income working households.

These findings accord broadly with the results of our survey of the enabling infrastructure attributes of the world cities – see Figure 5.7 (page 166). London's ratings by both London and overseas businesses on national and international transport links and especially on intra-city mobility were well behind overseas business' ratings of their own cities. The reverse was the case with regard to the available stock of commercial property and housing

LONDON: WORLD CITY MOVING INTO THE 21ST CENTURY

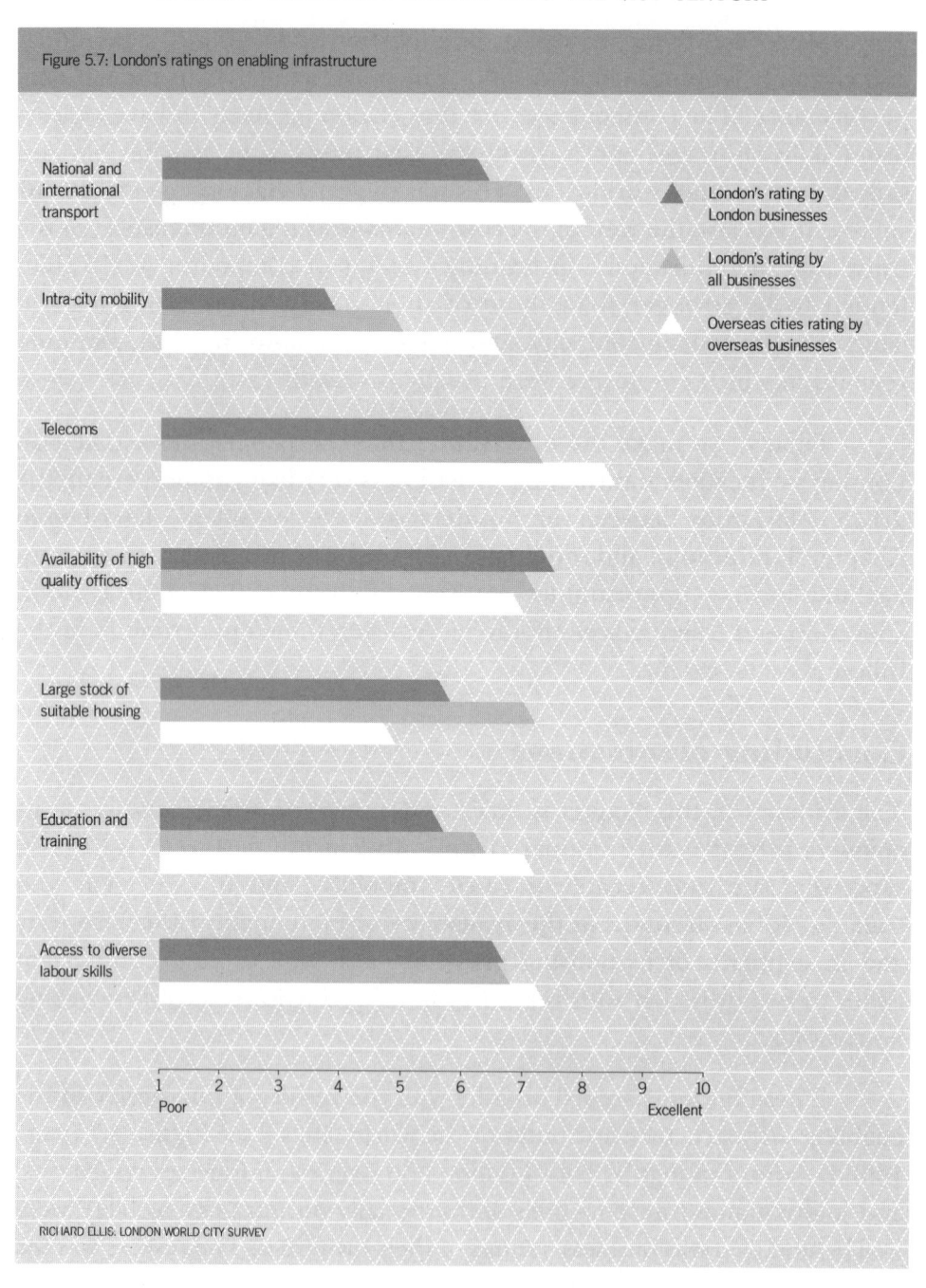

Figure 5.7: London's ratings on enabling infrastructure

- National and international transport
- Intra-city mobility
- Telecoms
- Availability of high quality offices
- Large stock of suitable housing
- Education and training
- Access to diverse labour skills

▲ London's rating by London businesses

▲ London's rating by all businesses

△ Overseas cities rating by overseas businesses

1 (Poor) — 10 (Excellent)

RICHARD ELLIS, LONDON WORLD CITY SURVEY

where London was seen to be advantageously placed. However, on education and training and the accessibility of diverse labour skills, London was rated less favourably than other world cities.

Summary

- ☐ Underpinning wealth creation, job generation and the quality of life in world cities is their enabling infrastructure. We define this to include transport and communications, land-use especially for commercial development and housing, and education and training provision.

- ☐ In terms of current and proposed transport arrangements, London's relative position lies below Paris and Frankfurt on the one hand and above Tokyo and New York on the other. Congestion on the road network is a problem in all world cities – New York, London and Paris are on a par in terms of rush hour traffic flow. Congestion and system constraints on the mass transport network are less problematic in Paris and Frankfurt. The strength and effectiveness of the transport planning regime is lowest in London and New York.

- ☐ London is now reaping both the negative and positive consequences of being the premier international air services hub in Europe and perhaps the world. Its capacity constraints are shared by New York and Tokyo but not by the other world cities. London has the potential to gain most benefit from the Channel Tunnel because of the opportunity it provides to participate in the renaissance of long-distance rail travel on mainland Europe.

- ☐ The sea and major rivers form a significant and visible part of the geography of all the world cities and contribute to the image of the city. The waterways and waterfronts, and their use, are of such importance that they require as much policy attention as is given to land and air transport.

- ☐ London ranks alongside Tokyo and New York in terms of telecommunications. London and New York lead the world in optical fibre deployment and London is only surpassed by New York on the proportion of major offices with digital switches.

☐ Our comparisons make it clear that in London more stock of modern office accommodation has been added in the City and Docklands than in Frankfurt, Berlin and the Tokyo and Paris central business districts. Rents for office accommodation in London are now falling but, on the most recently available comparisons, were higher than in any other world city except the Tokyo central business district.

☐ House prices in London are, on average, lower than those found in other world cities – once relative incomes are taken into account, the position is only slightly less favourable. The major difference between London and other cities is its tenure structure with a relatively high proportion of owner-occupation. Access to social housing is difficult everywhere but in other world cities there are large private sectors providing for new entrants and often for lower-income employed households as well.

☐ London suffers from being part of a British system of education and training which lags behind that of other countries in terms of vocational training and post-16-year-old education. Moreover, there are aspects of education and training in which London, especially inner London, is weaker than the national average, for example inner London participation rates in education for over 16-year-olds are significantly below the national average.

☐ Our survey respondents confirmed the assessment in this chapter – transport, especially intra-city mobility, and education and training are components of the enabling infrastructure which are particularly poorly provided for in London compared with other world cities.

BIG CITIES LIKE LONDON
ARE A CONJURING TRICK. A BENEFICIENT
ILLUSION, PROVIDING EVERYONE WISHED VERY HARD
THEY FLOURISH, BUT WHEN SELF CONFIDENCE EBBS
THE GAME IS UP. THAT IS WHERE
LONDON IS TODAY, SO
IS LONDON DYING?

TO SEE LIVING LONDON, IN FULL
VIGOUR, MEANS GOING ROUND ITS NOOKS AND
CRANNIES. STOP OFF IN NEWINGTON GREEN IN LITTLE
TURKEY, IN BRICK LANE THE RAG TRADE HUSTLES AND CHILDREN PLAY,
IN SOUTHALL FAMILIES STOCK UP ON SPICES, IN RICHMOND
CROWDS SAUNTER AND ENJOY THE NEW RIVERSIDE,
AND OFF DALSTON LANE, THE CLUBS HOT
UP FOR SATURDAY NIGHT.
LONDON LIVES!

The Evening Standard Magazine, 29th August 1991

County Hall
LONDON RESIDUARY BODY

6
PROSPECTS AND POLICY FRAMEWORKS

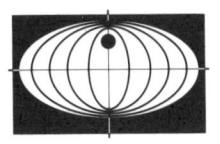

The findings of this study so far indicate that London is a city with recognised pre-eminent world city status. It has advantages over other world cities, but also major disadvantages. If it rests on existing advantages and pays too little and too late attention to its disadvantages, London may reach a plateau in its development. This is especially true of those London attributes which relate to its enabling infrastructure in intra-city mobility and in education and training.

In this chapter we examine first how the respondents to the special survey undertaken for this project saw the prospects for London's competitiveness and status in the 21st Century. We consider where action needs to be taken to strengthen these prospects, both in the view of the survey respondents and our own assessment of the evidence. We then report the findings of our survey on the role of the urban policy framework in contributing to the enhancement of world city status. The final section of the chapter describes the urban policy regime which prevails in each of the world cities and will close with observations on the prospects and policies for London in the 21st Century.

Prospects for increased competitiveness and status

In Figure 6.1 we summarise the results of our survey with regard to the perceived prospects for the world cities in terms of wealth

LONDON: WORLD CITY MOVING INTO THE 21ST CENTURY

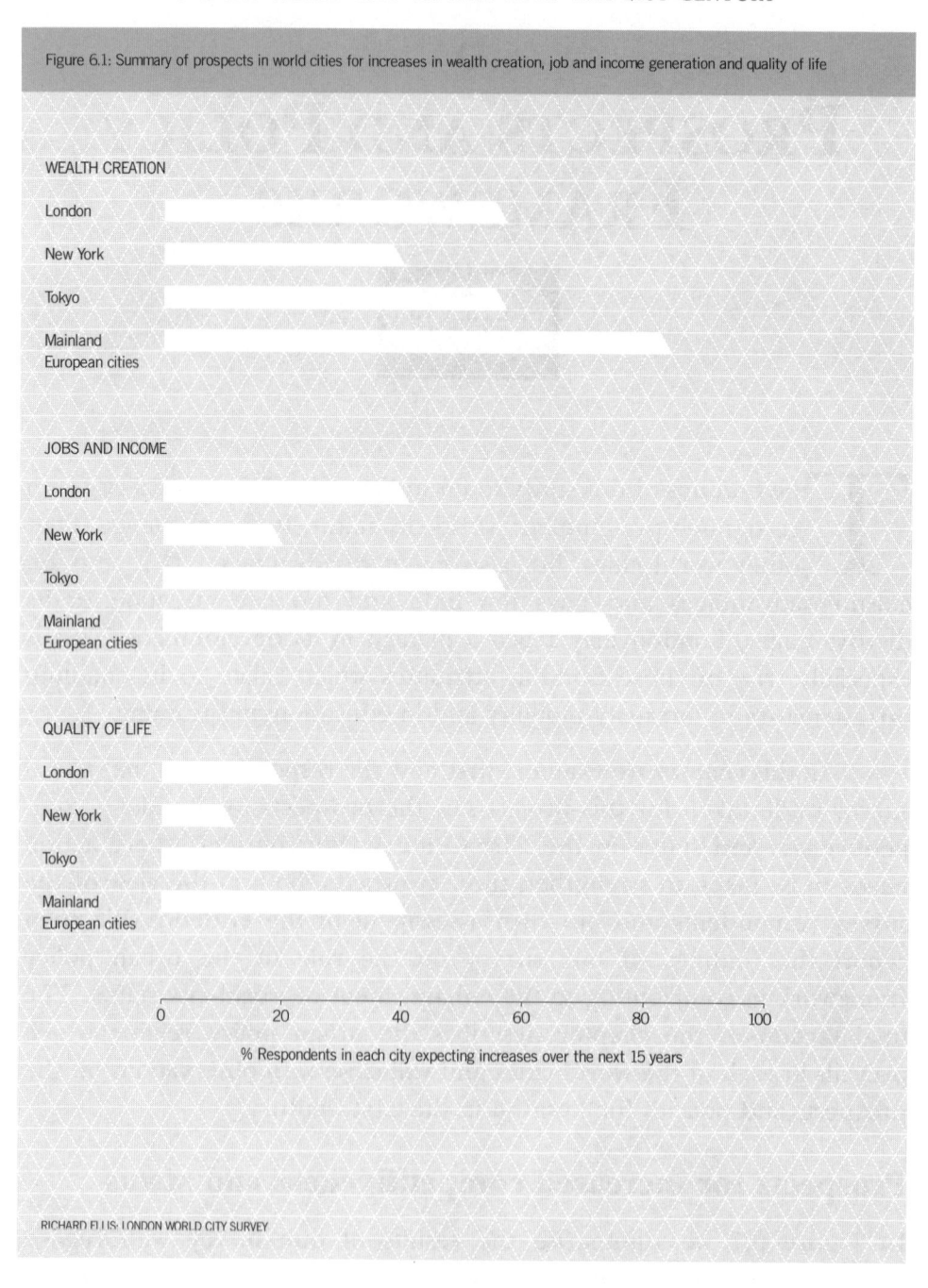

Figure 6.1: Summary of prospects in world cities for increases in wealth creation, job and income generation and quality of life

WEALTH CREATION
London
New York
Tokyo
Mainland European cities

JOBS AND INCOME
London
New York
Tokyo
Mainland European cities

QUALITY OF LIFE
London
New York
Tokyo
Mainland European cities

% Respondents in each city expecting increases over the next 15 years

RICHARD ELLIS: LONDON WORLD CITY SURVEY

creation, job generation and improved quality of life over the next 15 years.

London respondents were as bullish about the wealth creation prospects of their city as Tokyo respondents were about theirs, more bullish than New York firms and less so than the respondents from mainland European cities. But, on job generation and improved quality of life, London respondents were much less optimistic than other respondents except those from New York.

If we take a look at respondents' views on the prospects for increased competitiveness and world status, it can be seen from Figure 6.2 that the optimism in London's continued wealth creation capability is mirrored in the assessment of its future competitiveness. Over 80 per cent of London respondents thought competitiveness prospects were good or very good, although the proportion rating prospects as very good was

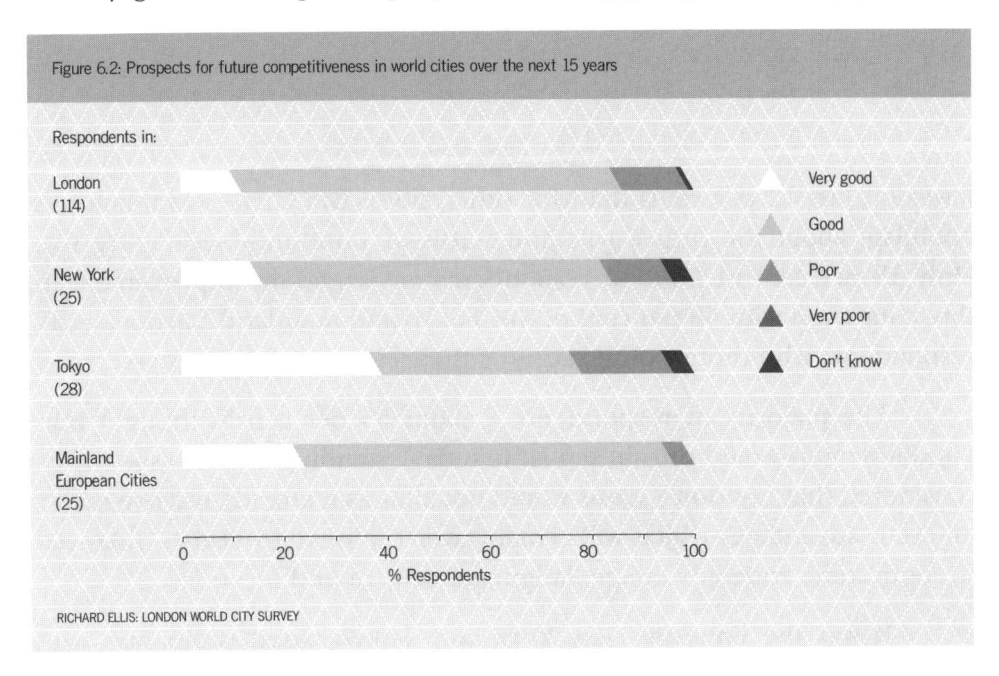

Figure 6.2: Prospects for future competitiveness in world cities over the next 15 years

RICHARD ELLIS: LONDON WORLD CITY SURVEY

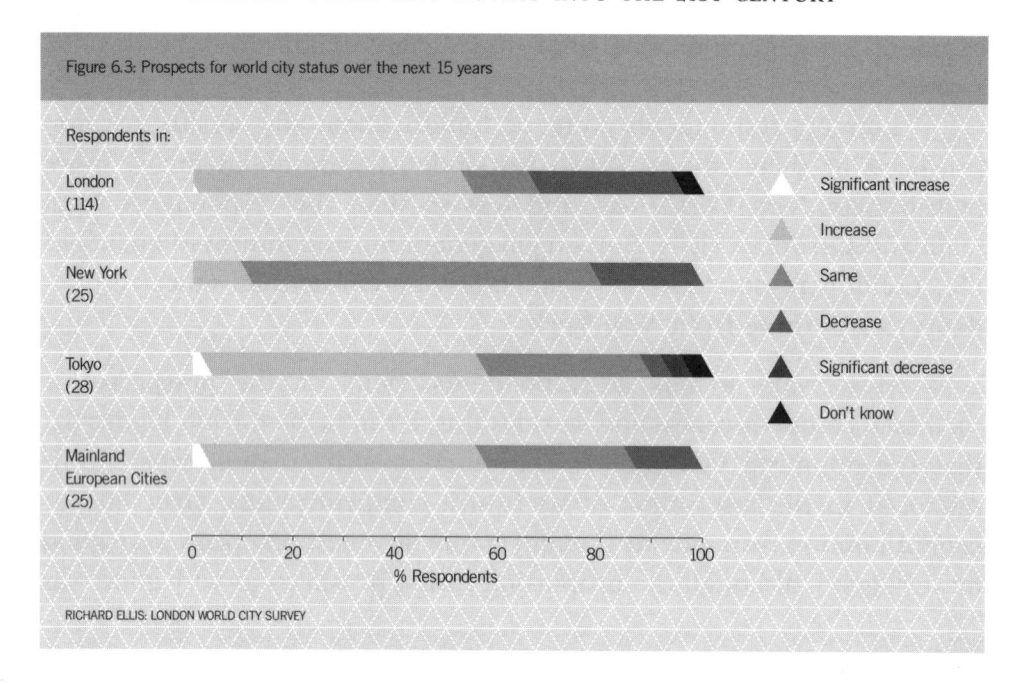

Figure 6.3: Prospects for world city status over the next 15 years

lower (at just 12 per cent) than for other cities. But there was much less optimism about the future role and status of London – see Figure 6.3. Only 13 per cent of London respondents envisaged an improvement in this, compared with 58 per cent of the Tokyo and mainland European city respondents who thought the status of their cities would improve.

The majority of respondents – about 55 per cent – thought that London's status would remain similar to today's standing. Many respondents considered that London's status would not alter as it already has five major inherent advantages which will remain over the next 15 years – financial strength, time zone advantage, language, culture and location.

It was the London, New York and Tokyo based companies who dwelt on London's advantages, whereas mainland European companies focused on the potential for London to lose out if it did not "get its act together". European companies in particular quoted the view that

London's geographical remoteness was a potential threat to its future status.

Almost one third of respondents believed that London's status will decline. The main reasons for the anticipated decline were twofold: first, the competitive challenge from other cities, particularly those likely to participate in European growth. As one American business put it, "it will be in relative decline – just a matter of economic shifting – as some areas rise, some decline". The second main reason for decline was seen to be the lack of any serious planning to enhance London's position relative to competing European cities. The point was succinctly expressed by a London business, "it will inevitably decline unless something is done to pull London together, especially its transport".

We asked respondents to identify the actions needed to enhance the competitiveness of their city. About two-thirds of the London respondents suggested improvements to the transport infrastructure. "The chaotic transport infrastructure makes London appear a less successful and significant place than it really is. This would have to be the starting point." Improvement of the transport infrastructure was also a priority in the other world cities, although in New York over 70 per cent of the respondents wanted improved security and reduced crime levels. Other less frequently mentioned tasks for London included "cleaning London up" and "better education for people from school age upward and on-the-job training".

However, the survey results indicate that London, as a major world city, had inherent advantages which, positively approached through strategic policy and promotion, could help London enhance its competitiveness and world city status. The findings also clearly suggest that London faces significant threats over the medium term from its peripheral geographical position and associated insular attitudes and from inadequacies in its transport infrastructure.

London's position is most likely to be squeezed by the competitive threat from Tokyo and from several centrally located European cities, notably Berlin, Paris and Frankfurt, which are expected to grow significantly in size, wealth and status. However, unlike New York which is likely to see a decline in its world city status, London's position is retrievable by building on its inherent strengths which are still currently recognised by overseas business. London-based organisations and businesses tend to be most negative about its attributes and prospects. These perceptions in particular need to be addressed and redressed quickly before overseas businesses come to share our own view of ourselves.

The results of our survey confirm the findings in our previous chapters. The relative strengths of London are there to be exploited – its potential for wealth creation in the "soft economy" of services, information industries and culture, its available skills and aspects of its quality of life. But the relative disadvantages of London do not appear adequately tackled in two important respects. First, those aspects of the enabling infrastructure typically associated with a co-ordinated approach through public policy – transport, land-use, education and training and longer term conditions for creativity and innovation – have not been addressed with the same vigour or thought as in other world cities. Second, there is no collective or co-ordinated voice for London to promote its interests and image, or any successful mechanism to address the infrastructural problems which contribute so much to urban stress and which are difficult for individuals to manage on their own.

City-wide policies in world cities

We designed our survey of companies based in the world cities to address key issues with regard to city-wide policies. We wanted to establish the importance attached by multi-national business and other organisations to a world city having integrated and forward-looking city-wide policies. We sought to identify the degree to which each of the world cities were perceived to have such policies, whether respondents considered there to be a role for an official strategic planning and transportation body to co-ordinate policy for the city and whether they were aware that their respective cities had a strategic plan.

How important is a city-wide policy? One fifth of respondents rated integrated, forward-looking, city-wide policies as a critical attribute and about 60 per cent thought it was an important attribute of a world city. Almost one third of businesses and organisations based in London thought city-wide policies to be a critical attribute, a much higher proportion than in the responses from the other cities. When the London responses were analysed in greater depth, it became evident that organisations and especially organisations in the cultural sector – considered this to be an even more critical factor than London businesses.

The degree to which city-wide policies exist London businesses and organisations were strongly of the view that integrated, forward-looking, city-wide policies were either absent or poor in London – about two-thirds of them believed this. The perception was particularly evident amongst organisations in London, who were considerably more critical of London's city-wide policy system than businesses located in London. About one quarter of the respondents from Tokyo and New York rated their city-wide policies as poor but over a quarter rated them as good. The mainland European respondents were the most enthusiastic about their city policies, with nearly one half claiming them to be good. Unlike London respondents, overseas businesses did not consider London's policy system to be below average. Indeed, their perceptions tended to assess the London system as good, especially amongst the Japanese, over 40 per cent of whom gave London this rating – a higher proportion than rated their own system as good. Very few respondents from overseas rated the London system as poor.

A role for an official strategic body in world cities A large majority of all respondents (some 85 per cent) considered that there was a role for an official strategic planning and transportation body to co-ordinate policy for their city. Respondents from London gave the most enthusiastic affirmative response to this question – 9 out of 10 considering there to be a role for such a body. Rather surprisingly the mainland European response was more muted – one quarter said there was no role for such a body. However, comments obtained by respondents (to an open question) provided useful insights on the reasoning behind the answers. London businesses and organisations were clearly of the view that transport within and to London needed to be co-ordinated and that the existing planning and co-ordinating regime was inadequate. A number of organisations and, in particular, businesses commented on the need for such a body as long as it was non-bureaucratic, effective and "not like the former Greater London Council".

The mainland European response emphasised their positive stance to planning and co-ordination – "there has to be a centre for co-ordination" – but also reflected some concern that there should be more private sector involvement in the planning process. The reason for the negative response from one quarter of respondents on the need for a co-ordinating body was simple – they already had one. The advantages the New York respondents saw in a co-ordinating body were the same as in London – primarily as a means to resolve transportation problems. In addition, they anticipated that a strategic body could address the financial problems of the city and help co-ordinate service provision. Transportation co-ordination and the easing of congestion were also high on the Tokyo respondents' list of reasons for a co-ordinating body. But some of them saw a wider purpose for it too in improving the city's efficiency and competitiveness.

There was a consensus amongst all respondents that there was a role for a co-ordinating authority and that, whatever else it might do, it would have to integrate transport provision.

Awareness of strategic plans in world cities "Does your city have a strategic plan?" This was the simple question we directed at our survey respondents. Nine out of ten London businesses and organisations said, "no". One quarter to one third of the responses from New York and Tokyo said "yes". A resounding 70 per cent of the respondents from mainland European cities were aware of their city's plan.

Summary

From the summary Figure 6.4, it can be seen that London businesses and organisations, along with respondents in other world cities, considered that strategic city-wide planning was an important world city attribute. An overwhelming majority of London's respondents thought that integrated city-wide policies were necessary for London's future development – especially because they would help to alleviate London's transportation problems and because the existing urban policy framework was not working to London's advantage. The majority of respondents were aware that their city did not have a strategic plan.

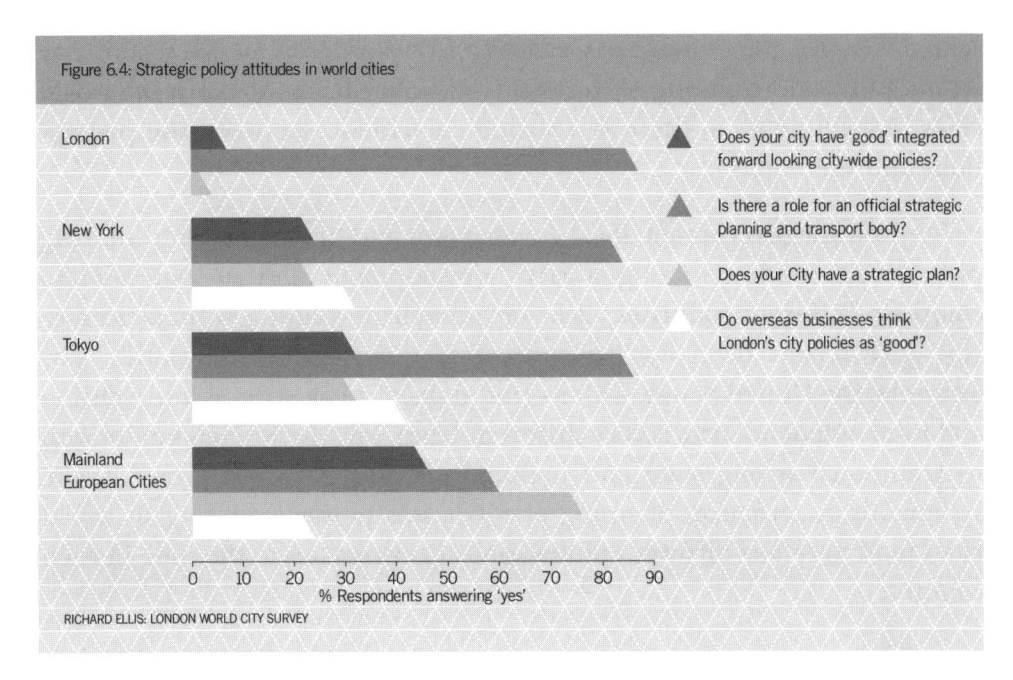

Figure 6.4: Strategic policy attitudes in world cities

- Does your city have 'good' integrated forward looking city-wide policies?
- Is there a role for an official strategic planning and transport body?
- Does your City have a strategic plan?
- Do overseas businesses think London's city policies as 'good'?

% Respondents answering 'yes'

RICHARD ELLIS: LONDON WORLD CITY SURVEY

Within Europe, there was a highly positive stance towards city-wide planning and an awareness that, not only did these plans exist, but on balance they were working well. Respondents in New York had similar perceptions to those in London – namely they recognised that their city did not have an integrated city-wide plan, and that its absence was exacerbating New York's transportation and management problems. Respondents in Tokyo, whilst recognising the importance of city-wide strategic planning were not entirely sure if their city had such a plan or if it was working particularly well.

Policy frameworks in world cities

In the previous section we reported the conclusions of our survey that London's competitiveness and world status prospects could be enhanced by appropriate coordination of city-wide policies. Clearly what was presented were the perceptions of a sample of respondents. In this section, we set out our understanding of the reality of policy frameworks in the world cities. As will be seen, there is a strong coincidence between the perceptions and the reality.

Central government, local government and private decision-making play a role in determining a city's development and its potential to compete. Different countries allow far greater devolution from central to city government or from city government to local communities. For example, the United States, with its traditions of weak federal intervention and local independence, is very different from, say, the French model with its traditional strong state and national planning. To some extent, the systems of governance, planning and administration operating in world cities tend to reflect different philosophical approaches to the state in each country.

Because of their scale, economic muscle and symbolic significance, the larger world cities cannot be ignored by their national governments. Indeed, they may well exert power beyond their "real" importance. French presidents have, in recent years, vied with each other to undertake "grands projects" in Paris, despite considerable provincial suspicion of, and competition with, the capital. Berlin has once again been chosen as national capital of Germany, and will probably become the focus and symbol of the strength and importance of that country's political, cultural (and possibly financial) life in Europe and the world. Despite its apparently imminent state of collapse for the last twenty years, New York remains a powerful political symbol of the freedom and opportunity offered by the United

States and, as the home of the United Nations, the whole world. London, like Paris, dominates the nation's decision-making processes. The importance of the effective governance of London to England and Great Britain is becoming increasingly a matter of political concern for all the major political parties – not surprisingly since it represents almost 20 per cent of national GDP.

The world cities vary in terms of the degree of national government control over their actions, in their structures of regional and local government and in the effectiveness of their political and planning systems. As with any international comparisons, there is a degree to which cultural differences explain why apparently similar institutions in particular countries produce quite different results. New York and Tokyo both have an elected city-wide leader – mayor or governor – for their populations of many millions of people, yet the appalling state of New York's government contrasts strongly with the relative effectiveness of Tokyo's administrative arrangements.

The degree of freedom for locally-independent action offered to individual world cities differs considerably. New York City has, in theory at least, greatest independence. It can raise, through its own local tax income, the finance for its expenditure programmes and is free of much control from higher-tier governments. There is some potential control over budgets by the state government, but virtually no federal involvement. As a result, the mayor and other elected officials have enormous discretion over the spending and, to a lesser extent, the raising of resources. But when New York suffers dire social and health problems, it is on its own. We suspect that London, Paris or Tokyo would always, in a last resort, be able to rely on some degree of national government assistance.

Under the constitutional arrangements operating in Germany, Berlin and Frankfurt have considerable freedom from the Federal Government. However, in both the allocation of resources and in influence over planning, the States (Lander) have powers over German cities.

Nevertheless, as far as services and provision are concerned there is a constitutional principle in Germany that powers should be operated at the lowest possible level. Thus, the city governments in both Berlin and Frankfurt enjoy considerable local discretion to use resources and to make plans.

However, land-use planning is a three-tier process involving federal, state and local government. There is, by British standards, considerable consensus in the relationships between different levels of government. This is possibly because of the existence of a strong constitutional structure in Germany giving each tier of government clear responsibilities and relative financial freedom, perhaps a consequence of the system of electoral proportional representation which encourages coalition government.

Tokyo enjoys less independence from central government than New York City, Frankfurt or Berlin, but by virtue of the city's massive population (over 12 million in the city area) and the concentration of powers over public services in the Tokyo Metropolitan Government, the machinery of government has huge power which is enhanced by the close links between the Governor of Tokyo and national government. The Tokyo Metropolitan Government's strength can be measured by its capacity to undertake projects like the massive waterfront subcentre development or the move to its prestigious new offices at Shinjuku. Most public services in Tokyo are controlled or influenced by the metropolitan government. About three-quarters of Tokyo's resources are raised from local taxation, giving the city considerable financial independence. In addition, the nature of Japanese culture coupled with the single party hegemony of the post-war years has contributed to the stability of Tokyo's development.

Of the world cities under consideration, Paris and London are probably most directly under the control of their national governments. This said, in recent years Paris has become more independent, while London has lost powers to Central Government. The French state has traditionally been highly-centralised, with national government founded in an educational system which is focused on producing a highly-trained bureaucracy making day-to-day decisions over most aspects of public life, particularly in Paris. Only relatively few, very local services fall within the control of local government. In recent years, decentralisation policies have increased the powers of the Paris city government and its mayor. Indeed, the high visibility of the Mayor of Paris and the fact that, more often than not, his politics are at odds with those of the government, has created pressures within central government to weaken the powers of the city. There are government-imposed restrictions on local tax-raising.

By contrast, for the last century London has had a local government system with greater powers than those enjoyed by Paris local government. Moreover, from 1965 until its abolition in 1986, the Greater London Council's powers, although intentionally weak, extended over virtually the whole built-up area of London, whereas the Ville de Paris is responsible for only the centre of the metropolis. With its abolition, the GLC's responsibilities for guidance on strategic planning, decision making in public transport and major roads and for major developments were transferred to central government. Many responsibilities – including education in inner London – were transferred to the thirty-two Boroughs and the City of London. London's local authorities now raise only about 15 per cent of their revenue income from local taxation and are subject to tax limits, which inevitably reduces freedom to manoeuvre.

The structures of government also vary from city to city. New York and Tokyo have arrangements for city government which are extensive but do not cover the full metropolitan area. Each has a directly-elected civic leader – in New York, a mayor and in Tokyo, a governor. In both cities, there are lower-tier systems of government. New York City comprises five boroughs, which have no service-provision functions, though borough mayors have some powers of patronage. Tokyo consists of twenty-three special wards, each of which has some responsibility for services provision. But, in each city, the metropolis-wide authority has by far the greatest powers.

Berlin and Frankfurt also have city-wide local government, although of course the cities are far smaller than New York and Tokyo. Berlin has a population of about 3.5 million and Frankfurt well below 1 million. Paris has a city council with responsibility for the core area of the metropolis: the old city within the inner ring road (population 2.5 million). Beyond this Ville de Paris area, there are many smaller communes, which are grouped into "departments". Each department is headed by a government-appointed prefect, who provides government oversight of policies and public funding in the area. There is a department solely for the Ville de Paris. Eight departments, including Paris, constitute the Ile de France region. Land use and transport planning in Paris is handled by a joint body which has representatives from national government and all levels of local government. This region has a population of about 10 million. Berlin, Frankfurt and Paris have mayors who are appointed by the elected councillors for their respective cities.

Thus, New York, Tokyo, Berlin, Frankfurt and Paris all have some kind of city-wide local government. Each of these cities has a mayor, although not all are directly-elected and their functions vary. London is significantly different from all the other cities considered because it has neither a central government minister, nor a city-wide elected local government nor a mayor. London's local government – covering much of the built-up area of 6.5 million people – is split between 32 directly-elected Borough Councils and the Corporation of the City of London. As in Paris, some of London's local service provision is controlled by central government.

Individual boroughs have unpaid indirectly elected mayors, with a largely ceremonial role, who change each year. The City of Westminster has a Lord Mayor and the City of London has a civic leader, known as the Lord Mayor of London, who represents the people and businesses of the small and historic core and financial centre of the metropolis. Looking at the other world cities, Tokyo and Paris (Ville de Paris) are run by centre-right administrations: Governor Suzuki is a member of the governing Liberal Democratic Party, while Paris' Mayor Chirac has been Prime

Minister of the rightist RPR. Thus, in addition to being (in British terms) "Conservatives", the civic leaders of both Tokyo and Paris are closely aligned with national politicians. New York City, by contrast, has (by American standards) a left-leaning mayor. Currently, David Dinkins and currently thirty-four out of thirty-five city council members are Democrats. In recent years, London's boroughs have split almost evenly between the Conservative Party and the Labour Party, usually with fourteen or fifteen under the control of each party. The centrist Liberal Democrats generally hold three or four, while the City of London is "independent" of party politics.

The comparison between London and other world cities is stark: the biggest metropolitan area in Europe has no city-wide authority or agency, and its major strategic decisions are in effect in the hands of central government with its day-to-day controls being run by individual London Boroughs. Yet, it would be simplistic to infer that this unusual form of government is inevitably worse than others in use. For example, New York has a relatively strong, easily-identified, city-wide but not wider metropolitan government, and its public services are hopelessly inadequate and in a state of decline because it has no financial help from the Federal Government or the State. The government of Paris, which is often held up to Londoners as a model of good practice, has social problems in the suburbs beyond the affluent areas of Ville de Paris.

Looking forward, it is clear that city-wide governments and mayors are seen as providing a focus for the promotion and development of other world cities. Putting aside the best way of administering public services such as transport, the capacity to promote the city and to provide a framework for development is widely seen as giving Paris, Frankfurt and Tokyo an edge over London, while a united Berlin has all to play for in terms of effective city-regional government.

Land-use planning in world cities

Land-use and development is subject to the same varying degrees of government control. Figure 6.5 illustrates the degree to which the controls

Figure 6.5: Assessment of land use planning regimes

	LONDON	NEW YORK	PARIS	FRANKFURT	BERLIN	TOKYO	
National	3	NSR	2	9	9	4	
Regional	NSR	NSR	2	9	1	2	
Local	4	4	4	2	1	2	
Degree of integration	1	NSR	1	9	4	3	NSR = No Statutory Regime
Overall assessment	8	4	9	29	15	11	Maximum score for each component = 9

RICHARD ELLIS

are perceived to be strong and/or effective from city to city as assessed in Richard Ellis' work. The results suggest that Frankfurt and Berlin are subject to stronger and more effective planning controls than other world cities. To the extent that their respective planning systems lack effective integration, London and Paris appear remarkably similar. However, they differ markedly in terms of administrative structure because, unlike Paris, London does not have an effective regional (metropolitan-wide) tier of land-use control. Within Tokyo, planning policies and controls are strongly influenced by central government and, when compared to London and Paris, show a relatively higher degree of administrative integration. Conversely, within New York all planning controls are at the local level, with no integration with either Federal or State governments.

The planning and development strategies for the world cities are set out in Figure 6.6 as outlined by their respective statutory metropolitan planning agencies. While London has no statutory metropolitan wide plan. The Government in September 1989 has issued Strategic Planning Guidance for London (known as Regional Planning Guidance No. 3). This provides the statutory strategic planning framework for the preparation of Unitary Development Plans by the London Boroughs. The Government Guidance does not include geographically specific policies. In contrast, LPAC's policies in advice advocate consolidation and restraint in the overheated west, and growth and development in Inner and Outer east London, particularly in the Growth Points identified along the London end of the East Thames Corridor. The City of New York has also designated growth and restraint areas. However, unlike LPAC's strategy the city's zoning regulations are effective and statutory. The city therefore encourages office developments to locate to the West side of Midtown, whilst growth is being stabilised to the east with preservation orders being enforced on Upper East Side.

London's Docklands provides London with a unique opportunity to enhance its status as a world city by enabling it to respond more easily to future world city demands. However, the experience and attitudes of other world cities also shows that each (with the exception of Berlin so far) has the planning intentions to encourage major new commercial development in areas within close proximity to the existing central business district. For example:

Paris: La Defense outwards to Gennevilliers and Montesson is identified for commercial development, while growth of the area around Roissy/Charles de Gaulle is confined to international business development.

Frankfurt: The planning and development strategy for the city is provided by a point-axial system by which development impulses are transmitted along designated axes, the space between the axes being rural areas protected from new development and providing mutual access to urban and rural communities.

New York: The Public Development Corporation has launched specific world city projects (for example, the New Commodities Exchange and the

LONDON: WORLD CITY MOVING INTO THE 21ST CENTURY

Figure 6.6: Summary of strategic plans in world cities

National Land-use strategies

City and national body		Status	Spatial Planning Aims
London	Department of the Environment	Statutory	Coordinated framework for regional and local planning. London Docklands, Isle of Dogs Enterprise Zone, Planning Policy Guidance 9
Frankfurt and Berlin	Standing Conference of State Ministers	Advisory but binding statements of principle	Focused development on: — key centres — populated, under-developed areas (Ranking of Structural Areas) Coordinated development to protect rural areas
Paris	National Government	Statutory	Decentralisation of commercial activity away from Paris and L'Ile de France with tax and other incentives
	DATAR	Advisory	Large scale public developments and investments
New York	Federal Government	Statutory	N/A
Tokyo	Ministry of Construction	Statutory	Decentralisation out of Tokyo with greater regional integration
	National Land Agency	Statutory	Multi-centre core strategy for Tokyo Metropolitan Region — Regional Development Plans — Comprehensive Development Plans

Regional Land-use strategies

City and regional body		Status	Spatial Planning Aims
London	London and the South East Regional Planning Conference	Advisory	Economic growth, revitalised older urban areas, whilst conserving the countryside. A New Strategy for the South East, 1990.
Frankfurt	Interior Ministry for Hessen	Statutory	Focused development on: — key centres — existing populated, under-developed areas Coordinated development to protect rural areas
	Regional Planning Authority for South Hessen	Statutory	Frankfurt, Wresbaden and Darmstad identified as urban areas
Berlin	Senator for Town Planning and Environmental Protection	Statutory	No formal policies announced since unification but suggestion that greater emphasis be placed on regional centres (including Frankfurtoder) to ease city congestion in Berlin
Paris	Prefecture de la region d'Ile de France with assistance of local government	Statutory	Closure of gap between east and west of Paris region and between central Paris and parts of the periphery: Le Livre Blanc, 1990
New York	Regional Planning Association	Advisory	Regional Plans for New York Metropolitan Area
Tokyo	N/A	N/A	N/A

Urban Land-use strategies

City and urban bodies		Status	Spatial Planning Aims
London	London Planning Advisory Committee	Advisory	Strategic growth points and centres: Strategic Planning Advice for London 1988.
	London Planning Authorities: 33 Boroughs, London Docklands Development Corporation	Statutory	Major office employment in the Central London Activities Core Zone and Docklands: Borough plans, Unitary Development Plans
Frankfurt	Umlandverband Frankfurt	Statutory	Adequate land provision for commerce in Frankfurt and surroundings: Preparatory Land-Use Plan (1985-2000)
	Frankfurt City Planning Department	Statutory	Detailed plans for specific areas: Binding Land-Use Plans
Berlin	Senator for Town Planning and Environmental Protection	Statutory	'No formal policies at present'
Paris	IAURIF and DREIF	Statutory	Development of zones for commerce away from the Central Business Districts; Le Livre Blanc, 1990
New York	State of New York	Statutory	N/A
	New York City	Statutory	Development of west-side of Midtown; decentralisation of business to neighbouring Boroughs: zoning resolutions
Tokyo	Toyko Metropolitan Government	Statutory	Multi-centre core plan strategy, development of Tokyo Bay and Tama New Town: Long Term Plans for Tokyo
	Ward Areas	Statutory	Preparation of plans with Tokyo Metropolitan Government and Ministry of Construction: zoning of urban promotion and control areas

RICHARD ELLIS

Audubon Research Park) and advertised specifically for back-office sites to be located on Staten Island.

Tokyo: The objective is to switch from a single-core concentration of office activities in the central business district to a multi-core system. In particular, it is intended that the Tokyo Bay development will provide a completely new world city business environment based upon its teleport. The core is to be further sub-divided into "subcentre cores" (for example at Tama New Town and Shinjuku) while peripheral and associated activities are to be decentralised even further (for example, Tsukuba Science City).

It is worth emphasising two particular aspects of the land-use strategies which have been planned for Tokyo, New York, Paris and Frankfurt. The first is that they are couched in world city terms. This is certainly the case in New York and Tokyo where both city governments have expressed their intention to defend and sustain their respective global roles. The second aspect which should be highlighted is that the land-use planning of these cities is merely one element of a broader-based strategy for development which embraces many of the issues we have discussed so far – for example, the knowledge base of the city, communications, market access and competition, the labour force, human resources and the environment in its widest sense.

CONCLUDING OBSERVATIONS

The global dimension provided by our comparative assessment of world cities has brought home to us very strongly that London's prospects will be intimately bound up with its ability to cope with a rapidly changing world – characterised by increasing competition from new sources and more complex trading relationships. For a mature world city like London, its experience in international markets and trading relationships will stand it in good stead.

But trade integration and convergence will bring competition and rivalry both from new geographical sources – the rapid rise of Frankfurt on world financial markets – and from markets that were previously distinct. Banks, securities firms, insurance companies, advertising agencies, building societies and accountancy firms are now seeking to rival each other in new, and within each others' core lines of, business. In the cultural sector, theatre, film, video, opera and popular and classical music, sport and entertainment are to an increasing degree converging on and competing in the same markets.

The changing nature of competition will require alertness and flexibility on the part of world cities, especially the more mature ones. They will need to cultivate their agglomeration economies and creativity through the clustering of key market players, sophisticated support services, and a high quality professional labour force. The businesses which thrive on proximity to world affairs and to each other in face to face communication will include financial and business services, media and publishing, cultural, sports and entertainment activities, higher education and research provision, design, fashion and advertising, conference and tourism management. Convergence amongst these players will create a potential for some interesting and innovative packages of products.

This new global melting pot will provide a harsh competitive environment. The world cities who emerge triumphant will be those whose enabling infrastructure provides them with the resources to be flexible and creative. They are those which provide a seed-bed where innovation, production and service delivery can flourish. That means – as was recognised by our survey respondents – good intra-city mobility, a strong creative centre, high quality education and training provision and integrated city-wide forward-looking policies. There seems to be a clear consensus from our survey work and the reviews in our previous chapters that London is disadvantaged by the lack of regionally focused policies for the development of the city in these respects. Moreover, the capacity to promote the city and to provide a framework for its development is widely seen as giving Tokyo, Paris and Frankfurt, and even New York, an edge over London.

SUMMARY

☐ Our survey respondents confirmed our own assessment – prospects for London's future competitiveness are good, sustained by its wealth creation capacity, but prospects for enhanced world status were diminished by the poorer prognosis for job generation and improved quality of life in London.

☐ The relative strengths of London are in its potential for wealth creation especially in financial and business services and cultural activities – manufacturing remains a vulnerable component of economic activity.

☐ There are two key areas of relative weakness. First, there are those aspects of the enabling infrastructure typically associated with public policy, provision or regulation, notably transport, environmental quality, education and training and the conditions for creativity and innovation through the knowledge base. Second, there is no city-wide, forward looking strategic body for London – embracing wealth creation, job generation, the quality of life and the enabling infrastructure.

☐ The results of our survey were emphatic on the role of urban strategy and for an official strategic body in world cities. Nine out of ten London respondents affirmed that such a role would be beneficial. Improved transport coordination was seen to be the most important benefit.

☐ Our comparison of London with the other world cities in terms of their arrangements for governance was stark. The biggest metropolitan area in Europe has no city-wide authority or agency and its major strategic decisions are in the hands of central government.

☐ The land-use strategies of other world cities have two general characteristics which should be emphasised. First, they tend to be couched in world city terms (eg, Tokyo and Paris) or they contain world city initiatives (eg New York). Second, they tend to be linked with other city-wide policies with regard for example to the knowledge base of the city, its labour force and the environment.

☐ As part of city-wide, forward-looking strategies, the other world cities have the intention and mechanisms to promote themselves in the world and to act as ambassadors in the global urban community giving them an edge over London.

WE'VE GOT
TO KEEP THE SEED-BED FERTILE,
SO THAT LONDON IS READY TO CHANGE
AND GROW IN THE RIGHT PLACES
WHEN OPPORTUNITIES PRESENT
THEMSELVES.

Heather Kerswell,
Chair of the Association of London Borough Planning Officers, June 1991

Tender Shoots for Future Growth
COOPERS & LYBRAND DELOITTE, THE IMAGE BANK

7
STRATEGIES FOR THE 21ST CENTURY

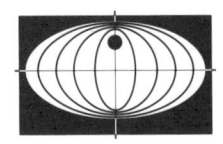

In any study of this kind the profusion of facts can smother the situation they seek to describe. In this final chapter, our intention is to clear the decks a little – to put the comparative assessments behind us and concentrate on laying the foundations for a strategic policy agenda for London. In the next section we set out what our assessment suggests are the key issues for London. In the final section we describe our proposed strategic priorities.

KEY ISSUES FOR LONDON

Wealth creation

Our comparative assessment gives us no reason to doubt the Agnelli Foundation's strategies for wealth creation in a world city. These were that a world city must:

- **draw on the past to develop the resources of the future** – it must have the ability to turn its traditions and culture into a competitive edge in global markets;

- **prepare for change and anticipate new developments** – there must be both a willingness and the opportunity to take account of longer term trends in global trade and investment; *and*

☐ **develop and enhance global links and relations** – it must work to further international links and the transfer of knowledge and experience between cities to foster integration in the urban community.

To develop these characteristics, London must be able to provide for those businesses which benefit most from the agglomeration economies of a world city – affordable offices in appropriate locations, a large and diverse pool of labour skills and world-class communications. It is a hard and unpalatable fact of London life that start-ups, small firms and the cultural sector may well find it more difficult to maintain a foothold in the capital against the larger, more well entrenched and more profitable interests. The current situation in London's property market offers a window of opportunity for such businesses to re-assess the viability of a central London location and to keep or gain a place there.

The results of our survey emphasised that London businesses must adopt bold, innovative attitudes in global markets. A common theme was that other European cities would fare better than London in taking up the opportunities of change in Eastern Europe because they were less insular and more positive in their approach to the challenge. With perhaps the exception of the financial services sector, there was a general impression that the business community had an aversion to medium-to-longer term risk. This is a characteric which inhibits the translation of creativity into production and plagues many aspects of London's cultural sector as much as it constrains British manufacturing performance.

Relative to other world cities, London as a whole appears less inclined or able as a city to develop and capitalize on international links and relations. Very simply, this is because London does not have institutional representation in the world arena. As a consequence, it seems to others to be lukewarm about engaging in the international debate on the future of the world cities and unadventurous in advancing bilateral relations with other major urban centres to pave the way for commercial developments and cultural exchange.

STRATEGIES FOR THE 21ST CENTURY

There is no shortage of conventional ways of doing this – trade missions, cultural exchanges and co-operation agreements. But the Agnelli Foundation report suggested that the city-state itself might develop further the capability for international cultural and possibly economic initiatives. In the light of the European Commission's recent Green Paper on urban environment, it seems clear that environmental issues should be added to this list. The significance of developing ambassadorial and more informal relations between world cities is not merely symbolic. Such dialogue both generates direct commercial opportunities and increases exposure to the cultures of new and different markets and in the process expands commercial attitudes and potential.

Our analysis suggests that there are three key infrastructure components that underpin wealth creation in London:

- ☐ transport;
- ☐ innovation and enterprise; *and*
- ☐ the means by which London's global wealth creating image is presented and promoted.

As far as the transport infrastructure is concerned, we draw an important distinction between international transport links and "intra-city mobility" – which covers everything from journeys on foot to travel by Tube to trips down the Thames. It is better mobility within London to which we attach most significance for two reasons. First, good international links need to be complemented by convenient access from the airport or rail terminal to the destination within the city. Business trips are not made from one airport or rail terminal to another but from one workplace or home to another. Second, good intra-city mobility is the oil that prevents agglomerations from grinding to a halt. It facilitates the face-to-face communications over a meal or in a cafe or at the theatre or at an international conference or sporting event. It enables business to call on an adequate labour pool from within the metropolis. It becomes part of the overall day-to-day experience of delight or despair.

Jobs and income

All the world cities in our sample experience severe labour market problems. New York illustrates the destructive polarisation which can leave the city centre inhabited mainly by the very rich and the very poor while the remainder move to the city periphery and beyond. The economic, social and, for the New York authorities, financial costs are progressively damaging.

The process is progressive because, as the regional metropolitan area widens, it encompasses other local government bodies determined to reap the advantages of such expansion while resisting the costs. Thus, increasingly local self-interest becomes embodied in the status quo.

The process is damaging because the longer the problem is allowed to deteriorate the more difficult it becomes to tackle. The polarisation is reinforced, the infrastructure and urban fabric eroded. This makes the city less attractive to residents and business. And, before long, both begin to leave and the destructive spiral accelerates.

Three issues have been identified with regard to London's labour market. The first is that labour demand and supply conditions in London are not analysed and understood in a comprehensive way. Nor are the labour market implications of major developments systematically examined and fed into policy considerations for the metropolitan area as a whole. Insofar as there are London wide labour market issues and local ones not geographically defined, they are not likely to be fully addressed through the Training and Enterprise Councils and the boroughs alone.

The second issue is that of "mismatch" – the dichotomy of unemployment and unfilled vacancies – and the need quantitatively and qualitatively to increase the effective labour supply. The most obvious, albeit problematic, option is for increased training (especially modular and accredited courses) and more enlightened recruitment policies. Other measures are needed on a significant scale to enhance local recruitment and enterprise, especially for the disadvantaged. This must include improved intra-city mobility, community based outreach and referral/guidance agencies, and the development of ethnic minority businesses and community voluntary groups.

The third issue relates to tracking and monitoring labour market developments. There is no system in place which allows continuous assessment of the extent to which supply and demand for labour is, or is likely to be, mismatched. Both public policy makers and the private sector could benefit from a system which puts them in a better position to assess the labour market implications of such projects as Canary Wharf and the Kings Cross development. London Boroughs wishing to use the new spending powers for economic development are required to draw up Economic Development Plans. There would appear to be a case – since the Plans will involve labour market initiatives – for a London wide summation and review of them in the context of guidance from central government.

Our analysis suggests that four key infrastructure components underpin jobs and income generation in London:

- intra-city mobility;
- education and training;
- housing; *and*
- a comprehensive information base and analysis of London's labour market.

Quality of life

World cities are bustling, hectic environments in which to live and work. This can be a source of stress. The key to the continued efficient functioning of world cities is the effective management of such stress.

In practice, stress within a world city is related to the overall quality of life it is able to offer its inhabitants. Our assessment is that the key negative dimensions are dirt, discomfort and danger. These are most closely associated with levels of air pollution and cleanliness, noise generation, access to "green" or public space and levels of crime.

It is clear that environmental quality is as much a matter of perception as it is of reality. The evidence suggests that London has a marked advantage over other world cities in terms of available "green" space and tends to feature among the middle order of the rankings on the other criteria used to evaluate environmental quality. Yet the perception of Londoners and others of the quality of London's environment is rather different. The results of the survey of businesses undertaken as part of this study indicates that, in terms of having a "clean, safe and pleasant environment", London is seen as having a position inferior to that of the comparator cities except New York.

The inconsistency between perception and reality suggests that action could be taken to improve the level of information and awareness of environmental quality in London. This could be targeted on individuals and businesses in London as well as opinion formers in the rest of the world. In particular, there is scope to promote London generally as a city providing a good quality of life; to highlight specific favourable comparisons between London and other world cities to reveal its key environmental strengths; and to promote examples of successful action taken to enhance environmental quality in London.

Of course, a policy of altering perceptions for the better, by increasing awareness, could and should not be pursued in isolation. By clearing away the environmental red-herrings, London will be better placed to tackle the all too real effects of city stress.

Our analysis suggests that four key infrastructure components underpin an enhanced quality of life in London:

- safe and reliable mobility within the city;
- a clean and pleasant environment;
- personal safety; *and*
- comprehensive information and audit on the state of the environment.

Strategic Priorities for London

We have now identified the key infrastructure components relevant to the strategic issues for London. These are:

- transport, particularly intra-city mobility that is safe and reliable;
- innovation and enterprise;
- education and training;
- housing for lower income households; *and*
- a clean, pleasant and safe environment.

In addition, we identified the need, under each of the key issues, for means to be found by which the image of London – and information on its attributes – could be more systematically presented and promoted.

During this study, it has become clear that the reality of London life is all too often blanketed by misconceptions; the ability to act is constrained by a dearth of reliable information. We concluded that wealth creation, jobs generation and the quality of life would be enhanced by the city wide delivery of carefully focused intelligence gathering, information dissemination and promotion functions.

Rather than attempt to outline a policy framework to encompass all the issues raised, we think it is more productive to build on the key infrastructure components to propose strategic priorities for sustaining London's future competitiveness as a world city. We have grouped these priorities under three distinct categories: planning, the policy context and promotion.

Planning This concerns strategic, city-wide land-use and transportation decisions within a broad level of funding which London can obtain from the national cake. In other words, we recognise that resources are in short supply and that, in opting for one priority, we either exclude another option or limit the extent, nature or speed of its implementation.

The policy context refers to the socio-economic policies implemented at a national level by central government or its agencies. There may be a justification to revise such policies, to adjust their delivery or to contemplate policy innovations which take account of London's distinct requirements. The issue is whether and to what extent London should receive tailored treatment because it is different from other parts of the UK by virtue of it being a world city in competition with other cities in global markets.

Promotion is the way in which London's image is projected in the world arena and how that image is determined and designed.

For each of these categories we have identified a "headline" urban policy priority plus two supporting priorities – see Figure 7.1.

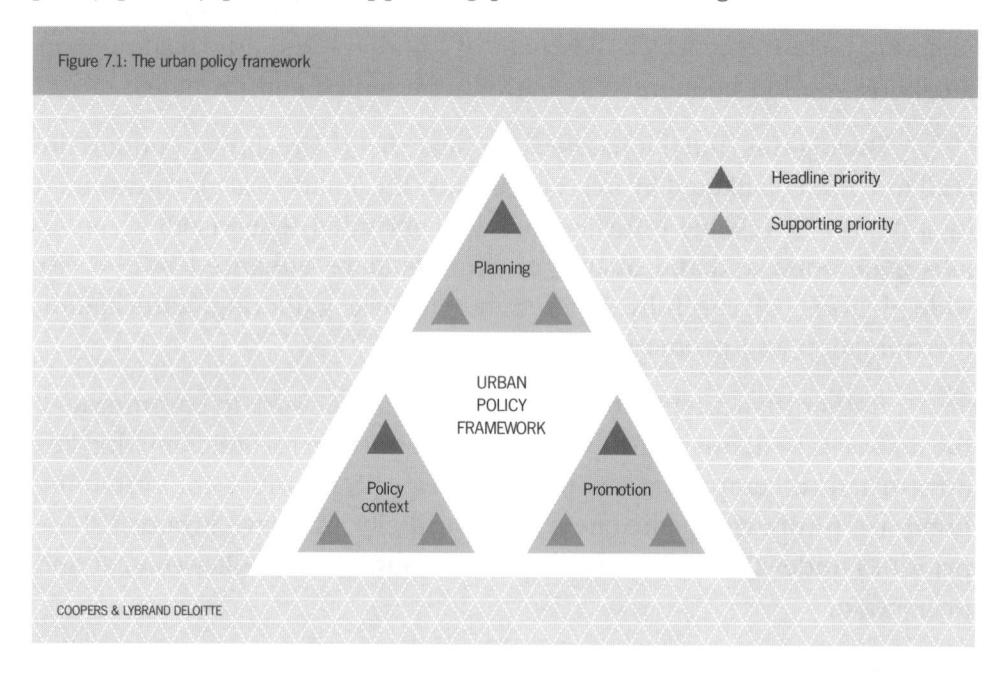

Figure 7.1: The urban policy framework

COOPERS & LYBRAND DELOITTE

The Planning Priorities
Headline priority: intra-city mobility

Our headline priority for **planning** is improving the reliability and safety of movement in London – "intra-city mobility". We place this ahead of

STRATEGIES FOR THE 21ST CENTURY

improving national and international transport links. We do so because we believe that London is particularly weak compared with other world cities in terms of its capacity for, and the quality of, intra-city mobility, and because we think that improvement in this attribute is essential to wealth creation, job generation and the quality of life in London, see Figure 7.2.

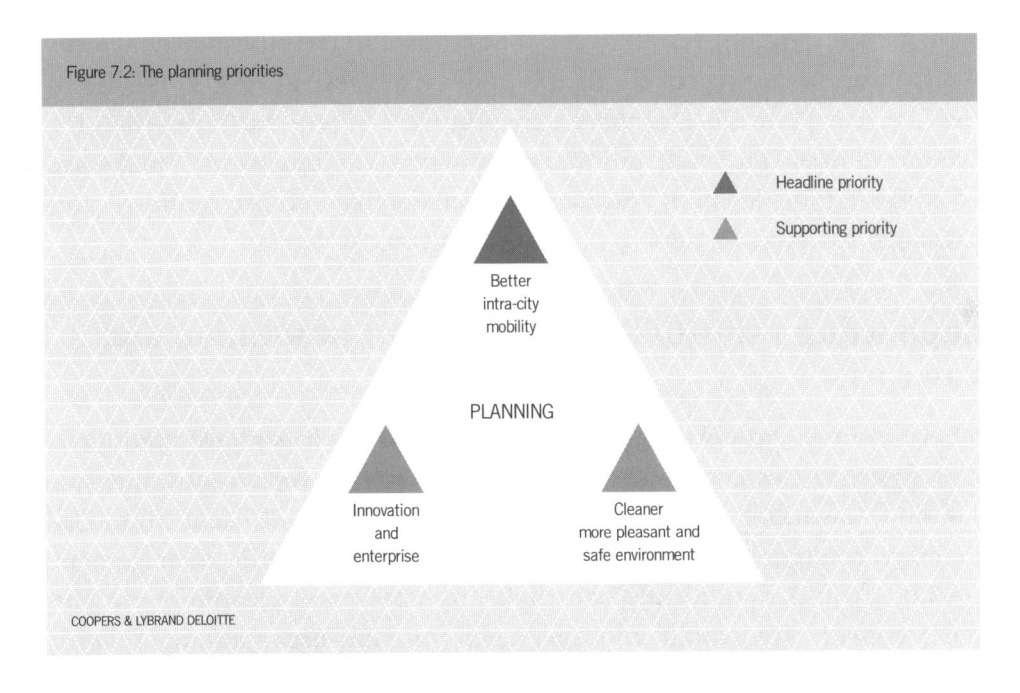

Figure 7.2: The planning priorities

- ▲ Headline priority
- ▲ Supporting priority

Better intra-city mobility

PLANNING

Innovation and enterprise

Cleaner more pleasant and safe environment

COOPERS & LYBRAND DELOITTE

The implication of this is that, assuming hard decisions have to be made, we would give priority, for example, to the cross-London rail lines over the "Heathrow Express" and the Channel Tunnel High Speed Rail Link, to the extent that these require public funds. Thus, by emphasising intra-city mobility as our transport priority, we have effectively selected to improve international transport through enhanced *air* rather than rail links (after all, three quarters of all overseas visitors to London travelled by air in 1989). The investment in cross-London rail therefore would need to be associated with improved conventional connections from Heathrow to the City of London and East London and with early consideration of the next site for major airport runway development. This demonstrates that, whatever transport priority is selected, there will be implications for the rest of the transport system which deserves to be assessed in a coordinated way.

Our priority on intra-city mobility also implies increased investment in the quantity, quality and overall attractiveness of buses and light rail systems. We were impressed by the commitment to the bus services in Paris (where the average age of the fleet is under six years), in New York (where the five year plan allocates more expenditure – $6bn – for buses than for the metro or surface rail) and in Tokyo (where the bus services make use of advanced bus location and information systems and are designed and managed to act as feeders to the metro and rail systems).

Supporting priorities – environment; innovation and enterprise

There are two supporting **planning** priorities which we have identified. The first is a clean, pleasant and safe environment for all movement in London, including pedestrians and cyclists. More efficient intra-city mobility combined with traffic calming and other traffic management methods could significantly contribute to safety and cleanliness of the environment. We would add the need for land-use planning to give priority to improvement in the quality and care of existing areas of public space, the development of new areas of public space for recreational, amenity and ecological purposes, and the protection of individual safety. We think it would be desirable to develop a London-wide approach to environmental monitoring and impact assessment so that action can be taken in a systematic way on consistent criteria at local levels.

Our second supporting planning priority is innovation and enterprise. Our comparative work suggested that the links between creativity and commercial exploitation were not well enough developed in London. This is exemplified by the conspicuous absence of science or technology parks in London and of any clear policy for the development of science and technology in London. Other world cities such as Paris, New York,

Tokyo and Berlin not only have such parks, but there is a declared commitment of the authorities in those cities to their significance in urban development. Most of the technology parks are sited on the city peripheries and in some cases (for example, Paris and Tokyo) were established as sub-cities associated with planned strategic transport infrastructure. Potential sites exist for such parks within the growth points already identified in East London as appropriate by LPAC, and in the London Boroughs' Unitary Development Plans.

It can be argued that London has its science and technology base already established scattered through its urban fabric, down the reaches of the M4 motorway corridor to the west and in the phenomenon of Cambridge to the north-east. But there are two points to make. First, this is not how London's technological infrastructure is perceived or presented. Second, the London research community does not have its own park perhaps because it sees its role as a national rather than local research centre. And London's growth points – notably to the east – are not currently associated with any specific proposals for a technology park.

We have used the terms science and technology park interchangeably. In fact, there are important differences and, without going into details, our foremost planning priority is for a park directly linked to London's educational and research sector to incubate science-based new ventures.

We recommend that these planning priorities need to be recognized at the national, regional and local government levels. London Boroughs and central government ought to consider, and attach priority to, initiatives which enhance London's world city status.

The policy context priorities
Headline priority – education and training

The headline priority we have identified for the *policy context* is education and training. This is critical if London's labour market is to operate more efficiently and London is to make the most of its own resources, see Figure 7.3.

Figure 7.3: The priorities for the policy context

- ▲ Headline priority
- ▲ Supporting priority

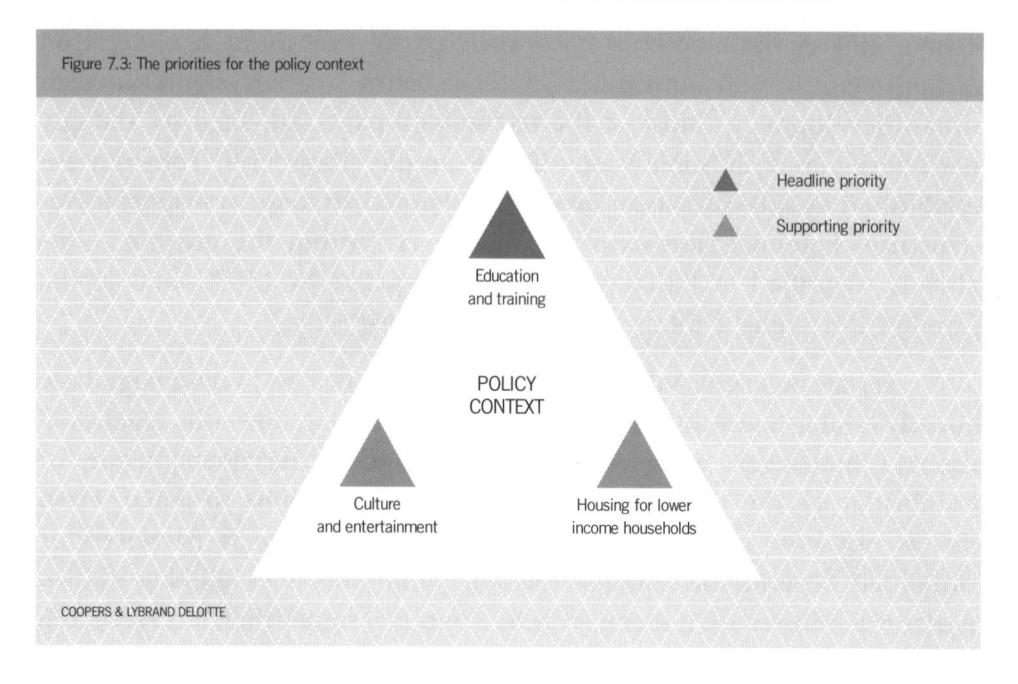

POLICY CONTEXT
- Education and training
- Culture and entertainment
- Housing for lower income households

COOPERS & LYBRAND DELOITTE

We make three distinctions in our assessment of priorities for London with regard to education and training. First, London is well-endowed with higher-education. But there does not appear to be the integration with business, for example through technology and science parks, that characterises the other world cities. The recommendations of the previous section on innovation and enterprise are clearly relevant to this issue.

Second, London's education and training, particularly for the age range of 16–18-year olds, is provided in a fragmented way through the local authorities and the Training and Enterprise Councils. This seems likely to make it more difficult to develop a comprehensive policy for London even though for a significant proportion of employment opportunities London could be regarded as a single labour market. Possible scale economies and a London-wide view of priorities will be difficult to achieve. Furthermore, those employment opportunities which are related to local labour markets may cut across the geographical boundaries of the authorities and the Councils. In such circumstances any tendency for inter-agency rivalry and border disputes will adversely affect the speed and extent to which local labour market problems can be addressed.

The disadvantages of this fragmented approach will be exacerbated where the resources to manage and implement education and training provision are in scarce supply and have to be distributed across a large number of agencies. We take the view that the task of these local agencies would be eased if some resources could be devoted to developing and maintaining a comprehensive view of London's labour market to provide a strategic and information framework within which local issues could be considered.

The third distinction we make in our assessment of London's education and training provision concerns particular segments of the labour market. Clearly definitive conclusions on this will require a detailed and comprehensive analysis of labour market conditions which we have not undertaken. However, from our world city perspective we are persuaded that London's global wealth creation capability will only be sustained if skills are developed appropriate to financial and business services, knowledge based manufacturing, the cultural sector, and the conference and tourism business. Moreover, we take the view that the social and physical infrastructure of world cities would be much less subject to stress if more of these skills could be provided from the indigenous labour supply. This suggests continued and enhancd efforts to bring the "outsiders" and the disadvantaged of London into the effective labour supply.

Supporting priorities – housing and the cultural sector

We have two supporting priorities for the **policy context**. The first concerns housing. If London is to compete with other cities, developing an accessible supply of affordable housing for employed households is a major priority. London's growth sectors must be enabled to recruit key staff who can secure affordable housing readily; if this is not available, then as with inadequate training facilities, expansion of London's key strengths will be seriously constrained.

In particular, we note the need for an easily accessible rented sector of reasonable quality homes. All other world cities have largely deregulated private markets and tax regimes which at least do not discourage landlords. Clearly, the policies by which such a market could be achieved are national in scope. For more local policies the options are with respect to the planning system, for example, enabling the conversion of existing stock, both of dwellings and property in other uses, into suitable units to sell or rent to lower income households. This process is observable in all the major cities, except perhaps central Paris, and should be regarded as a priority for central London. The consequent loss of larger family accommodation would need to be monitored.

The problem of homeless families has almost as significant implications for the labour market. Such households are housed by the social sector as a priority call on available accommodation. Consequently access to social housing based on employment requirements is virtually ruled out. Clearly there are many such trade-offs in allocating scarce housing resources between the needs of employment, community care and other purposes. The impact of these choices on London's competitiveness needs to be recognised.

There is no example of a world city where adequate housing is provided for lower income working households without direct or indirect intervention by the government. The evidence from other cities suggests that while the market can provide for middle and upper income households effectively, only the social sector, with assistance from both central and local government, can hope to maintain and expand the provision of adequate and affordable housing for London.

Our recommendations are that the dimensions of the present tax regime which inhibit the private rented sector should be reassessed, that the allocation of scarce housing resources should take full account of labour market and employment needs as well as of community care objectives, and that the market's inability to provide housing for lower income households should be recognised as an impediment to London's development prospects.

Our second supporting **policy context** priority relates to the cultural sector and has some similarities to our assessment of housing, namely that different segments of the market are more or less amenable to market forces. In both the housing and cultural sectors we encounter the trade-off between private and public gain. We think the mistake is to assume that one should always prevail over the other.

A wide range of empirical studies have demonstrated that, worldwide, investment in cultural activities can be highly effective in terms of wealth and job creation and in enhancing the quality of life, in the development of tourism image building and in city marketing. Yet, in London, the cultural sector continues to be perceived as an indulgence, the icing on the cake of economic success and not as a major employer and wealth creator in its own right. As with so many of the issues we have described in this study, it is this perception which must be overturned if London is to make the most of its rich and diverse cultural base.

Not only do cultural activities create wealth and jobs and enhance the quality of life of the city's inhabitants, but they also play a significant role in presenting the depth and diversity of London's culture to the world. In short, culture and entertainment add value and can be profitable. If encouraged, they can enhance further London's status in the global community. As a consequence, this sector demands long-term strategic *investment*, not reluctant intermittent *funding*.

Once we have severed the link which tethers arts finance to benevolence, the strategic imperatives for this sector become clearer. Established mainstream art not only represents commercial potential, but with imagination it can be used to promote more innovative endeavour. The radical and innovative side of the arts should be regarded as the sector's research and development testing ground, the area in which new ideas will be developed which could ultimately enhance and consolidate the commercial status of more mainstream activity.

Our research suggests that, in spite of London's leading position in many aspects of cultural provision, there are consistent failures to translate creativity into marketable products. There is a tendency to rest on the city's cultural heritage rather than to provide a supportive environment for the start-up phase of artistic product development. We see no reason why this stage in the creative process should not be supported by the kind of infrastructure normally associated with more conventional industry – for example, business advisory services, managed workspaces and the development of links with education and with other industries which might ultimately benefit from innovation in specific types of artistic endeavour, so that the vibrancy of London's diverse sub-cultures can be maintained. Indeed, for tourists, especially the young, this remains one of the prime reasons for coming to London.

Finally, if this sector is to develop it must be visible. But over the last two decades, artistic endeavour has been edged to the periphery of London life. The sector needs to take full advantage of the slump in the commercial property market to bring active artistic enterprise back into the centre of London where its merits can be demonstrated and its products more effectively marketed.

The promotional priorities

Headline priority – global promotion

The headline priority for **promotion** centres on the need to promote London in the global market. By this we mean promotion in its broadest sense – selling London's enterprise and culture, services and potential to the world at large, inverting that British self-deprecation which is all too often taken for complacency in the rest of the world, see Figure 7.4.

The simplest resolution of this priority would be to increase the funding and coordination of existing agencies like the London Tourist Board and putting London as a separate and higher priority in government's overseas promotional efforts. We suggest that a more robust solution

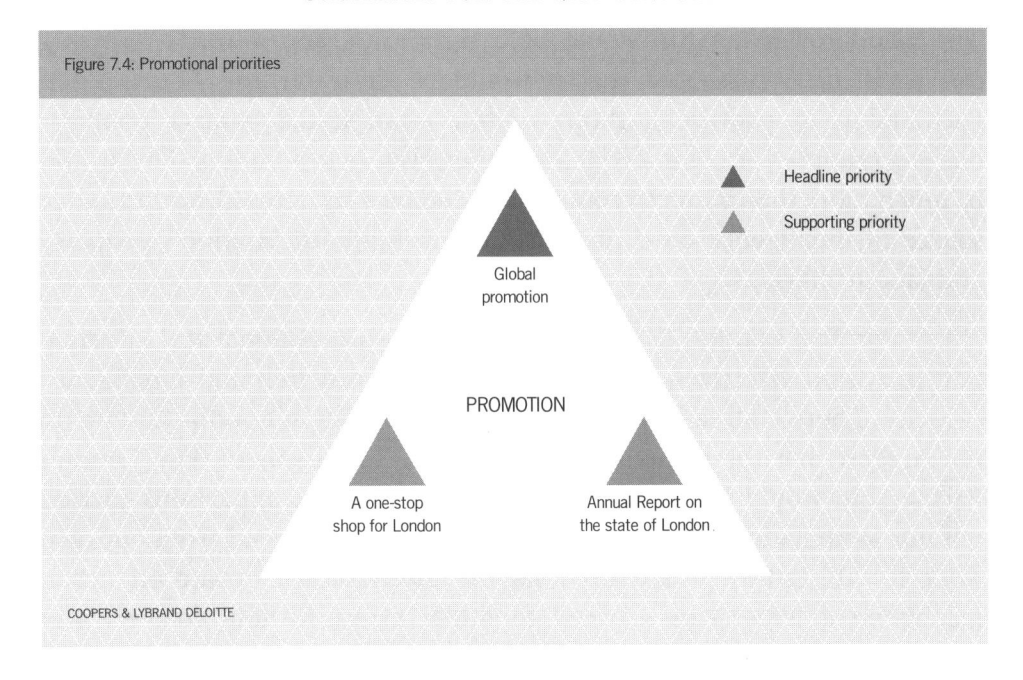

Figure 7.4: Promotional priorities

- ▲ Headline priority — Global promotion
- ▲ Supporting priority — A one-stop shop for London; Annual Report on the state of London

PROMOTION

COOPERS & LYBRAND DELOITTE

might be the founding of an agency which would combine public and private sector concerns in the interests of London as a whole. Such an agency could be called The London Partnership.

We envisage its primary purpose to be the co-ordination of existing promotional efforts and the development of new initiatives. There are a range of functions which might be involved – from goodwill and cultural exchanges with other world cities; international conferences on urban issues; information exchange on urban management practices and experiences; to the more commercially oriented functions of trade missions and the promotion of inward investment and tourism in London.

Supporting priorities – a one-stop shop and an annual report on the state of London

Henry Kissinger once complained that he could never call London. Centrally located and a genuine fusion of public and private interests,

The London Partnership would be a significant step towards resolving this problem. We suggest that it would be desirable for The London Partnership to provide a shop window – an initial contact point or one-stop shop – for commercial and other visitors to London. This would be much more than a tourist centre. It would be a recognised, authoritative source of intelligence on conditions, for example, in London's property and labour markets.

For The London Partnership to fulfil its promotional and information provision effectively, it would also need a research and intelligence capacity. There is already a range of such capabilities in London and we do not suggest that these should be duplicated. The focus of The London Partnership would be particularly on international comparisons carried out in a systematic way. We are only too aware of this need from our own work for this study. We doubt that the international debate on urban management issues can proceed to much effect without focused and carefully selected statistical data for comparably defined cities. We do not think The London Partnership should be charged with this task, but anticipate that it might offer advice, carry out or commission surveys and provide research work on a contract basis.

Finally, we propose that The London Partnership should produce an annual report which would set out how it is performing against its objectives and should assess London's performance in the global context. Such a report should not merely serve as a promotional showcase, but must identify trends and opportunities by which London and its residents can profit – a resource for enterprise rather than a receptacle for rhetoric. It would need to build on the LPAC Annual Review and that of the London Research Centre and of the London Tourist Board. From our work for this study, we suggest that the following aspects of London's performance should be regularly monitored: bilateral and multilateral global events which London hosted, initiated or participated in; developing patterns in London's housing and labour markets, education and training and the support of innovation; perceptions and facts on the quality of London life; cultural, scientific and creative developments in the city;

STRATEGIES FOR THE 21ST CENTURY

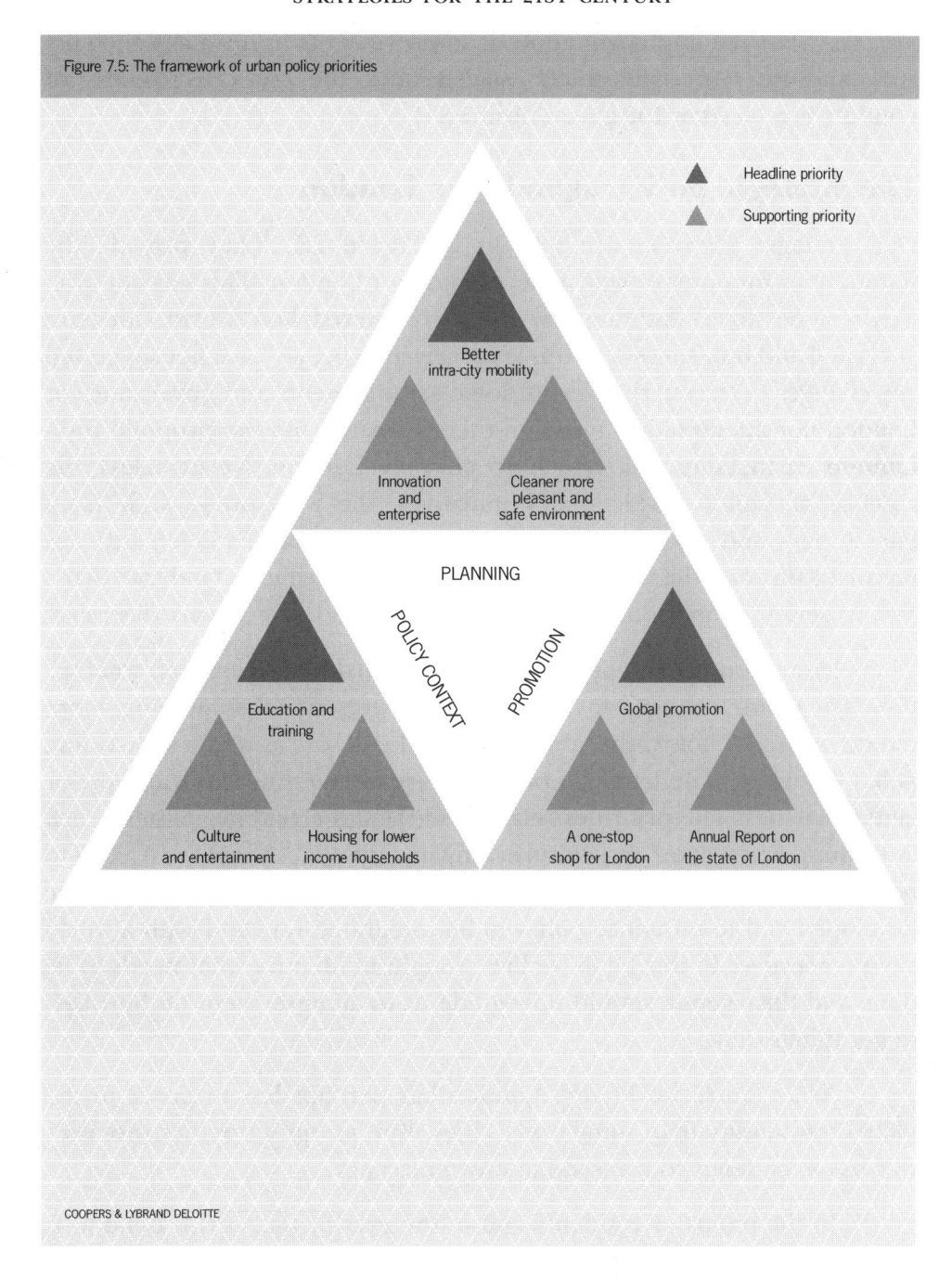

Figure 7.5: The framework of urban policy priorities

▲ Headline priority
▲ Supporting priority

- Better intra-city mobility
- Innovation and enterprise
- Cleaner more pleasant and safe environment
- Education and training
- Culture and entertainment
- Housing for lower income households
- Global promotion
- A one-stop shop for London
- Annual Report on the state of London

PLANNING
POLICY CONTEXT
PROMOTION

COOPERS & LYBRAND DELOITTE

progress with the implementation of improvements in intra-city mobility and land-use, especially public spaces; and the cost-effectiveness of London as a location for global business.

The strategic policy agenda for London

Our strategic priorities are set out in Figure 7.5. They provide the foundations for our strategic policy agenda for London. This sets out what needs to be done. Although we have considered how world cities are governed and how successful this is perceived to be, we have not suggested any changes to the current institutional arrangements and governance of London nor attempted to redesign them – apart from the proposal for a London Partnership as a vehicle to promote London. Nevertheless, the absence of London wide policy initiatives, the widespread view from our surveys and elsewhere that current institutional arrangements are unsatisfactory and the world city initiatives of other cities, all indicate that a serious review of and some changes to current arrangements are desirable.

Discussion about appropriate institutional arrangements, whether they are minor changes to what exists at present or something more radical, should follow rather than precede the debate as to the over-riding policy priorities. The latter, in our view, are not confined to transport or land-use issues. The priorities relate to social and economic matters, such as training, innovation and culture. Any institutional changes are likely to be more effective if they allow the broad view of London's needs to be developed and to influence policy in an integrated way and with a world city perspective. In this book we have sought to identify what needs to be done and this agenda should now guide us to an agreement on how best to get things done.

As a mature world city, London has perhaps less to prove to the global community than some other cities. But, as our study has revealed, this has a tendency to translate into complacency.

In the minds of residents and in the eyes of the world, London is often perceived as a loose cannon amongst world cities. Somewhere along the line, London appears to have lost direction and a sense of its own worth. In our comparative analysis of world cities we have illuminated the strengths which London must promote and develop to consolidate and enhance its status as a world city.

The strategies outlined in this final chapter are intended to neutralise the weaknesses we have identified and to provide the first steps towards harnessing London's world-class potential. They can help establish London at the centre of the global community as we move into the 21st century, build a new confidence in London by Londoners and enhance its reputation for innovation and enterprise in the rest of the world.

BIBLIOGRAPHY

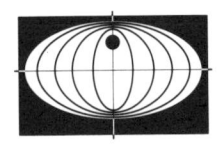

1. Abe, H & Allen, J D, *Regional development planning in Japan.* Regional Studies, October, 1988.
2. Abercrombie, Patrick, *Greater London plan 1944.* HMSO, London. 1945.
3. Age (Melbourne), *Melbourne is best place in the world to live study shows.* Age (Melbourne), November 20th, 1990.
4. Agnelli Foundation, *The city effect: the new central role of urban areas.* Agnelli Foundation, Turin. 21st Century, September, 1990.
5. Amt fuer kommunale Gesamptentwicklung und Stadtplanung, *Regional development plan for South Hessen (Regionaler Raumordnungsplan fuer Sued-Hessen).* Amt fuer kommunale Gesamptentwicklung und Stadtplanung, Frankfurt. 1986.
6. Attinger, Joel *et al., The decline of New York.* Time, September 7th, 1990.
7. Audit Commission, *The management of London's authorities: preventing a breakdown in services.* Audit Commission, London. 1987.
8. Audit Commission, *Urban regeneration and economic development.* HMSO, London. 1989.
9. Bachtler, J & Clement, K, *Inward investment in the UK and the Single European Market.* Regional Studies, April, 1990.
10. Bank of England, *The gilt-edged market since Big Bank.* Bank of England Quarterly, February, 1989
11. Bank of England, *The Single European Market: survey of the UK financial services industry.* Bank of England Quarterly, May, 1989.
12. Barchard, David, *London's strength revealed by Bank study.* Financial Times, London. Financial Times, November 9th, 1989.
13. Barclays de Zoete Wedd Research, *Tokyo's office market.* Barclays de Zoete Wedd, December, 1986.
14. Beckman, M, *Location theory.* Random House, New York. 1968.
15. Begg, I and Cameron, G C, *The regional distribution of high technology activity.* University of Cambridge, Dept of Land Economy, 1990.

16. Berlin Economic Development Corporation, *Berlin: An ideal location for your business – Now and after 1992*. Berlin Economic Development Corporation, 1991.
17. Black Horse Relocation, *Corporate relocations within Great Britain*. Black Horse Relocation, London. 1987.
18. Boggan, Steve, *London transport fares most expensive in Europe*. Independent, April 22nd, 1991.
19. British Airports Authority, *Airports traffic statistics 1989/90*. BAA, London. 1990.
20. British Invisibles – Economist Advisory Group, *Overseas earnings of the arts, 1988/89*. British Invisibles, London. 1991.
21. Buschel, C and Stonham, P (eds), *Jane's urban transport systems*. Jane's Publishing Company, London. 1989.
22. Business Strategies, *London: International financial & business centre: the role and contribution of Docklands*. Business Strategies Ltd, London. August, 1990.
23. Byrne, Therese E & Kostin, David J, *London office market II: breaking the code*. Salomon Brothers, New York. August, 1990.
24. Cambridge Econometrics, *Regional economic prospects – Region 1 (South East)*. Cambridge Econometrics, January, 1990.
25. Chaline, Claude Henri, *International handbook on land use planning*. International Society of City and Regional Planners, The Hague. 1984.
26. Cheshire, Paul, *Explaining the recent performance of the EC's major urban regions*. Urban Studies, June, 1990.
27. Cheshire, Paul, *London's performance in Europe: or avoiding becoming the 21st Century's Naples*. November 15th, 1990. (Prepared for LWT London Programme)
28. Cheshire, Paul, *The outlook for development in London*. Land Development Studies, July, 1990.
29. Chugani, Michael, *Hong Kong: HK ranks 33rd in world league*. South China Morning Post, November 20th, 1990.
30. City of Paris, *Parking in Paris*. City of Paris, 1984.
31. City of Westminster, *District plan*. City of Westminster, London. August, 1988.
32. Clarke, Rory, *The future of the Paris region*. European Trends, September, 1990.
33. College of Estate Management: Joint Centre for Local Development Studies, *Planning control in Western Europe*. HMSO, London. 1989.
34. Colliers Stewart Newiss, *London second to Tokyo in occupancy costs according to international office survey*. Colliers Stewart Newiss, London. May 24th, 1990.
35. Commission of the EC, *Green paper on the urban environment*. Commission of the EC, Brussels. 1990.
36. Commission on the Year 2000, *New York ascendant: report of the Commission*. Commission on the Year 2000, New York. June, 1987.

BIBLIOGRAPHY

37. Confederation of British Industry/Business Strategies Ltd, *Regional trends survey*. Confederation of British Industry, London. November, 1990.

38. Confederation of British Industry/PA Consulting Group, *Waking up to a better environment*. Confederation of British Industry, London. March, 1990.

39. Confederation of British Industry, *Transport in London: the capital at risk*. Confederation of British Industry, London. March, 1989.

40. Cooper, Wendy, *Berlin faces fresh siege, by investors*. Independent on Sunday, April 22nd, 1990.

41. Coopers & Lybrand, *British Telecom: 1992 – summary of telephone interview results*. Coopers & Lybrand, London. June, 1989.

42. Coopers & Lybrand, *State policy and the telecommunications economy in New York – Appendices*. Coopers & Lybrand, New York. 1987.

43. Coopers & Lybrand, *State policy and the telecommunications economy in New York – Study*. Coopers & Lybrand, New York. 1987.

44. Coopers & Lybrand, *State policy and the telecommunications economy in New York – Summary*. Coopers & Lybrand, New York. 1987.

45. Coopers & Lybrand, *State policy and the telecommunications economy in New York – Technical Proposal*. Coopers & Lybrand, New York. 1987.

46. Coopers & Lybrand/British Telecom, *London as a financial centre in the 1990s*. Coopers & Lybrand/BT, London. February, 1990.

47. Corbett, Anne, *France: Paris plans for the future*. Guardian, May 2nd, 1990.

48. Corporation of the City of London, *City of London local plan*. Corporation of the City of London, May, 1986.

49. Corporation of the City of London, *City of London local plan*. Corporation of the City of London, January, 1989.

50. Corporation of the City of London, *London's transport – a plan to protect the future*. Corporation of the City of London, 1990.

51. Crampton, GC and Evans, AW, *Myth, reality and employment in London*. Jnl of Transport Economics and Policy, January, 1989.

52. Crampton, GC and Evans, AW, *The determinant of total employment in Central London*. University of Reading, 1990.

53. Dagnand, Monique, *A history of planning in the Paris region*. Int Jnl of Urban and Regional Research, 1983.

54. DATAR (Delegation a l'Amenagement du Territoire et a l'Action Regionale), *Les villes "Europeennes"*. DATAR, Paris. May, 1989.

55. Davis, EP, *International financial centres – an industrial analysis*. Bank of England Quarterly, September, 1990.

56. Davis, EP & Latter, AR, *London as an international financial centre*. Bank of England Quarterly, November, 1989.

57. Dept of Education and Science, *Education statistics for the UK, 1990*. HMSO, London, 1991.
58. Dept of Employment, *Ethnic origins and the labour market*. Employment Gazette, February, 1991.
59. Dept of Employment, *The London labour market*. HMSO, London, 1988.
60. Dept of the Environment, *Guidance on the protection of strategic views for London: Consultation paper*. DOE, November, 1990.
61. Dept of the Environment, *Regional guidance for the South East (Planning policy guidance note 9)*. DOE, February, 1989.
62. Dept of the Environment, *Strategic planning guidance for London*. DOE, July, 1989.
63. Dept of Transport, *Statement on transport in London*. DTp, (No Date).
64. Dept of Transport, *Traffic in London*. DTp, 1990.
65. Dept of Transport, *Traffic management guidance in London (Circular 2/ 87)*. DTp, 1987.
66. Dept of Transport, *Transport statistics Great Britain, 1979–1989*. HMSO, London. 1990.
67. Dinkins, David, *The Mayor's management report 1990*. City of New York, 1991.
68. Donnison, David and Soto, P, *The good city: a study of urban development and policy in Britain*. Heinemann, London. 1980.
69. Duce, Richard, *Low crime rate and level of vandalism are most important factors for quality of life*. Times, August 21st, 1990.
70. EC Harris, *Construction industry economics survey: no 33*. EC Harris, London. January, 1990.
71. Economist, *An Apple that has lost its sheen*. Economist, June 1st, 1991.
72. Edward Erdman, *London's office market: the overseas influence*. Edward Erdman, London. January, 1989.
73. Eleftheriou, Gillian & Sweeney, Fiona, *Treading softly*. Chartered Surveyor Weekly, January 17th, 1991.
74. Erd, Rainer (ed), *Kulturstadt Frankfurt – Szenen institutionene, positionen*. S. Fischer, Frankfurt. 1990.
75. ES Magazine (London), *Why are we whingeing*. ES Magazine, December, 1989.
76. Estates Gazette, *Development control in New York City*. Estates Gazette, London. 1986.
77. Evening Standard, *London is second to Tokyo in office costs*. Evening Standard, November 23rd, 1988.
78. Fainstein, Susan, *Economics, politics and development policy: the convergence of New York and London*. (Paper prepared for Conference on Urban Policy and Economic Restructuring in Comparative Perspective, State University of New York, April 1989)
79. Feist, Andrew *et al.* (eds), *Funding the arts in seven Western countries*. Cultural Trends, March, 1990.

BIBLIOGRAPHY

80. Fielding, Tony and Halford, Susan, *Patterns and processes of urban change in the UK.* HMSO, London. 1990.
81. Financial Post, *Wealthy "wessies" and poor "ossies" face off in Berlin.* Financial Post, October 3rd, 1990.
82. Financial Times, *FT Survey: City of London property.* Financial Times, September, 21st, 1990.
83. Financial Times, *FT Survey: European finance & investment: London.* Financial Times, November 29th, 1990.
84. Financial Times, *FT Survey: European finance and investment: France.* Financial Times, October 22nd, 1990.
85. Financial Times, *FT Survey: European investment locations.* Financial Times, June 5th, 1990.
86. Financial Times, *FT Survey: Frankfurt.* Financial Times, September 17th, 1987.
87. Financial Times, *FT Survey: Relocation.* Financial Times, April 26th 1990.
88. Financial Times, *Japan's quality of life way behind the West.* Financial Times, July 18th, 1990.
89. Financial Times, *London's pre-eminence as a business centre confirmed by survey.* Financial Times, November 30th, 1990.
90. Friedman, John & Woolff, Goetz, *World city formation: an agenda for action and research.* International Journal of Urban and Regional Research, September, 1982.
91. Frost, ME and Spence, NA, *Employment changes in Central London in the 1980s: I The record of the 1980s.* Geographical Journal, March, 1991.
92. Frost, ME and Spence, NA, *Employment changes in Central London in the 1980s: II Understanding recent forces for change and future development constraints.* Geographical Journal, July, 1991.
93. Fujita, F, *The technopolis: high technology and regional development in Japan.* Int Jnl of Urban and Regional Research, December, 1988.
94. Gaudin, Francoise and Lephay-Merlin, Catherine, *Les depenses culturelles de la Ville de Paris en 1987.* Ministere de la Culture, Dept des etudes et de la prospective, Paris.
95. Glancey, Jonathon, *Gap between expectations and reality of city life.* Independent, August 14th, 1990.
96. Goldstein, Alfred, *Travel in London – is chaos inevitable?* London Regional Transport, London. 1989.
97. Greater London Arts, *Arts plan for London 1990–95: Arts in London – a qualitative research study.* Greater London Arts, October, 1989.
98. Greater London Arts, *Arts plan for London 1990–95: Arts in London – a survey of attitudes of users and non-users.* Greater London Arts, February, 1990.
99. Greater London Arts, *Arts plan for London 1990–95: Arts survey – technical appendix & tables.* Greater London Arts, October, 1989.

100. Greater London Arts, *Arts plan for London 1990–95: Illustrated summary*. Greater London Arts, February, 1990.

101. Greater London Arts, *Arts plan for London 1990–95: Vol 1: Main report*. Greater London Arts, November, 1989.

102. Greater London Arts, *Arts plan for London 1990–95: Vol 2: Appendices*. Greater London Arts, November, 1989.

103. Greater London Arts, *Building the arts in London*. Greater London Arts, 1990.

104. Greater London Council, *Greater London development plan*. Greater London Council, 1976.

105. Grigsby, John, *Perth is top in quality of life league*. Daily Telegraph, October 2nd, 1990.

106. Guillaume, Teresa, *How do we compare*. ES Magazine, (London.) December, 1989.

107. Hall, Peter, *Land-use change and transport policy*. Habitat International, London. 1983.

108. Hall, Peter, *Lets make London into Paris, England*. Evening Standard, January 12th, 1989.

109. Hall, Peter, *London 2000*. Faber and Faber, London. 1963.

110. Hall, Peter, *London 2001*. Unwin Hyman, London. 1989.

111. Hall, Peter, *The world cities*. Weidenfeld & Nicolson, London. 1984.

112. Hall, Peter, *Urban and regional planning*. Pelican, London. 1976.

113. Hamill, Gans et al., *How to save New York*. New York Magazine, November 26th, 1990.

114. Harris Research Centre, *Life in London Survey (1–10.10.90)*. Harris Research Centre, London. November, 1990.

115. Hayter, Martin, *France – the agency view*. Estates Gazette, March 10th, 1990.

116. Headland, Jane and Relph, Simon, *The view from Downing Street (UK Film Initiatives I)*. British Film Institute, London. 1991.

117. Healey & Baker, *European network property report: no 2*. Healey & Baker, London. July, 1989.

118. Healey & Baker, *Office locations across the world*. Healey & Baker, London. November, 1990.

119. Hebbert, M & Nakai, N, *How Tokyo grows: land development and planning in the urban fringe*. London School of Economics, London. 1988.

120. Henley Centre, *London 2000*. Association of London Authorities, London. March, 1990.

121. Hessisches Ministerium des Innern, *State development plan for Hessen (Hessiches Landesentwicklungsplan)*. Hessiches Ministerium des Innern, Wiesbaden. 1970.

122. Hessisches Ministerium des Innern, *State planning act for Hessen (Hessiches Landesplanungsgesetz)*. Hessiches Ministerium des Innern, Wiesbaden. 1970.

BIBLIOGRAPHY

123. Hessisches Ministerium des Innern, *State spatial planning programme for Hessen (Hessiches Landesentwicklungsplan)*. Hessisches Ministerium des Innern, Wiesbaden. 1970.

124. Hillier Parker, *International property bulletin*. Hillier Parker, London. April, 1990.

125. Hirmis, AK, London in the European dimension: key planning issues, PTRC 18th Summer Annual Meeting, September, 1990.

126. Holmans, AE, *House prices*. Dept of Environment, London. 1990.

127. Honigsbaum, Mark, *Grime busters*. Time Out, (London) June 7th, 1989.

128. Independent, *Majority of Britains are satisfied with life*. Independent, August 24th, 1990.

129. Industrie-und Handelskammer – Frankfurt, *Various tables/articles on Frankfurt's commercial activities*. Industrie-und Handelskammer – Frankfurt.

130. Institut d'Amenagement et Urbanisme de la Region d'Ile-de-France, *La region d'Ile-de-France en bref*. Institut d'Amenagement et Urbanisme de la Region d'Ile-de-France, Paris. 1985.

131. Institut d'Amenagement et Urbanisme de la Region d'Ile-de-France, *Les cahiers supplement 91*. Institut d'Amenagement et Urbanisme de la Region d'Ile-de-France, Paris. 1989.

132. Institut d'Amenagement et Urbanisme de la Region d'Ile-de-France, *Principaux amenagements routiers*. Institut d'Amenagement et Urbanisme de la Region d'Ile-de-France, Paris. 1978.

133. Institut d'Amenagement et Urbanisme de la Region d'Ile-de-France, *Schema directeur d'amenagement et d'urbanisme de la region d'Ile-de-France*. Institut d'Amenagement et Urbanisme de la Region d'Ile-de-France, Paris. 1976.

134. Institut d'Amenagement et Urbanisme de la Region d'Ile-de-France et al., *Le livre blanc d'Ile-de-France*. Institut d'Amenagement et Urbanisme de la Region d'Ile-de-France, Paris. January, 1990.

135. Institute of Practitioners in Advertising, *Advertising services 1990*. Institute of Practitioners in Advertising, London. 1990.

136. Jackman, R et al., *Labour market mismatch: a framework for thought*. Centre for Economic Performance. 1990.

137. Japan Economic Journal, *Japan: Success taking toll on Japanese*. Japan Economic Journal, January 13th, 1990.

138. Jenkins, Samantha, *Hillier Parker call for London planning body*. Estates Times, April 12th, 1991.

139. Jones Lang Wooton, *Decentralisation of offices from central London*. Jones Lang Wooton, London. November, 1989.

140. Knight Frank & Rutley, *International executive housing 1990*. Knight Frank & Rutley, London. December, 1990.

141. Krings, Eva, *Kultur macht politik: Wie mit kultur stadt/staat zu machens ist.* Kolner Volksblatt Verlag. 1988.
142. L'Atelier Parisien d'Urbanisme, *Paris project no 27/28, 29.* L'Atelier Parisien d'Urbanisme, Paris. 1989.
143. Labour Party, *London: a world class capital.* Labour Party, London. 1991.
144. Le Monde, *France: Japanese and American firms prefer London and Brussels to Paris as location for European offices.* Le Monde, January, 16th, 1990.
145. Leigh-Pemberton, Sir R, *Europe, 1992 & the City.* Bank of England Quarterly, May, 1989.
146. LEPU, *Change in Spitalfields: a survey of residents' skills and proposals for training.* LEPU, London. 1991.
147. Levine, Richard, *New York region faces slowdown in economy.* New York Times (Metropolitan), February 25th, 1990.
148. Lipscombe, R, *White book propels Paris towards 21st century.* Estates Times, March 30th, 1990.
149. Lipscombe, R, *White hot strategy for Ile de France.* Estates Times, March 30th, 1990.
150. Lomas, Graham, *London in prospect.* Institute for Metropolitan Studies, London. May, 1991.
151. London Boroughs Association, *Capital killer: air pollution from road vehicles.* London Boroughs Association, London. August, 1990.
152. London Boroughs Association, *London's airports.* London Boroughs Association, London. May, 1990.
153. London Boroughs Association, *Road pricing for London.* London Boroughs Association, London. July, 1990.
154. London Chamber of Commerce and Industry, *A bus strategy for London.* London Chamber of Commerce and Industry, London. May 13th, 1991.
155. London Chamber of Commerce and Industry, *London and the implications of the Single European Market.* London Chamber of Commerce and Industry, London. 1990.
156. London Chamber of Commerce and Industry, *London's economy: trends and prospects.* London Chamber of Commerce and Industry, London. April, 1991.
157. London Chamber of Commerce and Industry, *Planning for London's future – the views of business (supplementary survey report).* London Chamber of Commerce and Industry, London. October, 1990.
158. London Chamber of Commerce and Industry, *Statement on public expenditure 1991/92.* London Chamber of Commerce and Industry, London. July, 1990.
159. London Chamber of Commerce and Industry, *Survey of company planning in preparation for the single European market.* London Chamber of Commerce and Industry, London. October, 1990.

160. London Docklands Development Corporation, *Information circular*. London Docklands Development Corporation, London. October 27th, 1990.

161. London Regional Transport, *Annual report & accounts, 1988–89*. London Regional Transport, London. 1990.

162. London Research Centre, *London at work: an analysis of the Census of Employment, 1981–87*. London Research Centre, London. 1991.

163. London Research Centre, *London in need: a review of needs, policy and legislation affecting London*. London Research Centre, London. September, 1989.

164. London Research Centre, *Review of London's needs: report for the London Boroughs Grants Cttee*. London Research Centre, London. October, 1989.

165. London Research Centre, *Skill implications of employment change in London*. London Research Centre, London. 1991.

166. London Tourist Board, *London tourism statistics 1988*. London Tourist Board, London. January, 1989.

167. London Tourist Board, *Residents opinion survey*, London Tourist Board, London. October, 1986.

168. London Tourist Board, *Survey among overseas visitors to London – Summer 1990*. London Tourist Board, London. August, 1990.

169. London Tourist Board, *The economic impact of tourism in London*, London Tourist Board, London. February, 1987.

170. London Tourist Board, *The tourism strategy for London action plan 1990–1993*. London Tourist Board, London. 1990.

171. London Tourist Board, *Visitor expenditure survey in London*. London Tourist Board, London. November, 1986.

172. London Tourist Board/LPAC, *Tourism impact study*. London Tourist Board, London. 1988.

173. London Weekend Television, *London into Europe (London Programme, Nov 90)*. London Weekend Television, London. November 9th, 1990.

174. LPAC, *1990 round of employment projections for London (11.9.90)*. LPAC, London. September 11th, 1990.

175. LPAC, *London's skylines and high buildings*. LPAC, London. March, 1989.

176. LPAC, *Scenario testing exercise TASTE III*. LPAC, London. May, 1990.

177. LPAC, *Strategic planning advice for London*. LPAC, London. 1988.

178. LPAC, *Strategic planning for London: policies for the 1990s*. LPAC, London. October, 1988.

179. LPAC, *Strategic trends and policy 1989 – Annual review*. LPAC, London. December, 1989.

180. LPAC, *Strategic trends and policy 1990 – Annual review*. LPAC, London. December, 1990.

181. Macdonald, Alistair, *Pay patterns*. Corporate Finance, January, 1990.
182. Mammen, David, *Making Tokyo a world city*. National Institute for Research Advancement, Tokyo. 1988.
183. Martin, R and Tyler, P, *Local disparities in unemployment and regional wages in Great Britain*. University of Cambridge, Dept of Land Economy, Cambridge. 1990.
184. Matthews, Virginia, *Britain's quality of life fall blamed on 4 evils*. Daily Telegraph, August 24th, 1990.
185. McAhlone, Beryl, *British design consultancy: anatomy of a billion dollar business*. Design Council, London. 1987.
186. METROPOLIS (World Association of Major Metropolises), *Working groups and special assignments – Summaries*. METROPOLIS, Paris. 1990.
187. Metropolitan Police, *Report of the Commissioner of the Metropolis*. Metropolitan Police, London. 1991.
188. Monopolies and Mergers Commission, *London Underground Ltd: a report on passenger and other services supplied by the company*. HMSO, London. 1991.
189. Moore, Barry & Townroe, Peter, *Urban labour markets: reviews of urban research*. HMSO, London. December 1990.
190. Morgan Grenfell & Co, *Morgan Grenfell and continental European property*. Morgan Grenfell & Co, London. August, 1990.
191. Moynihan, Brian, *Now Paris aims high*. Sunday Times Magazine (Business World), 1990.
192. Muccini, Peter, *Cities with a future*. World Property, October, 1989.
193. Murray, Callum, *The civilising of a world city*. Architects Journal, January 10th, 1990.
194. Myers, Paul, *Londoners priced out of the good life says survey*. Guardian, March 22nd, 1990.
195. Myerscough, John, *Economic importance of the arts in Britain*. Policy Studies Institute, London. 1988.
196. New York City Partnership, *From schools to skyscrapers: building an effective development process for New York City*. New York City Partnership, New York. April, 1990.
197. New York City Partnership, *Meeting the challenge: maintaining and enhancing New York City as the world financial capital*. New York City Partnership, New York. June, 1989.
198. New York City Partnership, *The $1 trillion gamble: telecommunications and New York's economic future*. New York City Partnership, New York. June, 1990.
199. New York City: City Planning Commission, *Midtown zoning handbook*. New York City: Dept of City Planning, 1982.
200. New York City: Dept of City Planning, *New York City: Community district needs, fiscal year 1991*. New York City: Dept of City Planning, October, 1989.

BIBLIOGRAPHY

201. New York City: Dept of City Planning, *New York City preliminary strategic policy statement*. New York City: Dept of City Planning, January, 1991.
202. New York City: Dept of City Planning, *New York City zoning resolution*. New York City: Dept of City Planning, July, 1990.
203. New York City: Dept of City Planning, *Plans, programmes and policies 1980–85*. New York City: Dept of City Planning, October, 1985.
204. New York State: Governor's Advisory Panel on Financial Services, *New York's future in financial services*. New York State: Governor's Advisory Panel on Financial Services, June, 1989.
205. Newman, PWG and Kenworthy, JR, *Cities and automobile dependence: an international sourcebook*. Gower Technical, Aldershot. 1989.
206. OECD, *Cities and transport*. OECD, Paris. June, 1988.
207. OECD, *Cities and transport*. OECD, Paris. August, 1991.
208. OECD, *Environmental indicators: a preliminary set*. OECD, Paris. 1991.
209. OECD, *Environmental policies for cities in the 1990s*. OECD, Paris. 1990.
210. OECD, *Urban policies in Japan*. OECD, Paris. 1986.
211. Ozanne, J, *Report on Paris property market*. Estates Times, London. Estates Times, September 1st, 1990.
212. PA Cambridge Economic Consultants, *The south east London economy and the Single European Market*. PA Cambridge Economic Consultants, Cambridge.
213. Pieroni, C, *The impact of information technology on the location of financial services in England and Wales*. University of Cambridge, Dept of Land Economy, Cambridge. 1990.
214. Policy Studies Institute, *A statistical profile of the arts in London*. Policy Studies Institute, London. January, 1990.
215. Population Crisis Committee, *Cities: life in the world's 100 largest metropolitan areas*. Population Crisis Committee, Washington DC. 1990.
216. Port Authority of New York/New Jersey – Cultural Assistance Centre, *The arts as an industry: their economic importance to the New York/New Jersey metropolitan region*. Port Authority of New York/New Jersey, New York. 1983.
217. Porter, Michael E, *The competitive advantage of nations*. Macmillan, London. 1990.
218. Porter, Shirley, *A minister for London: a capital concept*. FPL Financial Ltd, London. 1990.
219. Prefecture de la region d'Ile de France, *Les transports de voyageurs en Ile-de-France – 1984*. Prefecture de la region d'Ile de France, Paris. 1985.
220. Prescott, Michael, *The need for tax incentives (UK Film Initiatives 2)*. British Film Institute, London. 1991.

221. Price Waterhouse, *Moving experiences: Volume 1*. Price Waterhouse, London. January 11th, 1989.
222. Price Waterhouse, *Moving experiences: Volume 2*. Price Waterhouse, London. January 11th, 1989
223. Punter, J, *Decentralisation of the planning system in France*. The Planner, April, 1989.
224. Rajan, Amin, *1992: A zero sum game*. Industrial Society, London. 1990.
225. Rajan, Amin, *Capital people: skills strategies for survival in the 90s*. Industrial Society, London. August, 1990.
226. Rajan, Amin, *Create or abdicate*. Institute of Manpower Studies, Birmingham. 1989.
227. Rajan, Amin, *How the City must hone its cutting edge*. Sunday Times, London. Sunday Times, September 30th, 1990.
228. RATP, *RATP – 1983*. RATP, Paris. 1984.
229. RATP, *Statistiques 1989*. RATP, Paris. 1990.
230. Regional Plan Association, (New York) *Job growth in the metropolitan region*. The New Century: Forecasts for the Tri-State Region, No 2, January, 1990.
231. Regional Plan Association, *Manhattan transfer*. Regional Plan Association, New York. 1989.
232. Regional Plan Association, New York, *The region in the global economy*. Regional Plan Association, New York. May, 1988.
233. Regional Plan Association, (New York) *The region tomorrow: a summary of RPA's economic & demographic projections to 2015*. The New Century: Forecasts for the Tri-State Region, No 2, April 1989.
234. Regional Plan Association, *Visions for the region tomorrow: toward a new regional plan*. Regional Plan Association, New York. 1989.
235. Renaud, B, *Housing affordability and housing finance*. World Bank, Washington DC, 1990.
236. Reuters, *Japan: Tokyo cost of living still leads foreign cities*. Reuters, July 24th, 1990.
237. Reuters, *London preferred as European financial centre, survey says*. Reuters, November 28th, 1990.
238. Reuters, *USA: Melbourne, Montreal, Seattle top ranking of world cities*. Reuters, November 20th, 1990.
239. Richard Ellis, *Berlin office market report*. Richard Ellis, London. 1991.
240. Richard Ellis, *World rental levels: offices*. Richard Ellis, London. January, 1990.
241. Roger Tym & Partners, *London jobs 1997: employment forecasts for Greater London, 1986–97*. Roger Tym & Partners, London. April, 1988.
242. Roger Tym & Partners, *London jobs 2001: briefing paper*. Roger Tym & Partners, London. January 30th, 1990.

BIBLIOGRAPHY

243. Rogerson, Robert, *Quality of life in Britain's intermediate cities*. Glasgow University, Dept of Geography, Glasgow. 1989.
244. Rogerson, Robert, *The geography of quality of life*. Glasgow University, Glasgow. November, 1987,
245. Rosen, S, *Human capital*. 1987.
246. Royal Society of Arts, *Beyond GCSE*. Royal Society of Arts, London. May, 1991.
247. Rudd, Roland, *Poor training practices 'pose threat to the City'*. Financial Times, September 22nd, 1988.
248. Sanko Estate Company, *Building and office rent data*. Sanko Estate Company, Tokyo. 1991.
249. Sanko Estate Company, *Office market Tokyo*. Sanko Estate Company, Tokyo. 1990.
250. Sapsford, Jathon, *Japan: Agency says good wages mean little in expensive Tokyo*. Reuters, September 26th, 1989.
251. Scherer, FM *et al.*, *The economics of multi-plant operation*. Harvard University Press, Cambridge, MA. 1975.
252. Scholz, Carol, *Frankfurt – eine stadt wirdVeskauft stadtent wicklung und stadtmarketing zur produktion des stadortimages am beispiel Frankfurts*. ISP. 1989.
253. Senatsverwaltung fuer Stadtentwicklung und Umweltshutz, *Preparatory land-use plan for Berlin (Flaechennutzungsplan)*. Senatsverwaltung fuer Stadtentwicklung und Umweltshutz, Berlin. 1984.
254. SERPLAN, *Developing South East strategic guidance: Regional statement*. London and South East Regional Planning Conference, London. October, 1985.
255. SERPLAN, *Into the next century: review of the South East Regional Strategy*. London and South East Regional Planning Conference, London. August, 1989.
256. SERPLAN, *A new strategy for the South East*. London and South East Regional Planning Conference, London. September, 1990.
257. Sharrock, David, *Scots ahead in the quality of life league*. Guardian, November 10th, 1990.
258. Simian, BB, *Land use planning in Japan*. The Planner, March, 1989.
259. Soldatos, Panayotis, *Model of analysis of the international deployment of modern cities*. Univerity of Montreal, Montreal. February, 1990.
260. Stadt Frankfurt am Main, *Statistisches Jahrbuch Frankfurt am Main*. Stadt Frankfurt am Main, Frankfurt. 1989.
261. Stevens, John, *Winning the war for safety on the streets*. Evening Standard, London. Evening Standard, November 7th, 1988.
262. Sunday Times, *Urgent: blueprint for saving a city slipping fast into chaos and decay*. Sunday Times, September 30th, 1990.

263. Takayama, A, *Development of the Tokyo Bay Chiba waterfront*. International Federation for Housing & Planning. Congress Report, 1989.
264. Tokyo Metropolitan Government, *City planning of Tokyo*. Tokyo Metropolitan Government, Tokyo. 1990.
265. Tokyo Metropolitan Government, *City planning of Tokyo*. Tokyo Metropolitan Government, Tokyo. 1983.
266. Tokyo Metropolitan Government, *Land price survey*. Tokyo Metropolitan Government, Tokyo. 1989.
267. Tokyo Metropolitan Government, *Second long-term plan for the Tokyo Metropolis*. Tokyo Metropolitan Government, Tokyo. November, 1986.
268. Tokyo Metropolitan Government, *Tokyo: yesterday, today and tomorrow*. Tokyo Metropolitan Government, Tokyo. 1990.
269. Tokyo Metropolitan Government, *Tokyo industry: a graphic overview*. Tokyo Metropolitan Government, Tokyo. 1989.
270. Training Agency, *Training in Britain*. HMSO, London. 1989.
271. Umlandverbund Frankfurt, *Preparatory land use plan for Frankfurt (Flaechennutzungsplan)*. Umlandverbund Frankfurt, Frankfurt. 1985.
272. Universities Statistical Record?, *University statistics vol 2: First destinations of university graduates*. Universities Statistical Record, London. 1990.
273. Van den Bos, Jim, *East axis turns to gold*. Chartered Surveyor Weekly, September 20th, 1990.
274. Van den Bos, Jim, *Paris takes command*. World Property, March, 1990.
275. Van der Cammen, H(ed), *Four metropolises in Western Europe*. Van Gorcum, Assen/Maastricht. 1988.
276. Vulliamy, Ed, *The Paris we can't match*. Guardian, February 8th, 1989.
277. Wakeford, Richard, *American development control*. HMSO, London. 1990.
278. Weatherall Green & Smith, *Central London office market*. Weatherall Green & Smith, London. October, 1990.
279. Weatherall Green & Smith, *Prospects: a City of London office survey*. Weatherall Green & Smith, London. November, 1990.
280. Webster, FV et al., *Changing patterns of urban travel*. Transport and Road Research Laboratory, London. 1985.
281. Which?, *Traffic in cities*. Which?, October, 1990.

INDEX

acid rain 94
accommodation
    see housing
air pollution 94–6
airport facilities 136–8
agglomeration economies
    significance of 26, 28–9, 31
    financial services and 61–2
Agnelli Foundation
    "complete" global cities, meaning 30
    "pure" global cities, meaning 30
    strategies for wealth creation 195–6
    world city definition 6
Annual Census of Employment (1989) 73
Arts Plan for London 45

Berlin
    cultural activities 48, 49
    demographic projections 79
    Economic Development Corporation 79
    German reunification 4
    green space 100–1
    labour market in 78–80
    Land-Use Plan (1984) 100
    manufacturing in 42–4
    pollution in 95
    population 78–9
    role in national economy 29
    strengths of 27
    urban design 103–4
building
    city planning restrictions 156–7
bus services 132

Central Business District
    influence on locational decisions 56
Channel Tunnel
    implications for European cities 3, 138
Cheshire, Paul 7
communications
    role in world cities 139–42
commuting
    into London 72–3
company cars
    UK tax concessions 134
Confederation of British Industry
    transport survey (1989) 127
congestion, transport
    in world cities 135
cultural activities
    as a production chain 46
    audio-visual industries 111–12
    design 113–14
    film 111–12
    high cost of 118
    in London 209–10
    in wealth and employment creation 44–9
    museums 114–16

music 113
promotion of 117
sports provision 116–17
theatre 110
visual arts 111

decentralisation
  manufacturing and 40
  world city trends 60
Docklands
  commercial development 187
  new housing development 156
  office accommodation in 151
  relocation and 62
  transport 134
  waterways link 139

Eastern Europe
  implications for world cities 1, 3
education
  in America 160–1
  in Germany 161–2
  in Japan 161
  in London 163–5, 205–7
  in the United Kingdom 162–3
EIDAN
  Tokyo transport system 130
employment 67–86
  Annual Census of Employment (1989) 73
  Department of Employment report (1988) 164
  education and training 157–63
  cultural activities 45
  key components 198–9
  manufacturing 38–44
  role of financial services 33
  skills mismatches 68
  transport and 127
enabling infrastructure
  airport facilities 136–8
  commercial property 142–9

communications 139–42
education and training 157–65
housing 152–7
intra-city mobility 53
key components 197
meaning 10, 125–6
rail facilities, international 138
waterways and waterfronts 138–9
European High Speed Rail Network 138
European Central Bank
  implications of location 35–6, 42

fares system
  public transport 132–3
financial services
  agglomeration economies and 61–2
  EC economic contribution 33
  growth of (1980s) 33
  in London 3–4, 22, 33, 37
  innovation in 32
  in the United Kingdom 33
  in Tokyo 22, 37
  in New York 31, 37
  liberalisation of 34
  role of national and economic development 34
  Single European Market, significance of 35–6, 50–1
Frankfurt
  as complete global city 30
  Bundesbank, location of 36, 42
  cultural activities 48, 49
  European Central Bank, location of 36
  financial services in 35
  German reunification 4
  green space 99–100
  high technology industry in 27
  housing in 152
  international transport links 81
  labour market in 80–1
  land-use planning 187
  manufacturing in 42

INDEX

population 80
urban design 103

Geddes, Patrick 6
Glass Steagal Act
    banking and securities legislation 35
government
    role in transport planning 128–9, 130–1
    of world cities 183–5
Greater London Arts
    Arts Plan for London 45
Greater London Council
    transport strategies 133
Greater London Development Plan (1976) 6
green space
    Berlin 100–1
    Frankfurt 99–100
    London 101
    New York 101
    Paris 101
    Tokyo 101

Hayklan, Steven 127
Heathrow Express 203
Hessisches Statistisches Landesamt 144
highways network
    shortcomings of 133–6
hinterland, economic
    role and significance of 29–30
homelessness 155–6
housing
    access 154–6
    homelessness 155–6
    in Frankfurt 152
    in London 207–9
    new building 156–7
    prices 152–4

Ile de France 2000 project 4
in-house training
    in Japan 181

Institute for Metropolitan Studies 56–7
integrated mass transport 131–2
intra-city mobility 53
    in London 202–4
    labour market mobility 67

land-use planning
    in Frankfurt 187
    in London 186–7
    in New York 187–9
    in Paris 187
    in Tokyo 189
litter pollution 97–8
Local Economy Policy Unit 71
locational decisions
    business priorities 56–60
London
    air pollution 95
    as pure command city 30
    Channel Tunnel, benefits of 167
    commuting figures 72–3
    competitive status 171–92
    crime, rising incidence 108–9
    cultural activities 44, 45, 47–8, 109–21
    decentralisation and 60–1
    demographic projections 70–1
    Docklands and corporate relocation 62
    European Bank for Reconstruction and Development 36
    financial services 3–4, 22, 27, 32, 37
    Greater London Development Plan (1976) 6
    green space 101
    homelessness 155–6
    intra-city mobility, weakness of 53
    labour market overview 70–5
    land-use planning 186–7
    locational decisions 56
    manufacturing in 22, 30, 38–44
    national role 2
    planning priorities 202–10

poor travelling environment 132
population 70
promotional priorities 210–14
rented accommodation 154
role in national economy 29
service sector 73
"short-termism" and 32
strategic priorities 101–2
telecommunications, perceptions of 53
Thameslink service 132
transport 126–42
urban design 107–8
West End development 148–9
Youth Training Scheme 163–4
London Chamber of Commerce 15
London Forum 15
London Planning Advisory Committee
land-use strategy 187
transport strategy 133
Los Angeles
film industry in 113

manufacturing
and economic diversity 39
decline of 22, 73
in world cities 22, 38–44
mayor
role in world cities 184–5
Mumford, Lewis 7

New York
as information centre 26–7
cultural activities 48
decentralisation and 60–1
demographic projections 75–6
environmental survey 98
Finance, Insurance & Real Estate (FIRE) 76
financial crisis 2, 4
financial services in 31, 35, 37
green space 101–2
labour market in 75–7

land-use planning 187–9
loss of corporate headquarters 31
manufacturing in 22, 38, 40, 76
population 75
Public Development Corporation 187–9
Regional Plan Association 26, 40
role in national economy 29
urban design 106
noise pollution 96–7

Pacific Rim
Tokyo's domination of 34–5
Paris
architectural style 104
as complete global city 30
cultural activities 48
demographic projections 77
financial services in 35
green space 101
hinterland, significance of 78
labour market in 77–8
La Defense 146
land-use planning 187
manufacturing in 41–2
mass transport system 132, 134
pollution in 95
population 77
role in national economy 29
urban design 104
vocational training in 78
pesonal safety
in world cities 108–9
planning
land-use 187–9
transport 128–31
pollution
air pollution 94–5
carbon dioxide emissions 95–7
litter 97–8
noise pollution 96–7
sulphur dioxide emissions 94–5

INDEX

property, commercial 142–52
    Berlin 144–5
    Frankfurt 143–4
    London 147–9
    New York 147
    Paris 145–6
    stock creation 149–52
    Tokyo 146–7
property, residential
    see housing

quality of life
    key elements 89–94, 199–200
    personal safety 108–9
    pollution 94–8
    public space 98–108
    urban design 98–108

rail network
    European High Speed 138
rented accommodation
    in world cities 154–5
risk management
    innovation and 32

Sellars, Peter 2
Single European Market
    financial services, implications for 35–6
    implications for world cities 1, 11, 12, 50–3
soft economy
    meaning 24
Soldatos, Panayotis 8

telecommunications
    advance digital switches 142
    in London 53, 140, 141
    optical fibre transmission 141–2
    role in world city 139–42
Thameslink service 132

Tokyo
    congestion in 81
    cultural activities 48–9
    EIDAN services 130
    financial services in 22, 37
    flexibility of labour force 82
    green space 101
    headquarters functions 81
    labour market in 81–2
    land-use planning 189
    manufacturing in 24, 39, 41
    national insularity 4
    noise pollution 96–7
    population 81
    recentralisation trend 61
    role in national economy 29
    "soft economy" and 24
    urban design 105–6
    Urban Parks Law 101
    workforce, aging 82
training
    see education
transport
    airports 136–8
    CBI survey (1989) 127
    carbon dioxide emissions 95–6
    employment and 127
    fares system 132–3
    funding public services 130–1
    government, role of 128–9, 130–1
    Heathrow Express 203
    highways network 133–6
    in Paris 78
    integrated mass transport 131–2
    international rail facilities 138
    international transport links 136–8
    intra-city mobility 5
    light rail systems 131
    private cars, restrictions on use 133–4
    significance for world cities 126–7
    waterways 138–9

urban design
    in Berlin 103–4
    in Frankfurt 103
    in London 107
    in New York 106
    in Paris 104
    in Tokyo 105–6

waterways and waterfronts 138
wealth creation 21–65
    agglomeration economies, significance of 61–4
    command and creativity 28–32
    cultural activities 44–50
    financial services 33–8
    future prospects 55–6
    global trends 50–62
    innovation and 31
    manufacturing 22, 38–44
    risk management 32
    strategies for London 195–7, 173
wholesale distribution
    in world cities 22

world cities
    agglomeration economies 28–9, 31
    as business location 21, 56–9
    city-wide policies 176–80
    command and creativity in 28–32
    "complete" global cities, meaning 30
    Eastern Europe 1
    economic diversity, value of 31
    global command 28–31
    global creativity 31–2
    hinterland, economic 29–30
    labour market attributes 67–9
    land-use planning 185–9
    manufacturing in 22
    mayor, role of 184–5
    meaning 5–11
    policy frameworks 180–5
    prestige location 21
    positive development of 4
    "pure" global cities 30
    quality of life in 89–123
    Single European Market 1, 11, 12
    wealth creation 21–65

Youth Training Scheme 163–4